Margaret Mee

MARGARET MEE's
AMAZON

Margaret Mee

Heliconia chartacea Lane ex Barreto
Cult. Rio de Janeiro,
Sitio Burle Marx
Proc. Venezuela (Amazonas)
1975

MARGARET MEE'S AMAZON

Diaries of an Artist Explorer

Kew

PLANTS PEOPLE
POSSIBILITIES

Antique Collectors' Club
in association with
The Royal Botanic Gardens, Kew

ISBN 1 85149 454 5

Frontispiece: *Heliconia chartacea*

British Library Cataloguing-in-Publication Data
A catalogue record for this book is available from the British Library

Printed in Spain
for the Antique Collectors' Club Ltd., Woodbridge, Suffolk

CONTENTS

Sarcoglottis

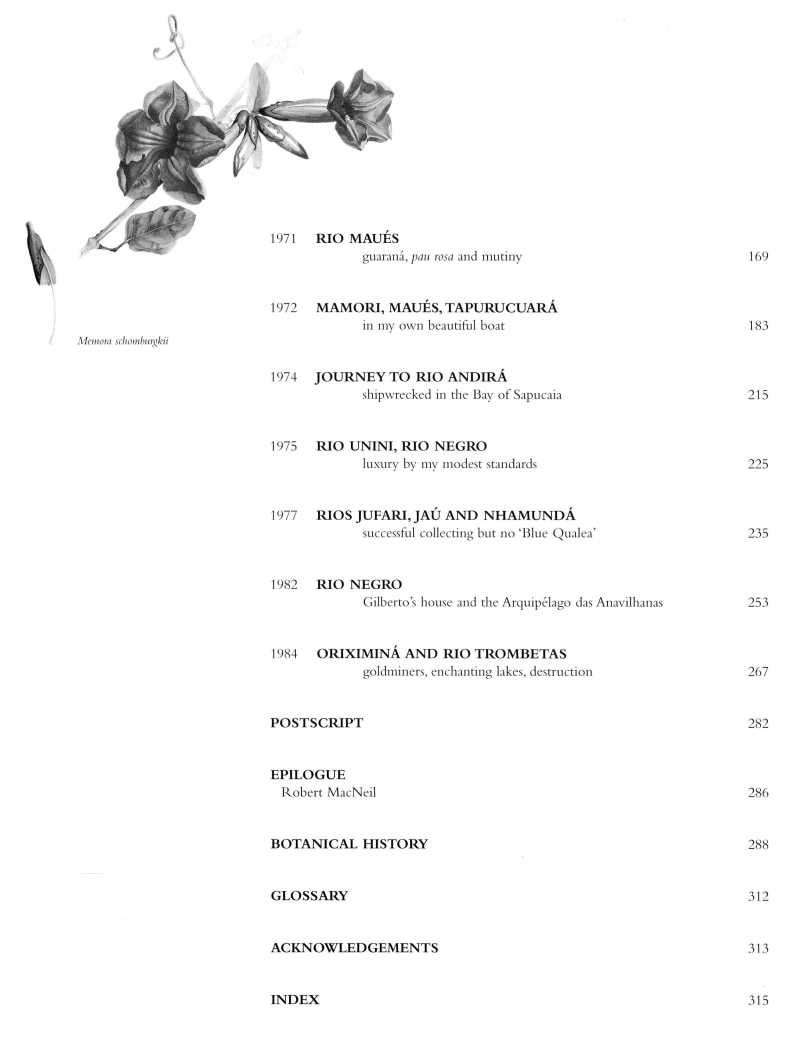

Memora schomburgkii

AUTHOR'S NOTE

My special gratitude to my husband Greville for his constant help and constructive criticism which has proved invaluable to my work; for his patience when I overstayed my time limit in the Amazon; his understanding and affectionate assistance without which this publication would not have been possible.

I am also indebted to: Dr. Roberto Burle Marx whose unquenchable love and enthusiasm for plants and nature inspired me over the years that I have known him as a wonderful friend.

Professor Richard Evans Schultes who has given me tremendous help and support in the scientific and academic field, which, combined with his great love and knowledge of the Amazon, has been a constant inspiration.

Ghillean Prance who, during my early journeys, was an almost legendary figure, for I heard of him in the remotest parts of the Amazon. His knowledge of the Amazon and its vegetation is impressive, as was his courage in penetrating the most difficult regions. He has been a constant inspiration to me.

Margaret Mee
Rio de Janeiro, Brazil
August 1988

Greville Mee, Uruguay, 1997

Mormodes buccinator

Margaret Mee combined a genius for painting in water colour with a passion for the flora of Amazonia. In the course of her fifteen expeditions to the region she amassed a wonderful record of its spectacular wild flowers, but she also became increasingly appalled by the damage being inflicted on this incomparable natural heritage. Every time she travelled through the area, she was dismayed to see how much of what she had seen and recorded during earlier visits had disappeared. It is dreadful to think that in the fifteen years since her death in 1988 it is estimated that a further 100,000 square miles of the Amazon rain forest has been thoughtlessly and violently exploited.

The growing demand by an ever increasing human population for space and resources threatens to create even more ecological disasters all over the world. The forests of the Amazon are one of the last and most important bastions in the battle to maintain an essential level of biological diversity for the wellbeing of future generations. Margaret Mee's wonderfully observed and executed paintings illustrate just what is at stake if humanity fails to provide adequate protection for these very special areas of the world.

Gustavia pulchra
Amazonas

Margaret Mee

An intrepid, gifted and sensitive artist …

Gustavia pulchra painted by Margaret Mee: symbol of the majestic, vulnerable region called Amazonia; a symbol of an intrepid, gifted and sensitive artist.

The large white flowers, tinged with yellow or pink, release their scent into the hot, still air. The tree that bears them stands in dark, flooded forest, the black water reflecting back every detail as in a glass darkly.

The Rio Negro region of Amazonia has called to the artist in Margaret Mee, with a call insistent and persistent. The ephemeral beauty, the light and shadow, the reflectance of the water, the magic of an opening flower bud have summoned her to ignore the frailties of body, and to face repeatedly the rigours and dangers of river journeys of Sprucean extension.

Many people have travelled Amazonian waters, many people have painted Amazonian plants, but Margaret Mee outranks those other travellers and artists simply because she, with her watercolours, went, saw and conquered the region. Margaret has been able to imbue her subjects with the reality of their own environments. She has seen, smelled and touched; she has travelled, itched, ached, perspired, been delayed, disappointed and remained; and then, she has painted. No wonder, that for us all her work bears authenticity as well as beauty. *Gustavia pulchra,* Gustavia the beautiful, a representative of forest beauty and an artist's dedicated skill.

Professor Sir Ghillean T. Prance
Director Royal Botanic Gardens, Kew, 1988–1999

Couroupita subsessilis

Artist, botanist and lover of nature ...

Artist, botanist and lover of nature, Margaret Mee has shared her matchless skills with countless folk not fortunate enough to have enjoyed personally the floral wealth of the Amazon rainforest. A woman of extreme modesty, she herself undoubtedly does not realise the impact that her talents have spread abroad. Nor does she understand, I am sure, the great heritage that she has created for the future of natural history.

Of very special interest to me – a botanist who for the past half century has studied the flora of the north-west Amazon – is her dedication to the forests of the Rio Negro area. She loves this region. Here she executed many of her most magnificent paintings.

It was here also that one of the greatest but one of the least appreciated explorers of all time, the Yorkshire botanist Richard Spruce, spent five productive years more than a century ago. In a very real way, Margaret has honoured Spruce's extraordinary contribution. For the two have much in common: she is shy and self-effacing as was he; and both, without actually realising the extent, have enriched our knowledge of the richest part of the Amazonian flora. And their very different material contributions – her life-like paintings, his dried herbarium material of hundreds of species new to science – have given a powerful impetus to the growing outcry against the uncontrolled devastation of the largest rainforest left on the globe. In more than one respect, Margaret, the quiet and unostentatious voice of the wilderness can be credited with one of the loudest voices for conservation.

She knows these species-rich woodlands well. She travelled miles in a dugout canoe with an Indian boy paddler. When she spied a flowering plant or a spot of colour in the all-pervading greenness, she stopped, set up her easel and painted. Mud, heat, insects weaned her not a whit from that fortunate plant and her brush.

It is not easy for me to choose any one of Margaret's paintings as my favourite – they defy such classification. Yet perhaps a painting like her *Aechmea rodriguesiana* strikes me strongly because it illustrates her appreciation of the interdependence of many of the plants in such an ecologically complex environment. This beautiful epiphyte is not portrayed as an isolated organism but as part of a vegetational whole. While this painting is but one in which the floral background of the principal subject is accurately and artistically depicted, the portrait of such a magistral bromel has always seemed to me to speak out its thanks to Margaret for appreciating its beauty and its life-style as part of a rich and in many respects a mysterious community of nature.

Receiving the World Wildlife Fund Gold Medal for Conservation, 1984

Richard Evans Schultes

Professor Richard Evans Schultes (1915-2001)
Director Emeritus
Botanical Museum of Harvard University, 1988

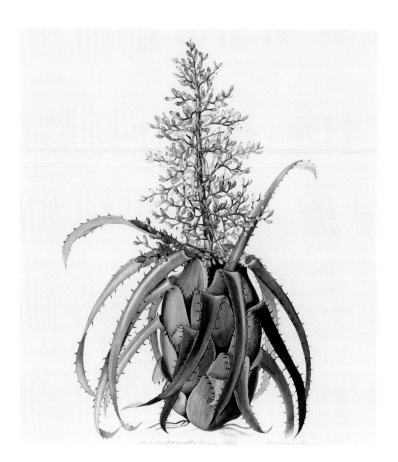

Aechmea polyantha

A specialist in scientific illustration ...

Velloziaceae

I remember an excursion I made not far from Rio to collect rare plants hitherto not cultivated. Margaret Mee, with her gift of keen observation, surprised us by always finding the rarest species. She has the desire to identify her discoveries and the joy of sharing them with plant lovers. It is this which takes her into the forests as an explorer, braving many dangers, illness and more, in order to arrive at the supreme moment of flowering, the moment when Nature seems to reveal herself in all her beauty, mystery and luxuriance. The artist takes advantage of this magic moment to discover and portray an infinite series of secrets and revelations, rich in colour and form.

As a specialist in scientific illustration Margaret Mee is the most efficient I have ever known. Her work achieves perfection without becoming stereotyped. Her organisation of design on the page is always well conceived. Minute details are so intelligently portrayed that they do not destroy the artistic conception of the whole; they are drawn with the greatest care and observation in order to analyse the complexity of structure and to reveal the beauty of the plants in their living manifestation. In fact Margaret Mee takes the plant form in its obscurity and shows its colour, rhythm, texture and form without ever becoming pretentious in so doing.

When I speak of the Brazilian flora there comes to my mind the numerous journeys I have made through the most diverse regions, each with its own character, where one always feels a new emotion, a sense of mystery about this extraordinary world, this world of plants. Once when I was in Amazonia, in those flooded forests where the water sometimes rises forty-five feet in a season, it was as though we were in a forested sea. Around the trunks lianas wound and clung like writhing serpents in a convulsive effort to reach the top. In this struggle for life and quest for light appear the most varied forms of life.

In hollows near the rivers the heliconias develop a theme of extraordinary richness and

Opposite. *Heliconia chartacea* var. *meeana*

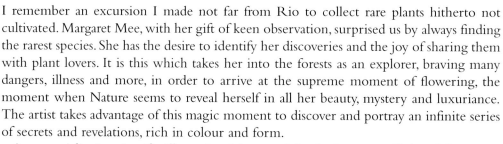

Heliconia uaupensis E.M.
Amazonas, Rio Uaupés

Margaret Mee

Catasetum saccatum

variety. Some of the pendent flowers have a dusty bloom on the bracts and leaves which combine vivid colours and unusual textures. To me their harmony is almost music. At other times I see them as sculpture, as forms projected in space, shapes enriched by the tension between flowers and leaves. Or I think of them as paintings of capricious shapes; I see them in sunshine and in rain when streams of light make them appear like precious stones. They are bird-like, as in *Heliconia imbricata,* at times parrot-like, as in *Heliconia rostrata;* or scorpion-like, as in *Heliconia mariae* where the jointed bracts resemble the segments of a centipede. At other times they have the delicacy of hummingbirds, as in *Heliconia augustifolia,* or they appear like a flight of green birds, as in *Heliconia sampaiona. Heliconia 'amazonica'* has the charm of an Impressionist painting; it hangs swinging in the breeze and, on a cinnamon-red stem, displays curving bracts of rose, purple, green and white, merging into unbelievable shades. The picture is completed by the leaves which seem to be intentionally split, giving the appearance of windswept hair. There are heliconias whose bracts are of extreme delicacy, taking the form of a chalice to protect the flowers. Sometimes they are red-orange merging into dark green with light, almost white, tips. Within the urn, cadmium yellow stands out in contrast with the ultimate blue of the fruits.

Brazil has been and continues to be the land of enchantment for the botanist. One can understand how these regions have fascinated and inspired Margaret Mee. This vast country has more than 650 species of bromeliads; some, like *Aechmea polyantha,* are known to us only from Margaret Mee's paintings. To seek out a plant, bring it from its obscurity and reveal it to those who are inspired by Nature, is a true discovery. Each plant is a mystery whose laws challenge us; whose reason for life, whose preferences, dislikes and interrelationships, teach us a lesson which should give us a better understanding of the world in which we live. I admire and respect Margaret Mee, who seeks to portray the intricate beauty of the many plants which have so far passed unnoticed in a world where greed and ambition ruthlessly destroy our wonderful heritage, the gift of life.

Roberto Burle Marx, Rio de Janeiro

Roberto Burle Marx (1909-1994) and Margaret Mee

Zo Office Supply
Post Office Box 900
Mendocino, CA 95460

11-16-12
12-42 0017

4   X
         •1·35 @
5   •5·40 ⏲
         •5·40 ⏲
         •0·39 ⏲

         •5·79 ⏲

INTRODUCTION

For thirty-two years, the artist Margaret Mee was enchanted by and lured back again and again to the massive, unpredictable and fertile rainforests of Amazonas. Her initial objective, to search out and illustrate the glorious flora growing in the tree canopies and along the innumerable waterways of the great rivers of the Amazon basin, was later combined with a growing concern at the commercial plunder of the great forests.

How did it come about that Margaret Ursula Brown, born 22 May 1909 in Chesham, Buckinghamshire, one of England's typical 'green and pleasant' counties, became the foremost botanical artist of Amazon flowers?

Influenced by an artist aunt and encouraging teachers, as a schoolgirl she showed early signs of talent, both in botany and drawing. The natural world of the quiet countryside in which her family lived and her ability to record it sowed early seeds. In her late teens, her artistic bent by now recognised, she attended the Watford School of Art, and subsequently taught art in Liverpool.

During her schooldays Margaret had become fascinated by all she read and heard of travellers' tales, and in 1932 she decided to travel herself, visiting Germany and France. During this time she spent little time drawing or painting since she had become closely and, as in all her projects, passionately involved in politics. After the war, when she worked as a draughtsman for De Havilland, she decided to retrain, first at St. Martin's School of Art, and later at Camberwell School of Art where she studied under Victor Pasmore. Artistic success there was complemented by meeting and marrying fellow student Greville Mee.

In 1952 on a visit to her sister in Brazil, Margaret was smitten by São Paulo. When Greville joined her, and since they found themselves at a watershed in their lives, they decided to stay and make São Paulo their home (they moved to Rio de Janeiro in 1986).

Cattleya bicolor

In São Paulo the seeds sown in Margaret's early life took firm root, for São Paulo was surrounded by countryside and landscape entirely new to her, where exciting plants and trees begged to be drawn. So began her career as a botanical artist, and in 1956, aged forty-seven, her first expedition and introduction to the wildlife and waterways of Amazonas.

It was at this point that Margaret began to keep the diaries that, along with her paintings, drawings and sketches, make up this book. As the reader is drawn into the record of her expeditions on the great Amazon and its tributaries, and in its large and towns and tiny settlements, it becomes apparent that, though plant hunting always came first whenever possible and practical, other events often took over. It seemed to be raining so often, so suddenly, so violently, that a small dug-out canoe could become a waterlogged if not dangerous place to be; rapids had to be got through – canoes were hauled overland to lighten the weight of the mother boat; recalcitrant boatmen were gently or sternly coerced; drunken prospectors were held off with revolver. After her first trip, when she and her companion Rita were unprepared both in dress and supplies - indeed near starvation – she quickly learnt the laws of equipment, but hated to see birds and beasts shot for food, and to avoid eating them kept supplies of packet soup rolled up with her hammock.

She was fascinated by the rich mix of Brazilians she came across and often lived with for a time; she was especially fond of the riverines she met, and over the years became friends with many of them. Slightly-built, blue-eyed and blond-haired, she felt it important not to let standards slip and kept up her appearance in the most out-of-the-way spots or after paddling for hours in sultry heat; she was enthusiastic to go to to any lengths to check out reports of a rare species, indeed discovered several new species, some of which were named for her; she fought losing battles with the dreaded biting insects – *pium* – in spite of wearing gloves and arranging an elaborate netting over her sun hat. But she never lost her sense of humour, and always saw the comic side after even the most dangerous or hostile situations.

Between expeditions, some of which lasted for up to four months, Margaret returned home to Greville, to teaching commitments, and to her own painting; for some time she was involved in research work at the São Paulo Botanic Institute, a job which took her all over Brazil and widened her knowledge of its plant riches. She was twice severely ill, with malaria and infectious hepatitis, not to mention the usual tropical illnesses which strike travellers, and underwent two hip replacement operations. Yet nothing daunted her determination to return to the Amazon to record its fabulous plant life.

Unpredictable weather and transport, and dependent as she usually was on cooperation from guides, meant Margaret often had to make hurried *in situ* sketches. She would then carefully note on the sketches every detail of the plants' forms and shapes, colours, environments and locations; these she might later work up into coloured sketches. She travelled with plastic bags and small collectors' baskets and boxes in which she kept plants, always concerned that they might not survive the long journey home to São Paulo or Rio where, working with her sketches, she would work up finished paintings. At Indian settlements where she spent some time, in order to preserve plants for as long as possible, she cultivated small gardens in which to grow collected specimens, many of which also ended up in research centres in São Paulo and Rio.

Recognition of her work came in the form of financial support from the Brazilian government, the National Geographic Society and a Guggenheim Fellowship. During her days in the Amazon Margaret met and was inspired by distinguished botanists and conservationists, and her developing interest, which became a passionate crusade, in preserving the fragile environments in which she travelled drew admiration and respect from the same experts who had been her first mentors, among them the orchid specialist Dr. Guido Pabst and the botanist Richard Evans Schultes. She counted the Brazilian landscape architect, Roberto Burle Marx, among her friends, for they shared a mutual admiration for the other's work in publicising the destructive commercial development throughout the Amazon region. After some dozen years' of travelling, Margaret had seen and learnt enough to be confident to write a report for the influential Institute of Brazilian Forestry Development, in which she highlighted the continuing and increasing devastation to the inhabitants and the plant and animal life of the great rivers. In 1976 she was awarded an M.B.E., and in 1979 the order of Cruzeiro do Sul (Brazil) for her services to botanical research.

Clusia

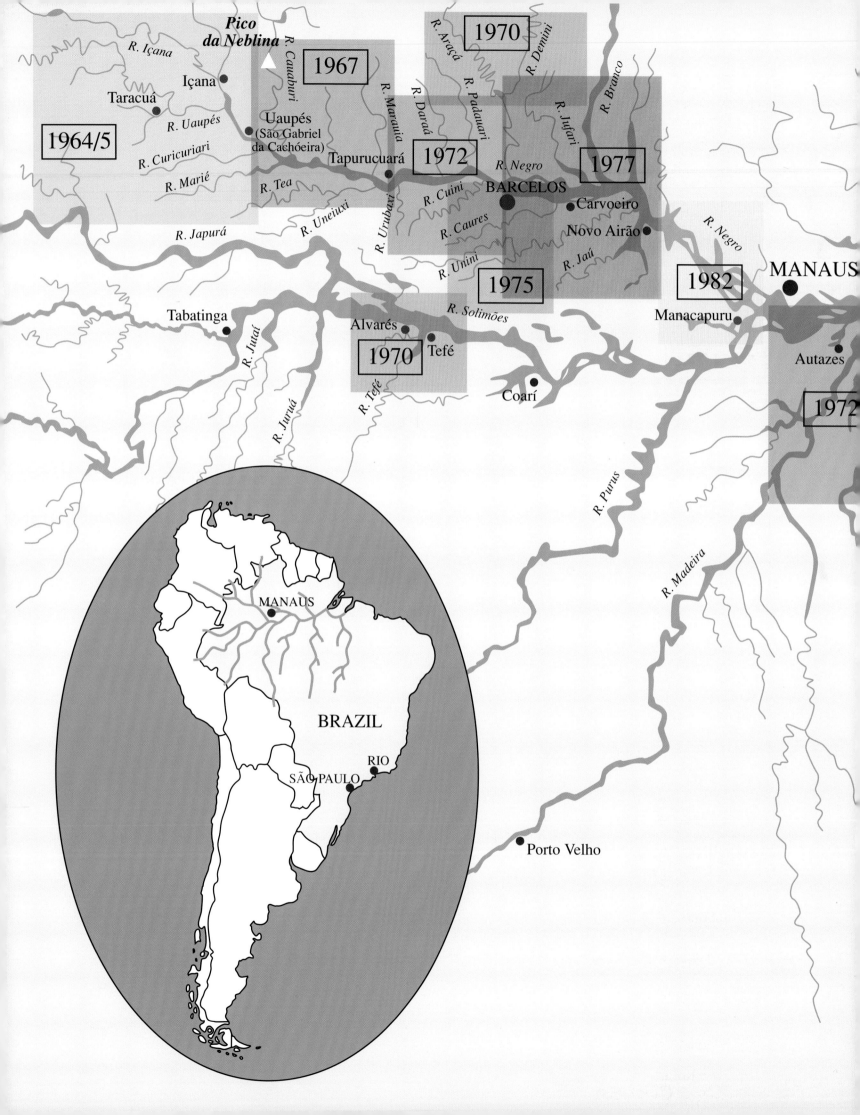

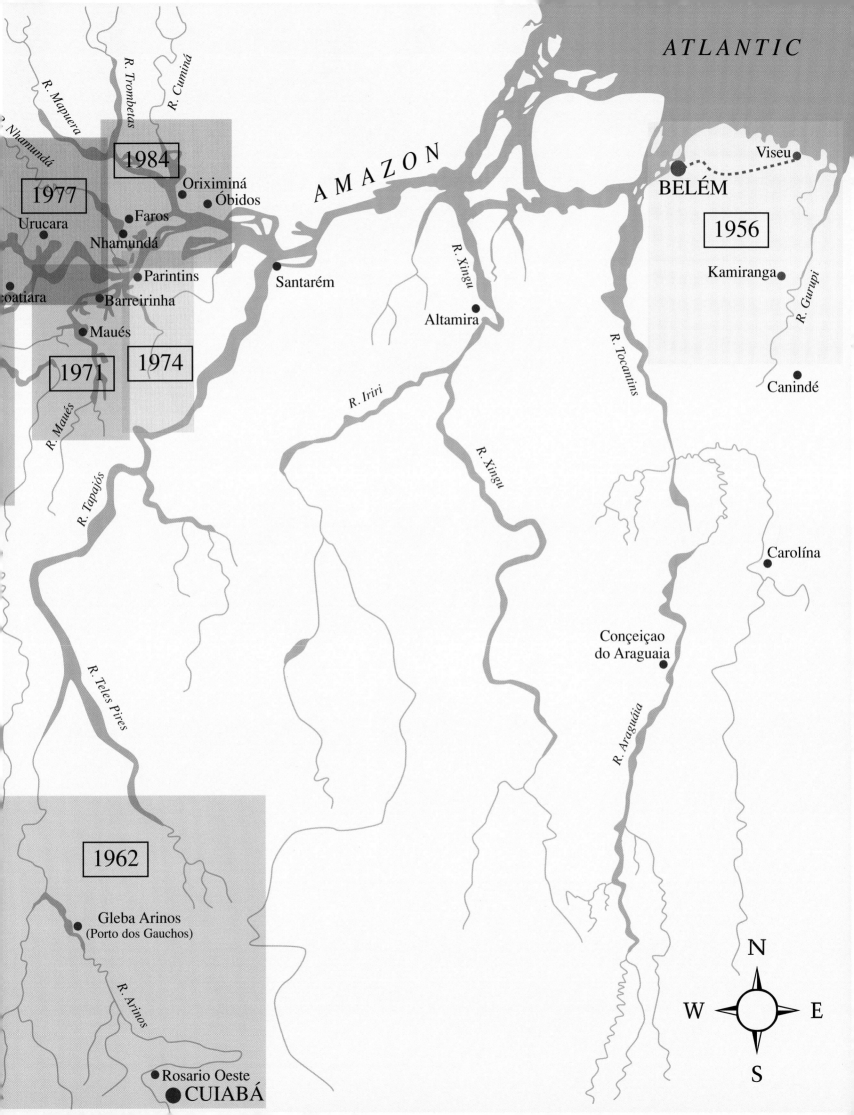

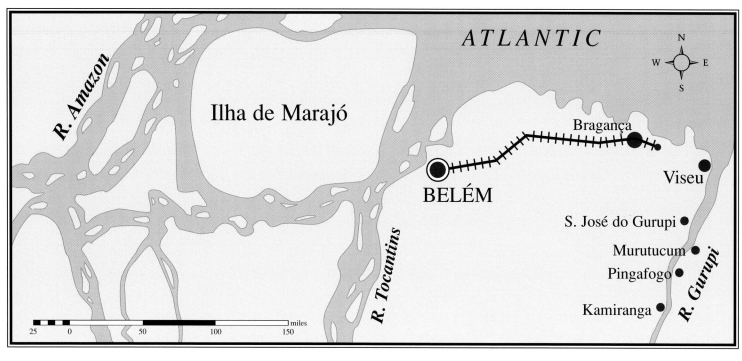

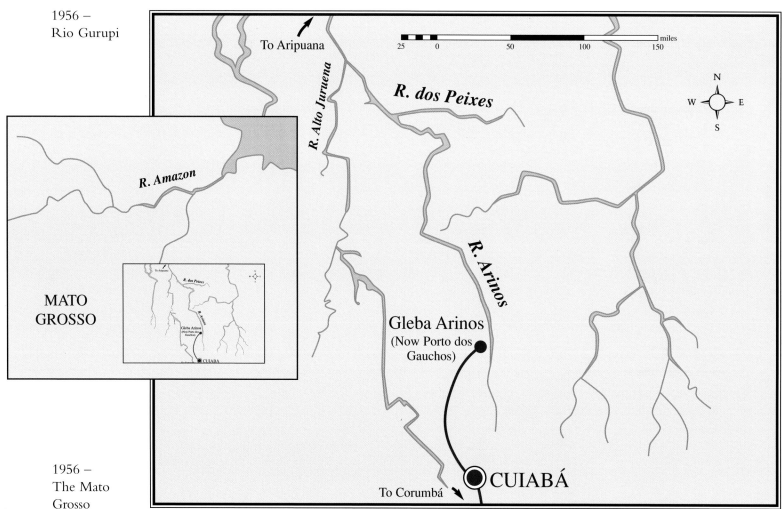

1956 –
Rio Gurupi

MATO
GROSSO

1956 –
The Mato
Grosso

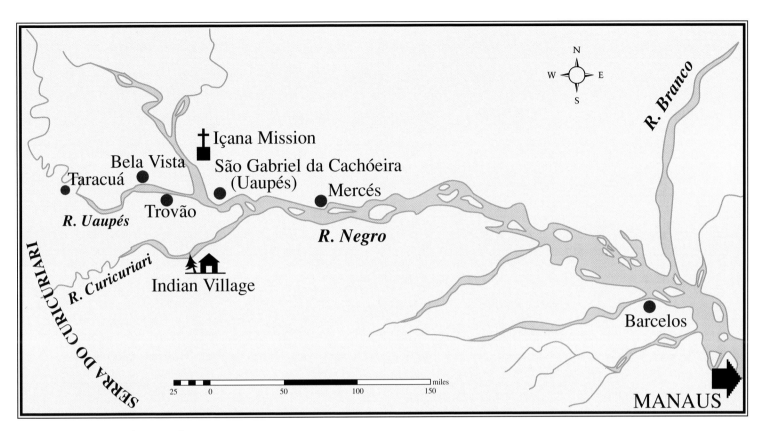

1964/5 – Uapés and Beyond

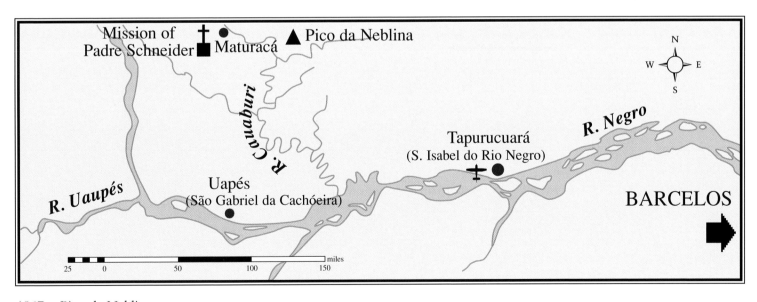

1967 – Pico da Neblina

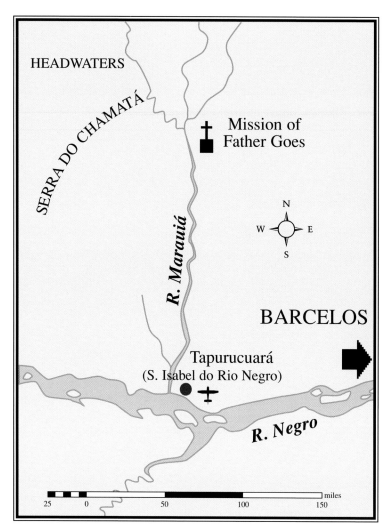

HEADWATERS

SERRA DO CHAMATÁ

✝
◼ Mission of
Father Goes

N
W ● E
S

R. Marauiá

BARCELOS

Tapurucuará
(S. Isabel do Rio Negro)

●
✈

R. Negro

miles
25   0   50   100   150

1967 − Rio Marauiá

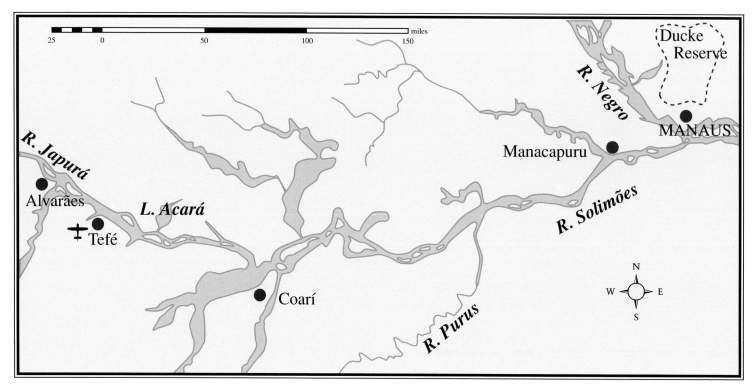

miles
25   0   50   100   150

Ducke
Reserve

R. Negro

MANAUS

R. Japurá

Manacapuru
●

●
Alvarães

L. Acará

R. Solimões

✝ Tefé

N
W ● E
S

●
Coarí

R. Purus

1970 − Rio Solimões

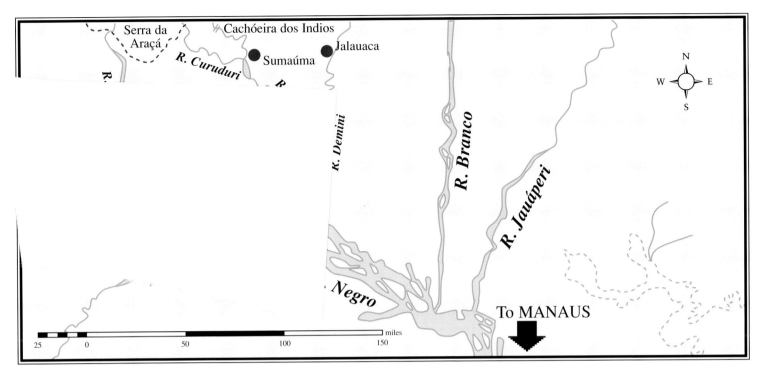

1970 – Rio Demini and Rio Araçá

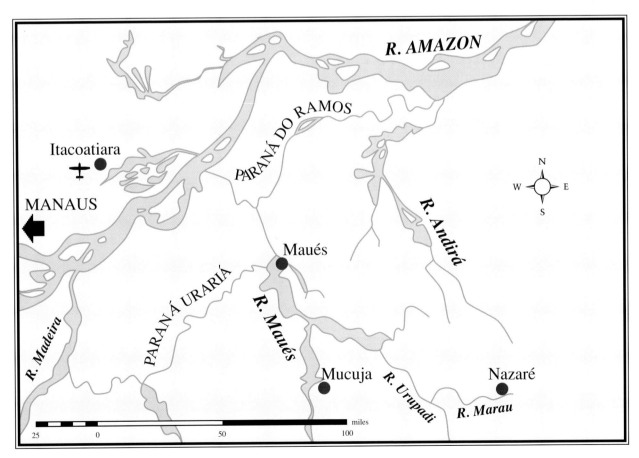

1971 – Rio Maués

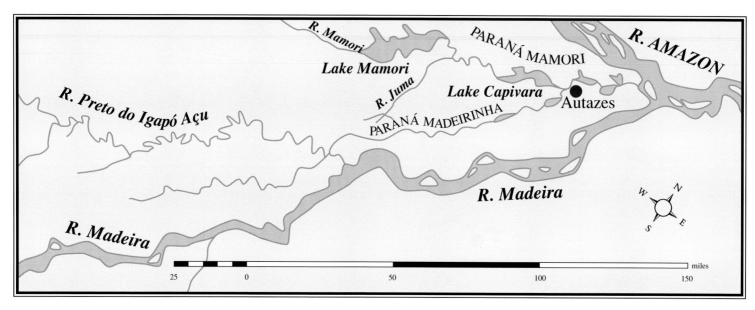

1972 – Rio Mamori

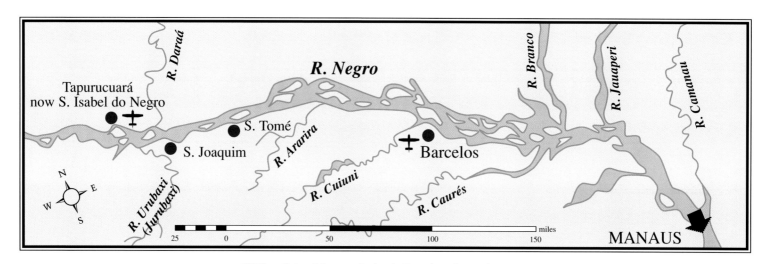

1972 – Rios Negro, Cuiuni, Daraá and Jurubaxi

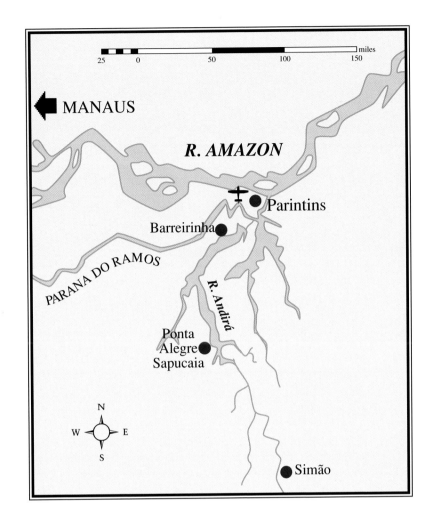

1974 – Rio Andirá

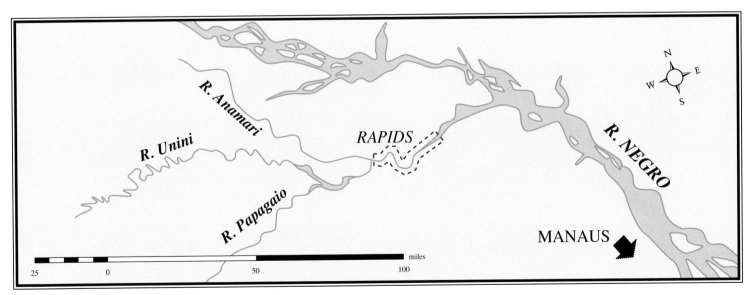

1975 – Rio Unini, Rio Negro

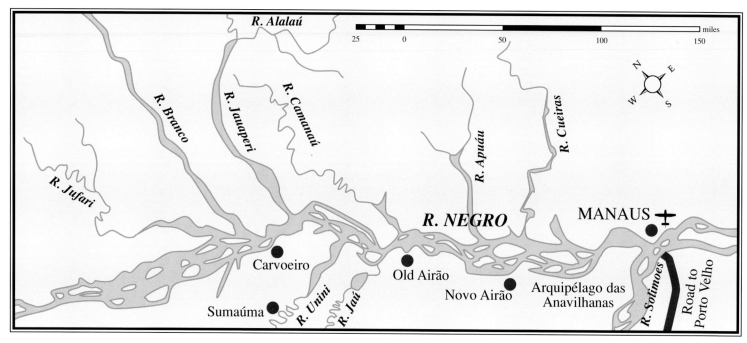

1977 – Rio Jufari and Rio Jaú

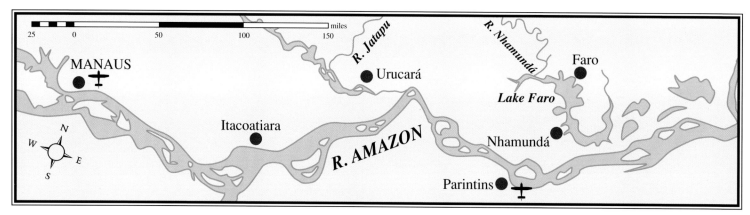

1977 – Rio Nhamundá

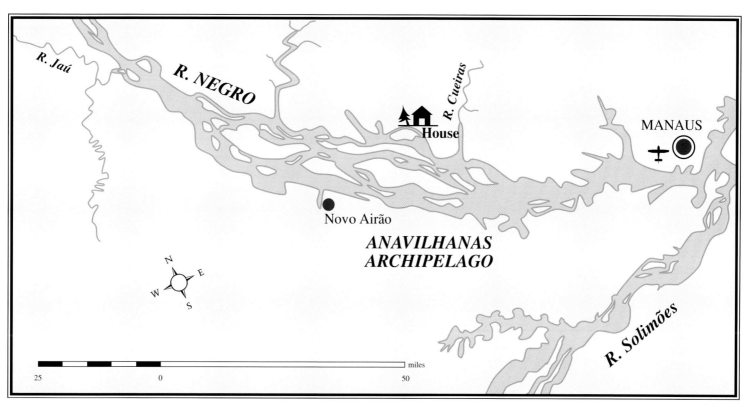

1982 – Rio Negro

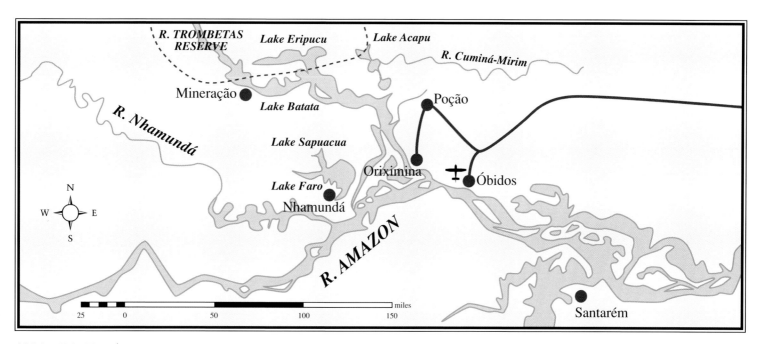

1986 – Rio Trombetas

Couropita
Rio Yamunda, Pará

Margaret Mee

Refuelling en route for Belém

1956

RIO GURUPI:

MY FIRST TASTE OF THE AMAZON

Opposite. *Couroupita subsessilis*

The small passenger-cargo plane left Congonhas airport, São Paulo, bound for Belém, capital of Pará. For myself and my companion Rita this was our first journey to the Amazon, and our excitement was intense. We were both dressed for the jungle – at least we thought we were: blue jeans, long sleeved shirts, straw hats and boots. Our strained purses did not allow for overweight luggage, and my rucksack was already heavy with tubes of paint and sketch books.

We sat intently watching the landscape slip by below, and with each stop our excitement grew. Uberaba, Carolína, then forest, threaded by meandering silver rivers. The pilot flew low over the great Rio Tocantins so that it seemed the tree canopies were above us and we could see the water flowing over its rocky bed. At last, as the sunset spread burning gold over sky and water, we reached the impressive mouth of the vast Amazon – so vast that we seemed to be flying over a mighty ocean.

Our first taste of tropical heat came as we stepped out of the plane at Belém airport, for even under the shade of the massive mango trees in which the little town abounded, the heat was intense.

We stayed in Belém for a few days, exploring, strolling through its fascinating port and market, and, when exhausted, sat in the shade outside our hotel drinking the delicious passion fruit juice of the region.

But the most interesting and useful of our activities was to visit the Goeldi Museum. Founded in 1866, the museum was instituted to study the natural history of Amazonia – its flora, fauna, natural resources and populations. Here we hoped to find out about journeying into the forests of the interior, and we were not disappointed, for the Director, Dr. Walter Egler, was not only sympathetic, but also gave us helpful introductions, advice and information. In his enthusiasm, he sent a keeper to cut flowers from a towering tree of *Couroupita guianensis* for me to paint. Whilst I was doing this, Rita explored the gardens and made friends with various animals, including a group of spider monkeys which decided to claim her as their property when she innocently held one of them by the hand.

Later, Dr. Egler showed us round the grounds where, with his natural ability with animals, he called a jaguar which came to have its head stroked, and then coaxed an angry wild pig to the fence. We also saw the first of a giant species of anteater held at the museum. While trying to substitute its natural diet of termites with eggs, the anteater's

In the shade, outside our hotel, drinking the delicious passion fruit juice of the region

31

Apocynaceae sp.

keeper had been wounded by its formidable nails and he appeared swathed in bandages. We also saw some fine Indian artefacts in the collection.

At the museum's Herbarium, the botanist Dr. Froes told us how, over twenty years or so before, he had flown low in a small plane over the mysterious, unknown region along the frontier between Brazil and Venezuela, where he had seen a spectacular waterfall and a great table-topped mountain in the Serra de Imeri. I felt very flattered when this experienced traveller, while showing us dried plants of the region, turned to me and asked me to look for a Strychnos vine, reputed to grow in the forests of Rio Gurupi – the river we were to explore.

In order to reach our destination on Rio Gurupi – Murutucum – we had to take a train from Belém to Bragança, a little coastal town not too far from Viseu at the mouth of Rio Gurupi. The journey from Belém in a small train with a wood-burning engine was painfully slow. There were interminable stops when local farmers appeared selling home-made food. Sparks from the burning wood poured through the open windows; suddenly, Rita sprang to her feet and began to hit me over the head, for she had spotted a chunk of burning charcoal in my hair which was about to go up in flames. When I arrived in Bragança, my dress was pitted with black holes.

In Bragança, a small port forgotten by the outside world, we aroused curiosity – even hostility – among the locals, for women wearing straw hats, jeans and boots were an unwelcome novelty. We soon found an unassuming commercial traveller's hotel, but the tiny room we were given, although cheap and clean, was certainly not comfortable. The only furniture was a broken mirror hanging over a rickety table and four hammock hooks. The cubicle showers were shared by all.

In spite of a good deal of inconvenience in Bragança – not to mention the noisy spitting in the room adjoining ours – we enjoyed these days of our adventure; but as time passed without news of the boat which was to take us from Bragança to Viseu, our spirits sank and boredom set in. I could find few things to sketch, for if we ventured any distance we became the centre of too much attention. So there was little to do but to wander around, disconsolately. On one

In the Estação Biologico, state of São Paulo

Stanhopea candida

occasion we met two lads who had made their way on foot from French Guyana. They told us the story of their fascinating journey, but, as elsewhere, we were constantly stared at: one of the locals had the audacity to ask the Frenchmen, who flushed scarlet, how much we cost!

After what seemed an eternity, in fact only five days, the boat for Viseu arrived. This was a rough little launch with a closed, wooden cabin tightly packed with at least twenty passengers, all from the region, together with a number of children. Conditions were far from ideal, and when we arrived in the choppy waters of the open sea, with the pitching and tossing of the boat some of the women were hysterical and the children crying. A *mulata* was in such distress that I offered her brandy from my precious hip flask, from which she drank too long and too eagerly. It was an offer I was to regret, for during the rest of the voyage she was perpetually worrying me for more.

Rita and I hung our hammocks side by side, mine against the cabin wall which I somehow felt would give me protection, but I suffered for this choice when we pitched and tossed in the strong currents off the rocky coast, and in the morning I saw I was bruised black and blue from buffeting against the wall. The kerosene hurricane lamp which hung over the foot of my hammock jumped from its hook during one stormy passage, falling on my feet, but fortunately extinguishing itself as it fell. After this disturbed night, I saw one of the loveliest sights by the morning light, flights of flamingoes rising against the dark green forests like a shower of geranium petals.

In Viseu we were introduced to João Carvalho, chief of the Indian Protection Service (IPS), whose headquarters were in Canindé, a village at the headwaters of Rio Gurupi. From him we learnt, among other things, that the area we were heading for was inhabited by Tembé Indians, whilst Urubu territory was on the lower reaches of the river.

In Belém the anthropologist Max Boudin had kindly given us an introduction to a

A house in Bragança

Sr. Raschid in Viseu, describing him as 'a retired gentleman farmer of Lebanese descent'. Once located, Sr. Raschid proved to be most kindly and helpful, and soon had our journey to Murutucum organised. We were to travel by a small trader's boat which would be leaving Viseu at 3a.m. the following morning. So, in readiness for our early departure, we packed that night, for our rucksacks were in some disorder, as two Urubu boys had looked through the contents when we arrived, their curiosity being greater than their shyness. I was fascinated by their soft voices speaking a strange language, their copper skin and blue-black hair.

We hung our hammocks in a small loft in the house where we stayed for the night and where not a sound could be heard. I fell into a deep sleep, awaking with a start, to see by the dim light of the kerosene flame that it was almost 2a.m. I had to pinch Rita to rouse her, and we dressed hastily and descended the precarious steps to call Sr. Raschid, as he had requested. A tall, sleepy figure in pyjamas and carrying a hurricane lamp, he led us down to the jetty, accompanied by the two Urubu boys. Dozens of wooden steps led down to the river, where we could see the dim light of the boat being prepared for the journey. At Sr. Raschid's command, the Urubus timidly took our hands and carefully led us down the dark precipice-like steps. A thick mist hung over the river, and once enveloped in the humid pall my teeth began to chatter. Eventually the boat slipped from her mooring and the 2½h.p. Archimedes motor began to splutter. We were on our way up Rio Gurupi! We searched our baggage for some protection against the bitter cold, pulled out plastic sheets intended for use against rain, and wrapped ourselves up like chrysalises until the sun rose and burnt off the mist.

The trader, Callandario, was a kindly middle-aged Portuguese, who sailed up and down the river, supplying the riverine population with everything from buttons to hammocks, and of course, rice, beans and sugar, etc. Malaki, a dusky young negro with a wonderful smile and character, was the senior member of the crew with the assistance of a young boy who helped him with, among other things, the cooking. When the motor failed (as it did frequently), or was not powerful enough to pass through turbulent rapids, Malaki would stamp and cry 'Vai, Motor, vai!' At times he and the boy jumped lithely into the foaming river, and hauled the hulk through the rapids into calmer waters. This set the pattern for our unforgettable voyage.

On the first night we hung our hammocks from trees beside an enchanted lake. I could not sleep for listening to the magic sounds of the sleeping forest. Only the trees slept, for the lake was alive with sparkling, splashing fishes, while the frogs' chorus mingled with the plaintive cries of night birds.

One of our first calls was at the village of São José do Gurupi, where the hospitable villagers entertained us with exaggerated adventures of encounters with savage animals, these tales 'washed down' with delicious fruit juices. Thus we meandered up the river,

Tembé Indians on the Rio Gurupi

Sobralia macrophylla

bathing in the warm water, stopping at huts and settlements until we reached the most dangerous and challenging falls of Rio Gurupi. There Malaki called an old negro to pole us over the falls. The gaunt old man stood in the prow like a giant ship's figurehead, swinging his bamboo pole from side to side, his dark face and body streaming with sweat. Once over the falls, Malaki departed, leaving Rita and me with Callandario and the boy to proceed to Murutucum.

The writer Francis Huxley had travelled through this region some months before, and memories of the young author were still fresh in the minds of the villagers, who recounted stories of him and his generosity in leaving his surplus food supplies for them. Huxley had journeyed far up the river and his book, *Affable Savages*, was the result of his experiences among the Urubu and Tembé tribes.

Max Boudin, who had given us our introduction to Sr. Raschid, had also kindly offered us the loan of his *maloca* in Murutucum where his 'housekeepers' Zico and Benedita lived. Unfortunately, as Zico was somewhat hostile and Benedita very demanding of our modest store of food and remedies, we avoided too much contact with the couple. Before Callandario left us – which he did with much hesitation – he gave us a large bunch of

Rodriguezia lanceolata

plantains and a good quantity of rice. The latter was invaluable during our last days in Murutucum, for with our lack of experience our provisions were inadequate or inappropriate, and at the end we had nothing to eat but rice and plantains. The plantains, however, proved a great disappointment as they never ripened, and uncooked were quite inedible; a problem compounded by the fact that we had no means of cooking except on Benedita's open fire, but, since this was constantly in use, we were only allowed to use it to boil water for rice.

Zico and Benedita's 'housemaid', a girl of four years old, had a bad case of chicken-pox. She always seemed to have a broom in her hands, sweeping, fetching and carrying the whole day long at harsh orders from Benedita. She dragged herself around, more dead than alive, appearing even too ill to heed the constant scolding.

Our hut, some distance away from the main dwelling, was tiny and primitive and open to the sky above the door. The roof was straw thatch and at night spiders invaded the ceiling. Fascinated, we watched them from the depths of our hammocks, though at first with some apprehension. Could they be venomous? But we soon learned that their only interest was in trapping insects which they seemed to attract by tapping with their bony front legs on the straw ceiling. Everything looked strange and mysterious by the flickering light of the kerosene flame which cast billowing shadows across the earthen floor and wattled walls.

Daily, and sometimes by night, we made a pilgrimage down to the *igarapé* which flowed into Rio Gurupi to fill our canvas bucket with water. By day we were able to bathe in the river and never a soul came near. However, on one occasion when we went down to bathe, we heard an outboard motor approaching. Wildly excited we hurried down the track, quite certain that it was João Carvalho coming to take us upriver to Canindé, an arrangement we had made in Viseu. To our chagrin, and their horror, a procession of *macumbeiras* appeared. A wizened old man beating a drum led the way, followed by men, women and children dressed in their best, ribbons fluttering, one woman carrying a figure on a red velvet cushion. Mastering our astonishment at this unexpected sight, Rita and I greeted them with 'Bom dia!' There was no reply and the old man with his head bent and gaze averted passed on, followed by the others who stared at us fearfully. Had we been mistaken for devils or evil spirits? It was an encounter between two different worlds.

We bathed rapidly and returned to our hut. There was excitement in the hut – loud talking and laughter. Benedita, animated and dressed in her best, came to invite us to the ceremony of killing a cockerel. Hiding our horror, we explained that our religion would not permit us to participate, but we gave her a small contribution to the feast which she clearly expected and took eagerly. The ritual of drum beating, accompanied by chanting, went on late into the night.

We spent our days in the forest, taking in the beauty of the shady trees and the creatures which lived under their canopy. A brown and furry bird-eating spider crouched on a tree trunk against which I was leaning; a chameleon, its throat extended to an orange ball, struggled to swallow a leaf insect as large and as green as itself; from the branches above, two curious toucans followed our antics with interested amusement as we struggled to reach a white flowering orchid, which had been dislodged by a previous night's storm and dangled on a liana. There were flowers to paint in plenty: the pink and white blooms of *Gustavia augusta*, red *Rodriguesia secunda*, perfumed *Epidendrum fragrans*, and many bromeliads.

During the frequent night storms, I lay in my hammock, listening to branches crashing through the forest, and in the morning collected the fallen plants. On one such search, I encountered a grey snake, stretched right across the track and no amount of tapping with my

Entertained by hospitable villagers

Gustavia augusta

Gustavia augusta
Amazonas Feb 1985

Margaret Mee

Prosthecia sp.

stick would make it move. Merely gazing at me insolently, it was daring me to step over it.

When our store of food was near an end, and Rita was lying unwell in her hammock, I began to worry – would João Carvalho ever arrive? On the third day of a boiled rice diet (and little of that), we were so weak with hunger that we decided we had to leave Murutucum at any cost. If we could get a boat we could go upriver to Pingafogo and take refuge with Antonio Carvalho, João's father, until his son came for us.

Zico had been away in the forest for some days, but was due back. His dog had already returned, with a high fever, covered with dried blood, its ears cut and pouring with blood. It came to our hut, drank quantities of water, and lay there, as though in need of our protection. We were horrified at its condition and asked Benedita what could have happened. Very casually, almost contemptuously, she replied that Zico had cut off the dog's ears because it refused to hunt. Appalled as we were by his cruelty, we realised that there was no alternative but to leave Murutucum with Zico as soon as he returned, for he was the only owner of a canoe. Without him we were completely isolated.

When Zico returned his dark face was more sullen than ever. We heard Benedita's gibes: 'Even your dog will not look at or obey you!' It was true, the dog resolutely ignored him, and no amount of threatening or shouting would make it respond. The animal was so aloof and contemptuous that Zico began to get alarmed and fearful of the huge beast, possibly thinking the dog was possessed of a spirit that would avenge his cruelty.

When I asked him to take us by canoe to Pingafogo, he blankly refused. I told him that we should die of hunger if we remained in Murutucum, and that he would be responsible.

Distictella mansoana

Psygmorchis pusilla

Drymonia coccinea

This seemed to perturb him, but nevertheless he began to make excuses until I showed him money – all that I possessed. Finally he wavered, then agreed to leave by canoe in the morning. The journey would take six hours. In spite of the fact that we were so hungry and weak, we packed our belongings joyfully that night.

Next morning, Zico's solid dug-out canoe was already moored near his hut, but before we could leave he had to bail out the evil-smelling and poisonous liquid which had come from an earlier cargo of manioc. When we at last set off, the canoe was alarmingly well down in the water with its unusually heavy load.

The river looked glorious in the sunlight, and our spirits rose as the paddle dipped through the water, bringing us nearer to our destination. About half-way and in mid-stream, the sky lowered, covered with inky clouds, and a sudden storm wind spun the canoe round and round with incredible force. I held my breath, praying that Zico's muscular arms would get us to the river bank. Straining every sinew in his arms, he reached the shore where the three of us hung frantically to low branches until the storm passed. We were drenched, as were our belongings – except for my sketch books which I had carefully covered in plastic wrappings. Shivering in our wet clothes we reached Pingafogo to be welcomed warmly by Antonio Carvalho and his Indian wife, Mocinha, who

Doing the washing

Heliconia sp.

immediately led us to an airy room, where we hung our hammocks and dried out. Later we wolfishly devoured a meal Antonio prepared for us. In fact, he was kindness itself, and all the more welcome after our experience in Murutucum.

Dear old Antonio Carvalho was the sage of Rio Gurupi. The peasants living up and down the river came to him to have their letters read or written, and to hear the news from the papers which he occasionally received from Viseu. His small market garden was flourishing, for he cultivated wisely. Instead of the usual practice of cutting and burning the forest around his home, he cleared some of the undergrowth from under the mighty forest trees and planted fruit trees using the leaf mould which the natural cycle continually renewed. His citrus trees, mangoes, coffee bushes and native fruit trees thrived under their forest protection. Possessing such a flourishing orchard had drawbacks as well as advantages, for his envious neighbours, seeing his trees laden with fruit, pestered him for supplies, although he repeatedly advised them how to create and plant smallholdings of their own. He cured many of the sick with the abundant medicinal plants to be found in the Amazon, for he had an amazing knowledge of their properties. Whilst we were there we witnessed the recovery of his old dog whom he had treated for shotgun wounds. When we arrived the animal was in a very poor way, but after treatment with a herbal mix devised by Antonio, it recovered, and on the day of our departure got up wagging its tail.

In spite of his knowledge of herb lore, Antonio was as superstitious as most of the locals. For him the 'evil eye' was very real, and the main character in one of the stories he told us. A young girl had visited him and had sat in the shade of a beautiful lemon tree. The following day the tree turned brown, withered and died. The girl came again, and sat under another lemon tree, with the same result. After that, she was forbidden to visit them. Rita listened to this tale of the 'evil eye' with some concern for, with one blue eye and one brown, she worried she would be considered a guest of ill omen.

At Pingafogo, besides Antonio and Mocinha, there were two youngsters, a girl and a boy, who fished, hunted and generally helped out. One evening the two went fishing in a distant *igarapé*, and as darkness fell and it grew later and later, Antonio began to fret that they had not returned. When at last they appeared, the girl looked like a spectre and the boy's short hair literally stood on end. They had surprised, and been surprised by, a jaguar. This encounter made Antonio very nervous when Rita and I went collecting in the forest alone, for we were always lured further and further afield by the wonderful plants: brilliant red spikes of *Heliconia glauca*, white bells of *Eucharis amazonica*, silver leaves of *Philodendron melinonii*, and the beautiful orchid *Gongora maculata* with its long inflorescences and

A *paca*, a small rodent rather like a guinea-pig

Margaret Mee

Gongora maculata var. bufonia
Rio Gurupi, Pará
February 1959

Solanum subinerme *Psychotria colorata*

powerful but fragrant perfume like hundreds of lilies. On one occasion we had completely forgotten the time when a shot rang through the forest, followed by Antonio's loud shouts. As he drew near we saw that he was angry and distressed, fearing something had happened to us. But he soon forgave us, and on the return took us to a settlement where the descendants of escaped slaves lived in isolation, never mixing with other races. Of African extraction, they were handsome people and seemed very independent in spirit. Antonio told us that many such communities exist in the jungles of Pará.

We heard that a launch was due to leave Kamiranga, a village some distance upriver from Pingafogo, and in the hope that it was heading for Viseu, Antonio offered to take us to Kamiranga by canoe. We left Mocinha and their beautiful home with regret, yet eager to return to São Paulo, for Rita and I were long overdue at the school where we both taught. We bid a sad farewell to Antonio who had literally saved us from starvation, and had become a good friend.

The launch in the port of Kamiranga was, indeed, sailing to Viseu. It was a passenger-cargo ship crowded with local farmers and peasants and loaded to capacity with *marva*, a highly inflammable fibre, similar to jute. We could scarcely find a place to hang our hammocks between the stacks of *marva*, and when more passengers and cargo piled in, we gave up in despair and decided to sleep on the *marva* instead, with as much leeway as rats in a hole. Among the passengers were a couple of young peasants, husband and wife, both bound for a hospital in Belém. It took no time for the man to show us the suppurating gash below his ribs, inflicted during a quarrel by a 'friend' high on marijuana, while the wife, in trying to defend her husband, had been badly cut about the face and arms. Both were smoking like chimneys, and the wife, a chain smoker, was throwing the lighted butts around, which, had we known at the time that *marva* was so flammable and prone to spontaneous combustion, would have kept us awake all night. As it was we slept like sardines in a tin, though I felt the hot soles of a man's heavy feet in my back throughout the night. The Raschid family were travelling on the same boat, but in a reserved cabin, so we saw little of them, and in any case felt our appearance too disreputable to visit them.

The captain of the launch was fond of the bottle. One night, when he had had more than enough to drink, he insisted, against the advice of the crew, on sailing through the night. Around midnight there was a horrible jarring crash as the boat hit and shudderingly landed at a steep angle against a rock. Rita and I, tense with claustrophobia, struggled out of our *marva* beds, put on our shoes, dragged out our rucksacks from the mêlée and prepared for the worst. Happily there was no 'worst' and the craft settled down, though with a considerable list. The captain, sobered by shock, called for calm, promising to right the boat by daylight. So we snatched a little more sleep, and before dawn heard the crew working feverishly to get the launch off the rocks; eventually they succeeded, with help from the river which was tidal at that level.

That day we sailed through mangrove swamps, a strange dream-like area, where little crabs ran about in the black mud through the roots of the trees. The heat was stifling, with a burning sun above, the torrid air not stirred by even a breath of wind. Then we learnt that the ship's drinking water had run out. Apparently there was a settlement nearby where water might be found, so one of the crew lowered himself into the black mud and struggled across. While we waited we watched some small boys catching crabs and coming up covered from head to foot in black mud. They passed the crabs to an old woman with frizzy, greying hair and a bony black face, who threw them into a pot for a moment or so and then strained them out and shelled them. She looked like a witch over a cauldron. The man who had gone

Dalechampia affinis, Kamiranga

Peccaries, hog-like animals

Neoglaziovia variegata

Bellucia pentamera

in search of water returned without having reached the settlement, which turned out to be a figment of the imagination. All we could do was to continue on our way until night fell.

At dawn there were loud shouts of dismay. Our launch was docked in the mud of the river bed and it was impossible to move her. During the night the tide had gone out and would not come in to lift the boat for several hours – some murmured 'perhaps longer'. The alternative was to chain haul the boat to where the water might be deep enough to float her again. All the men and a few women, including Rita and me, started hauling. It was back-breaking work, but after a long struggle we reached deeper water and loud cheers went up as we were waterborne again.

In Viseu we did not have to wait long for the boat to Bragança. Once again the cargo outweighed the passengers for it included twenty-four lean and hungry pigs resembling wild rather than fat, domesticated animals. A squealing, sorry band, they were driven into the hold with blows, waving of sticks and shouts. As the hold was open to the deck, they remained in view for the whole voyage, while their fleas deserted their skinny hosts for the passengers.

During the voyage an unfortunate pig got his hind leg trapped between two floorboards and uttered such unearthly screams that the passengers protested. Eventually one of the crew went down to release it, but was so brutal that the pig screamed in agony and sprang through a porthole into the river, swimming swiftly for the shore. Two of the crew rapidly lowered a canoe, and armed with bush knives, paddled madly in the creature's wake. But it swam like a fish, and soon landed and dashed through the dense vegetation bordering the river. The two men started to hack their way through this jungle, but retired defeated, much to my and Rita's delight. The animal was lost forever, but with his lack of jungle experience would he be a prey for the jaguar? No, he would probably become the leader of a herd, we were told, and the most savage when attacking man. Not without justification, we felt.

In Bragança we were greeted with a friendliness very different from our earlier reception. By this time we were bronzed and thinner, and our boots and clothes showed we had been travelling the hard way, so while we waited for the train to Belém, we were eagerly questioned about our journey. We left the little town in an atmosphere of goodwill, and had uneventful journeys to Belém and São Paulo.

On arrival in São Paulo airport all was noise and bustle. We felt conspicuous in our jungle clothes which contrasted strangely with the summer dresses of other women, while our large baskets of forest plants also attracted attention. Murutucum, that haven of green peace, where I had my first taste of the joys and hardships of Amazonas, seemed the other side of the planet.

Hibiscus bifurcatus Cav.

Guaruba

Catasetum sp.
Natural hybrid ?
Amazonas, Rio Negro 1972 ?

Margaret Mee

1962

THE MATO GROSSO:
ABANDONED IN THE DENSE FOREST

The journey up Rio Gurupi had been a hard one, but it had prepared me for future expeditions through the Amazon jungle. By trial and error I had learned what equipment was essential, what materials would be necessary for my work, what food and medical supplies were required, and the importance of comfortable and protective clothing. But, more importantly, my close contact with the vast forests and waterways of the Amazon had given me an overwhelming desire to go back for further discoveries and inspiration. Having caught a glimpse of the endless possibilities in those days in the forests of the Gurupi, I realised I was fascinated by that strange, exhilarating world where every tree and plant was new to me and which was teeming with animals, birds and insects. I was haunted by my wish to return, so when the opportunity presented itself in 1962 I eagerly accepted.

An anthropologist and his wife, who were planning an expedition to northern Mato Grosso to contact a tribe of Canoeiro Indians, the Ericksa, and study their way of life and culture, invited me to join them. John, the anthropologist, had gone ahead to contact the Indian tribe in Aripuana on Rio Alto Juruena and to prepare the camp there. Susan, his wife, and I were to follow later.

Opposite. *Catasetum*, possibly a natural hybrid

47

Velloziaceae

Tillandsia paraensis
(Bromeliaceae)

We left São Paulo by plane for Cuiabá, stopping en route at Campo Grande and Corumbá. Between Corumbá and Cuiabá the Pantanal lay below, a primeval landscape of lakes and waterways stretching to the horizon, with small hills isolated by flood water or linked by narrow necks of land. Nearing Cuiabá the landscape changed to table-topped mountains, extensive lakes, and forest clothing the plains and mountain slopes.

Cuiabá at that time was a small town, the outskirts relatively new and dull, but the centre old and charming with a church overlooking the main square and a row of graceful palms. From Cuiabá we were to fly to Gleba Arinos, a small staging post on Rio Arinos, but because of the threatening weather, we cancelled our plane reservations. Furthermore, we heard that the little plane we were intending to take had had at least eight forced landings or near disasters on previous occasions, and now it was long delayed in the interior, with no news of its whereabouts. So when we left Cuiabá two days later, on what was to prove a four-day journey, the station wagon we travelled in was so full of passengers that luggage was restricted to hammocks, rugs and food. The larger pieces, including my plant collecting tins, were to follow on by truck with a group of rough-looking rubber prospectors.

Later on we passed through the *cerrado*, or scrubland, just beyond the small town of Rosario do Oeste, and were still travelling through this region when night fell. A cool wind was blowing. The sand track into which the road eventually deteriorated became deeper and rougher, and the passengers had to help push the vehicle out of the deep sandy ruts, an activity we grew accustomed to as the track got progressively worse. Manuel, our driver, manoeuvered skilfully over seemingly impassable terrain and bridges consisting of loose logs.

We passed no houses, no people. It was the loneliest place imaginable. From time to time, wild animals appeared, dazzled by the car headlights. Two beautiful foxes, silver-grey ears tipped with black, ran across the track; four *jaguatiricas* vanished into the night. On one occasion whilst pushing the station wagon out of the sand I saw the imprints of jaguar pads.

Late that night we arrived at an extensive rubber plantation on the banks of Rio Arinos where we were shown to a hut. I hung my hammock from the rafters and Susan slept in rugs on the floor.

Before dawn we continued on our way towards Gleba Arinos, so that by daybreak we reached a wonderful *cerrado*. Unfortunately much of this glorious country had been reduced to ashes to satisfy the cattle-breeders' demands for new grass for their herds.

We passed the next night in a grand house on the plantation belonging to a well-known and influential Baiana. Here Susan and I had the luxury of a room to ourselves.

A sunny morning greeted us after the cold night, and from the tree tops I could hear parrots and macaws calling. That day we drove through an isolated region of virgin forest, which so far was still amazingly free from the destructive interference of the 'civilizados'. A few recent fires had thinned some areas, but there was still an abundance of plants, including the vines of scarlet passion flowers. This was the territory of an Indian tribe known as the Botacudos or Beço de Pau (lit. wooden lip), due to the discs worn by the men in their lower lips. This warlike tribe had never been subdued.

On arrival in Gleba Arinos we were directed to the house of Willi Meyer, a pleasant and hospitable man, who showed us to a room with a shower, the greatest luxury after the dirt and dust of the journey. This was to be our home whilst waiting to start our trip up the river to join John. Our host and hostess' main interest was cattle breeding, and Sra. Meyer also kept birds: two guans, three macaws, a parrot, and a fierce toucan who was cruelly isolated in a cage too small for him. My heart bled for the poor creature, who, imprisoned in the midst of his native forest, listened sadly to his companions singing as they flew free across the skies. Besides these birds, there were two emus who fed from the hand. The birds of the forests flying free were wonderful – *japims* (caciques) in bands, hundreds of *curicas* (a bird of the parrot family), parrots and macaws. But there was a strange lack of epiphytes. Maybe they were sprayed with DDT.

We dined with the Meyer family and an Indian boy of four years, a beautiful child who was being 'brought up' by Sr. Meyer. When venison appeared on the table the boy refused to eat it, since it was forbidden to his tribe, and our irritated host ordered him to leave the table, which he did with the dignity of a chieftain. We were shown photos of the Canoeiro Indians, a fine looking people to whose tribe I imagined the child belonged. And of course we were told disturbing stories of those who visited the tribe and never returned. . .

Passiflora sp.

A *jaguatirica*, a wild cat, smaller than a jaguar

Araeococcus flagellifolius

Before continuing our journey to John's encampment on Rio Alto Juruena, we had to wait for our baggage, so Susan and I passed the time by venturing into the forest where I collected a bromeliad. From its long and narrow mottled leaves it appeared to be an *Araecoccus flagellifolius*. In the midst of collecting we were startled by a heavy animal crashing through the bushes – possibly a tapir, of which there are many in this region.

Because the crew of the boat which was to take us up river were at wedding party, it was not till the afternoon when the interminable celebrations were over that they were ready to leave Gleba Arinos. As soon as this news reached us, Susan and I went down to the port and embarked on the small launch, the *Santa Rosa*. At least two of the crew were still mellow from the festivities, though not Candido, the pilot, a Munducuru Indian and by far the most handsome of the crew. He turned out to be a wonderful pilot, navigating the most perilous rapids with calm and confident assurance. Later in the journey I met Candido's cousin, Innocencia. She had the same serenity of face, fine features, and lithe movements. She paddled her little canoe, carrying Susan and me, over treacherous rapids with the same calm confidence, and on the island where we landed climbed seemingly impossible trees with an easy grace, throwing down orchids into my open arms. If these two are typical of the tribe, the Munducuru must be a wonderful people.

The *Santa Rosa* was a small working launch, used for collecting the rubber from the plantations scattered far up along Rio Arinos and Rio Alto Juruena. The sickening smell of crude rubber lingered throughout. Our battered luggage was piled in, my plant collecting tins still showing great dents in the metal, for they had arrived almost flat as pancakes after their journey from Cuiabá. When I first saw them in Gleba it was only with difficulty I restrained my tears. When opened they revealed my precious, and only, saucepan, hopelessly squashed, paint tubes oozing among my clothes, and many other sorry sights. But all this, and the sour looks of the guilty rubber prospectors who had used the tins either as seats or pillows on their four-day journey, were soon forgotten as the *Santa Rosa* began her voyage up the still waters of Rio Arinos.

One of the crew was a pale young man of German descent who told us how, on his first day as boat's engineer, he had been pierced between the ribs by an arrow fired by one of the Beço de Pau. The Indians had appeared in numbers, shooting arrows into the air as a friendly warning. These fell about the launch, and another member of the crew, also on his first trip, panicked and answered the shower of arrows with a rifle shot. The Indians retaliated and the young man was the unfortunate victim. As we passed the region where some of the tribe were to be found, he pulled down the canvas blinds of the boat's cabin in case of stray arrows.

That first night on the waters of the Arinos we slept aboard in our hammocks, the boat moored opposite the squalid hut of two rubber tappers. I slept little, enjoying the many sounds of the water and life in the tropical forest. Soon after dawn we moved on down river which gradually lost its placid aspect and grew more and more beautiful and dramatic. It was broken up by islands and numerous groups of huge stones on whose submerged surfaces grew rose-pink aquatic plants. These stones clearly showed the rise of the waters during the rainy season – white below the water line, black above. They were shaped with a purity of form that Henry Moore or Barbara Hepworth might have dreamed of. The country at this point was flat, small hills occasionally rising behind the forests where Assai and dark Buriti palms grew in profusion.

Diving birds were plentiful, their black heads with yellow beaks appearing just above the surface. In the evening light macaws flew overhead in pairs, the red sunlight glinting on their brilliant plumage. Silent, solitary storks, with enormous wing spans, flew to their shadowy homes in the jungles. I collected a beautiful *Galeandra juncoides* at the mouth of this river and Rio Alto Juruena.

Araeococcus flagellifolius

That evening we moored near the mouth of Rio dos Peixes, aptly named, as there the crew caught two enormous fishes, a barracuda and a *pirarucú* (a very large edible fish). By this time, our stodgy diet of stale bread, old cheese and soft chocolate, with occasional packet soup dissolved in cold river water, was replaced by many varieties of fish, fish and more fish.

Before dawn we left our mooring, but the mist over the river was so dense that we had to moor the boat to a giant half submerged tree, and wait until the sun rose and burnt off the mist before continuing on our way. The vista where the Rio Arinos and Rio Alto Juruena met was magnificent. Soon after we had passed this impressive watersmeet, suddenly the river widened, flowing swiftly around islets and groups of rocks leaving only

Heliconia sp.

narrow navigable channels. We were buffeted through what seemed like a swirling sea, and it was here that we lost two of the five convoy canoes we were towing and where Candido effected their spectacular rescue.

The Rio Alto Juruena flows through the northern Mato Grosso, and is difficult to navigate due to the frequent rapids and groups of rocks, rounded by the elements across the ages, which sometimes form barriers across the wide expanse of the river. We passed many islands, some large and densely forested, others of rock and sand, sparsely covered with tortured trees and bushes, moulded into strange shapes by the rise and fall of the waters and exposure to the raging storms which sweep the river during the sultry summer months.

My plant finds grew more and more interesting: Heliconias, Catasetums, Brassavolas, Tillandsias followed in swift succession. Trees were spectacular, and amongst the dark forest foliage gleamed leafless giants with shining white trunks and spreading boughs – Bombacaceae and Bignoniaceae. Golden Ipé and red Bombax were in flower, and from one tree's dark domed canopy hung long, deep red tassels of blossom.

While the crew prepared the boat to pass a great rapid, we moored to a giant fallen tree, and here we met a fly in the ointment – the minute blood-sucking fly (*pium*) which gets through the finest net and sucks until its victim is covered with little streams of blood, reminiscent of old oil paintings of martyred saints. They were so numerous and invasive here that I was forced to wear a veil, but I braved them to swim and wash away the day's sweat in the cool, refreshing river. Ipé trees, their slender white trunks bearing panicles of yellow flowers, lined the river banks.

At Seringal, a small settlement on the river trading with Gleba, Geraldo, a river pilot and overseer of the rubber tappers and the rubber tappers' launch, came on board. He was of European descent, blond and muscular.

Our next stop was at a lonely and mean hut which the crew laughingly told me was known as the 'house of the beautiful wife'. Poor woman, she was anything but beautiful. She stood in the dark doorway of her ramshackle hut, a strange figure – her dark face looking out from a once white headcover, her tatty long dress hanging sloppily over her trousers. She was obviously delighted to have visitors, smiled happily, showing large gaps between her teeth. Perhaps she had once been attractive but her hard life in a primitive hut had destroyed her beauty. In these distant jungles there is no question of medical or dental treatment, and malaria, parasitic illnesses and anaemia are common and debilitating.

From time to time, shots from the dense forest informed us that tappers wanted us to stop so they could buy merchandise. Then we would moor the launch while transactions took place. This was an ideal opportunity for collecting plants and Susan and I would become so absorbed that we wandered far from the boat until impatient shouts from the crew brought us hurrying back.

One day we picked up a rubber tapper paddling a dug-out canoe with two dogs in it. He was known as the Baiano, though his name was Jeronimo. Just as he and his large retriever stepped into our launch, his canoe listed and sank, leaving another, large black, dog struggling in the river. The crew pulled this dog into the boat, whilst Candido, calm and courageous as usual, jumped into the river and saved the Baiano's possessions, including his rifle. Later that day, three more rubber tappers with their hunting dogs came aboard. They were a wild looking crowd.

We sailed on late into the night after passing one of the biggest and most difficult rapids at sundown. The river here was magnificent, tremendously wide with scattered islands and groups of smooth stones, white above the waterline and black below.

At nightfall we arrived at the Baiano's isolated hut. A large powerful man, Jeronimo was a mulatto of about forty years old. His small beard, combined with a Moorish-type of headdress worn as protection against *pium*, gave him the appearance of a character from

Opposite. *Heliconia adeliana*

Tillandsia sp.

the Arabian Nights. He was rare for the type, for he said that he did not smoke, drink or fish, and certainly he lived in a very clean well ordered hut. He fed us on rice cooked in powdered milk – and very good it tasted as we were so hungry – and gave us condensed milk to drink. He was eager that we should visit him on our return and offered me an unlimited supply of *parasitas* (epiphytes) as bait.

The next day we called at four or five huts on the river where the rubber tappers, who were out working, had left notes of what provisions they needed. So, while the crew weighed out the rice and manioc, we went collecting.

Baracão was one of the largest villages we passed on the Alto Juruena. Although an

Indian village, the inhabitants were dressed in 'civilizados' clothes for they had been in touch with the outer world for some time. They were hospitable people and treated us to a delicious meal of turtle with rice. The children were most curious about the black veil I was wearing against the irritating flies, and one little girl timidly lifted it and, having done this once, seemed to find it an irresistible pastime. From these people we learned that John was in the neighbourhood.

The sound of an outboard motor broke the forest silence and our excitement grew as in the distance a large gleaming aluminium canoe came in sight. As it came nearer we recognised John. The greetings over, our baggage was transferred to the canoe and, piloted by an Urubu Indian, Pará, we sped off in the direction of the camp in Aripuana on the banks of Rio Alto Juruena. A small area of the forest had been cleared of underbrush, and here three hammocks with mosquito netting hung from the trees. There were crude racks for stores and equipment – with plenty of the latter (later it took two rubber tappers, each with a large canoe, several journeys to shift it up river).

I was introduced to other members of the expedition: Roberto, a tall heavily-built man of early middle age, the camp adjutant, and a boy of about twelve, who appeared to be pigeon-chested, but who afterwards I realised, like so many in this mosquito-infested region, was suffering one of the effects of malaria – an enlarged liver. His hammock was slung beside mine for he was supposed to help me with plant collecting. However, he stayed for only a few days and was replaced by a friendly Indian boy from Baracão called José. Pará, a young Indian married to a German girl in Gleba Arinos, was the occupant of the third hammock. He was an excellent pilot, a good hunter and, above all, had a wonderful sense of humour, a great asset when facing the frequent difficulties of these regions. Pará moved his hammock some distance away from mine and José's, which was fortunate, for every night, as he was addicted to rum, he was violently sick in the bushes.

John, Susan and Roberto slept nearby in a hut in the Indian village, about ten minutes'

Galeandra chapadensis

Pseudobombax sp.

walk away through the forest. When darkness fell at about seven o'clock, they left with the hurricane lantern. Then the only light in our camp came from two tiny kerosene lamps whose flickering flames threw eerie, moving shadows around. My diary was written nightly by this wavering light, sometimes eked out by the fitful flames from the fire, but usually by this time, cooking over, the fire was a heap of smouldering ashes.

That first night, lying in my hammock under the trees beneath the sky, in the heart of virgin jungle, I slept little, listening instead to the strange unfamiliar sounds and looking into the trees above. A brilliant moon shone through the leaves. A porcupine lived overhead in the canopy and night monkeys played nearby. They were our constant companions. Indeed I grew to love the company of the monkeys who haunted the camp after dark, and even became bold enough to play on my hammock. They were good guards, too, and always gave a warning if a jaguar or smaller wild cats were in the vicinity.

I felt singularly unprotected in my hammock with its transparent mosquito net, so covered the net with a plastic sheet, for the condensation from the trees fell like a shower of rain into my hammock and on to me. Otherwise, as there was no rain in July and August and the waters of the Alto Juruena were at their lowest, sleeping under the tree canopy presented no problem. Although the heavy dews kept the forest green, whilst camping on the banks of this magnificent river for two months there were only two storms which brought rain.

The following morning Susan called for me and we went together to the village. As we walked up the jungle path leading to the village, I noticed that the trees had been thinned selectively, while the palms had been allowed to develop, as had giant trees, towering out of sight, with roots like buttressed walls.

Nearly all the men of the tribe had left the village, looking for a particular type of bamboo to make arrows, for it was rumoured they were about to go to war with a neighbouring tribe. The Ericksa are a fine looking people, but warlike and with a tradition of cannibalism; they had recently eaten some of the rubber tappers who had ill treated Indian women. They all wore numbers of heavy necklaces, bracelets of monkey skin, and some of the men wore large discs in the lobes of their ears. The women were beautiful and petite.

The communal village hut was a large building, completely covered with palm leaves, and patches of sunlight fell on the dry leaves transforming the colour to a soft gold. The 'front garden' was decorated with various shapes and sizes of animals' skulls on sticks, which gave a rather grim impression in the shades of the dark forest. We were welcomed by a young woman who led us into the large hut, pushing aside the leaves which covered the entrance, saying softly 'Amor, amor', this being a sign of friendship and courtesy. The hut, which housed twenty-five people, was dark as night inside, so thankfully was free of *pium*. I strained my eyes to pierce the inky shadows, and gradually I made out the shapes of hammocks, some occupied by women. The children were playing silently on the earth floor amongst the ashes of the small, but ever-burning fires beneath the hammocks. A small, young woman, laden with ornaments was peeling yams; she was sitting in a sunbeam which gave the yams the colour of amethyst. She signed that I should come and sit beside her. From the shadows I was aware dark eyes were watching us shyly, curiously. The women spoke in hushed voices little more than whispers. Silence reigned, only broken from time to time by the laughter of the playing children or the cry of a baby. One of the women showed me her tiny, doll-like child, placing both my hands on the baby's head. Afterwards she blew softly over the infant's hair, as though to ward off any evil influences which I might have imparted with my stranger's touch. We were given sweet potatoes and chestnuts from the fire to eat, our hostess talking softly in her own language all the while. Later, accompanied by another woman and two men, all wearing

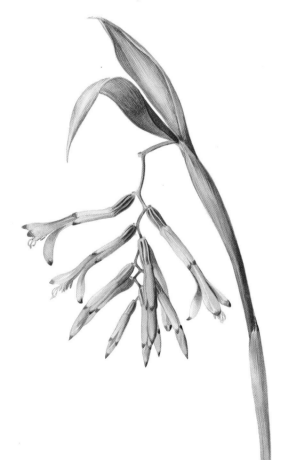

Billbergia distachia

knee-length necklaces and with beautifully groomed hair, she came into the forest to be photographed by John,

Aripuana stands on Rio Alto Juruena and, in shallow pools left by the river's overflow when the waters were high, we saw fish 'walking' considerable distances on their fins in the mud at the edge of the pools, depositing their eggs. They die as the mud dries, and the eggs eventually hatch out only when the rains return and the river rises. John was particularly interested in this for, besides being an anthropologist, he was a keen collector of ornamental fish.

It was on the west bank of this broad river, in forest which seemed to have been untouched since time immemorial, that I saw a lovely bromeliad (unclassified) for the first time, colonies spreading over the leafy ground. Unfortunately, the flowers were nearly over, and those which had not dried completely were beginning to fade. The large rosette, composed of orange pink bracts, was sunk in the centre of long thorny leaves. There were one or two ripe fruits, brilliant yellow and tasting of pineapple. From each mature plant radiated numerous offshoots. They were very different in appearance from the parent

I grew to love the company of the night monkeys who haunted the camp after dark

Hylocereus cf. setaceus (Cactaceae)

plant, the leaves being almost spatulate, purplish underneath and above. Indeed I hardly recognised them as bromeliads until I recalled that Tapiama, one of the Indians who often came to the camp, had brought me some of these young plants. These were being cultivated in the forest garden I had made, with other plants I had collected.

During the rains this area must be submerged, for the river rises at least three metres. This can be clearly seen on the great dome-like stones which stand in sculptured groups, again black below the waterline, white above. Walking inland, the ground became a maze of hummocks transversed by channels of black mud. The trees were tall, forming a dark canopy high above. In some parts of the forest there was little or no undergrowth. Where there was vegetation it was mainly marantas, heliconias and aroids. The trees varied considerably from fine and spindly to massive trunks supported by buttressed roots, like the walls of a fortress. Epiphytes were not abundant and were usually confined to the high branches of trees. Probably when the river overflows its banks the forest wears a very different aspect.

One day when John, Susan and I were busy collecting, we suddenly realised that our Indian guides had disappeared, and that none of us knew the track back to the canoe. Light was beginning to fail and John became alarmed and angry for he was aware of the dangers lurking in that part of the forest at night.

He ordered us into the *igarapé*, which would eventually flow into the Alto Juruena, but Susan refused on the grounds that it would spoil her only boots. I had no such excuse, and in any case was not going to argue with someone with such wide jungle experience, so I plunged into the water which at times was well above my knees. John, carrying his plastic bags in which swam new species of fish, hit a submerged hummock and fell on his face with a tremendous splash (he was tall and heavy), and the fish returned joyfully to their native habitat. John's outburst as he emerged covered with black mud was unrestrained. Drenched to the skin, we wandered through the forest calling loudly to the Indians. It was nearly dark when the distant voice of Pará responded. With great relief we

Tatupera (armadillo)

Streptocalyx poeppigii

emerged from the forest just as the sun disappeared over the river.

We were plagued by the biting flies all the time we were in Aripuana, and this made painting difficult. First I attempted working with a veil and wearing gloves, but both of these distorted my drawing and anyway the veil mesh was too open so the flies frisked in and out in triumph. My left eye suffered particularly badly, becoming very swollen. In the end all I could do to ward off the attacks was to wrap my hands in plastic. In spite of them I finished the painting I had set myself, but I had exhausted my supply of plants in flower and needed more to paint. So Pará and I went off in the canoe at break of day, crossed to the other side of the wide river, moored and walked into the forest.

Pará was armed with a rifle and a large hunting knife, the sheath stained with the blood of animals he had killed in the past. Almost immediately we left the river bank, on the leaf covered floor of this dark forest we saw colonies of plants and Pará climbed trees and lianas to collect Bromelias, Cattleyas and other orchids. Then we returned to the canoe, and found a still spot on the river which he said was the haunt of the enormous snake, the anaconda, and where we

Aechmea caudata

Radiokubi's wife was carried to the canoe

watched turtles and fishes in the clear depths until the heat of the sun became too much.

A convenient niche in a tree had been designated our post box, which the rubber tappers used as a collection and delivery point when their launch passed, but each time I looked my letters were still in the tree.

That night Geraldo called at the camp with the disturbing news of an intended Indian attack on the *Posto Indigena*, the area headquarters for Indian affairs and where a German pastor had a small mission. It would seem that the unpopular pastor was largely responsible for the situation, having absurdly insisted that the Indians should work an eight-hour day in his mission. Geraldo talked until dawn and I managed to snatch no more than an hour of sleep as dawn broke.

All in all it was a somewhat disturbed night. First a coati rushed screaming through the camp. Then there were strange noises in the river, plop! plop! and investigating by torchlight we saw an ocelot, then an alligator. After this the large porcupine started exploring in the tree canopies above. Finally, John and Susan heard a *jaguatirica* nearby.

But the following afternoon we were in a state of real tension when two rubber tappers met Pará and Roberto and passed on the news that the Beço de Pau Indians were attacking the *Posto Indigena* and that all the rubber tappers were leaving the area as quickly as possible. We thought it might be just a rumour, but then the rubber tapper Paraíba Doido gave his version of the story. According to Doido, who is not a well man (*doido* means crazy and I later learnt that, after a drunken brawl with a companion, he murdered the sleeping man with an axe), the attack by the Beço de Pau is an annual affair, and they do not leave their territory. However, after his departure John inspected guns and ammunition and we were warned not to go into the forest alone. Does this mean goodbye to my plant hunting? In the meantime I tried to adopt peace of mind and continued with my painting and cultivated my finds in my forest garden.

Shortly after some Indians visited our camp, among them Sheba, a pretty little woman with a large-stomached baby. She had about eight bracelets on either arm and was loaded with necklaces, including a small necklace of four jaguar teeth. Apart from this jewellery she wore nothing else but a palm fibre sling in which to carry the child. Sheba was accompanied by Tapiama who had been hunting with Pará, and as Tapiama ran all the time, Pará was quite exhausted. They had hoped to bring back wild pig but only succeeded in killing a poor little jacu, a game bird. I could not eat any.

I had happier encounters with other animals. I awoke early in the morning to hear what sounded like a dog barking. I jumped out of my hammock and ran down to the river from where the sound came, just in time to see six otters plunge into the water and swim away to an island where they stopped to sun and play. There were four adults with two young. From the island they swam across to the further shore which, because the river was so wide at that spot, was only just visible. These beautiful creatures were scarce as they were hunted for their skins. That same morning I walked from an *igarapé* into the middle of the forest. There, well hidden amongst the trees, was the communal hut of the chieftain Barari. His brother, Radiokubi was living there whilst Barari was away hunting. Radiokubi was handsome and lively, and wore a heavy necklace, feather ear ornaments and a loincloth of palm fibre. In the *maloca* lay Radiokubi's wife and her little son. One of her feet was swollen and painful and the leg half paralysed. She was very pretty, though dirty and thin. It appears a tree or branch had fallen and injured her leg. John persuaded Radiokubi to bring the woman and child to the camp so that her leg could be treated. She was carried in her hammock to the canoe, and eventually reached the camp and John's dispensary where a horde of people, mostly children, were waiting for remedies, mainly for dysentery and malaria.

Amazonian otter (*Ariranha*). These beautiful creatures were scarce as they were hunted for their skins

Our new Indian companion, Radiokubi, was a vivacious fellow and told us, mostly in sign language, of the many deaths amongst the Canoeira which had been caused by white men's diseases; of the revenge the Indians took on the rubber tappers who had introduced these illnesses; of gruesome details of cutting off heads and limbs, and eating eyes, cheeks and tongue. The tribe had five heads in the village and had made the teeth into necklaces. Radiokubi told many hair-raising stories about the anaconda and described how he had attempted to kill a young one about three metres long. But the wily reptile was too quick and hid under rocks in the river bed.

That night the newcomers slept in the open about fifty metres from the camp. But in the light of subsequent events later on in the night, they decided not to sleep in the open again, but to make a small sleeping hut nearby.

The first signs of trouble came when the night monkeys started to scream, the signal that some big cat was lurking in the neighbourhood. It was not long before I heard growling within a metre or so of my hammock. I lay cold with fear. It seemed as though the big cat passed underneath me. I heard Radiokubi calling frantically that there was a jaguar around, in spite of the brightly burning fire; then a shot from a rifle, and a loud crashing through the undergrowth as the animal fled into the forest.

Later I learned what had happened. A jaguar had attempted to seize his child and Radiokubi had thrown burning logs at it, but to no effect, for the creature merely retreated a little further into the shadows, waiting for an opportunity to return. In desperation, Radiokubi, unarmed, called Roberto, who reacted quickly by firing his rifle. I was restless for the remainder of the night, listening to the noise of the men building up the fires.

With the dawn Pará returned from hunting. He had been far away in the jungle for three days and nights, and had shot two tapirs. His back was covered with ticks as large as thumbnails. Susan and I had the greatest difficulty in removing them, and after trying spirit, lighted cigarettes, etc., we did it manually. The men went off to fetch the poor tapirs

Our new Indian companion, Radiokubi, and his son

Billbergia porteana (Bromeliaceae)

by canoe. I only saw them when they had been cut into pieces. Tapiama left the camp carrying an enormous bloody leg. Roberto told me two thousand tapirs had been killed in Gleba, and the numbers killed in Aripuana were probably as high. I wonder how long it will be before these beasts are extinct?

José, the Indian boy of seven assigned to help me in my collecting, was a charming child. He was extremely quick and intelligent and climbed trees with the ease and confidence of a marmoset, swinging to the more inaccessible ones on lianas. I shouted severely that he should come down before he broke his neck, but he only laughed mockingly and performed even more dangerous feats. Consequently he found me some lovely plants, including *Aechmea spruceii,* for which I had been searching all the time, and a *Billbergia* with a collar of red bracts and dark leaves mottled and striped with silver-grey.

Radiokubi and family established himself and his family in a small hut he had made of fresh green *babaçu* palm leaves. He also built himself a stove on which he roasted tapir, having received a share from Pará, as is customary with the Indians. But there was bad news from the Indian village further in the forest: the wife of the absent chieftain Barari had developed pneumonia, for which John gave her injections. Apart from humane reasons, we all hoped she would recover, as her death would put us under suspicion of practising witchcraft. In spite of the news that Barari would shortly return, the men of the tribe were all still away hunting or fighting, and John, impatient with their absence, had planned a five day journey, on foot, to a distant Indian village. However, he decided not to leave until Barari returned and before the the rubber tappers' launch had passed through Aripuana.

Bad news. John developed malaria. But in spite of this he had enough strength to fly into a rage when he heard that I had been into the forest collecting plants without leaving a message as to where I was going. And to make matters worse, that night a gang from the rubber plantation at Baracão arrived for medicines and stayed until next morning. They made sleep difficult, as they played a transistor radio at full blast until I asked for less noise because of our invalid. My head was raging and I just hoped that this was not a symptom of malaria. We now had two more invalids, Roberto with pains and sickness, and Paraíba Doido who fell ill as a result of drinking a litre of kerosene!

At last Barari returned, and he, his wife Talaao and child Tcherité came to our camp. Barari named many things for Susan who is making a vocabulary of indigenous words. He started to build a *maloca* beside that of Radiokubi, whose invalid wife I visited; I found the hut pleasant – cool and *pium*-free inside.

Early one morning, Susan came with the news that she and John were leaving for Gleba as John had developed a high fever. When the canoe had been loaded, the men went to fetch him and he could barely stagger along between them. He looked very sick, his face like greenish parchment. He had to lie flat in the canoe, and being tall and bulky there was only room for Susan and the pilot Pará. I had assumed that I would be leaving as well, and had quickly packed my plants in sacks and my hands were sore and full of thorns. To learn that I was to be left alone with Roberto and the Indian boy José stunned me. I said my goodbyes, but as I turned away, a feeling of loneliness and isolation overcame me and the tears rolled down my cheeks. The Indians had seen my distress and stroked my hair sympathetically, took my sacks back to the clearing and rehung my hammock. Then I replanted in my forest garden the plants I had recently dug up. Fortunately we were left a canoe, so would not be completely confined to the camp and its surroundings.

The days which followed were full of dangers and difficulties. Our food supplies were by now getting low, so José and Roberto went fishing but caught nothing. As soon as it was dark they set off again. As I was often left in the camp alone, Roberto instructed me how to use the rifle which hung on a tree near my hammock. The silence and darkness around made me feel very nervous and strained so I built up a good fire to drive away the shadows and loneliness. One day, one of the Indians came to the camp while I was alone and indicated that he wanted the gun, grabbing it from the tree and handling it carelessly. Although it was loaded, as calmly as possible I firmly took the rifle from him and explained as best I could that he could use it only with Roberto's permission. The Indians were a little in awe of Roberto who was well over six feet tall. At last the hunters returned, Roberto covered with terrible red weals that looked like urticaria. To make matters worse, an opossum raided our supplies and Roberto shot it. Poor creature! It looked so harmless and pretty in death.

As soon as night fell, the night monkeys were around us, quarrelling fiercely, while a loud-voiced owl sat in a tree above us, calling incessantly. Roberto, already nervous with his stings, jumped from his hammock, swearing and cursing the owl, took his gun and shot the poor creature. The noise awakened the Indians who came out to see what the trouble was. I was furious with Roberto and near to tears at this savagery. To placate me (so he imagined) he asked the Indians to make a collar of the feathers for me. Strange, that I, who hate all this killing, should be the recipient of the spoils. But I dared not refuse the collar for that would have given great offence to the Indians.

One day a horde of *mestizos* descended on the camp, and like a swarm of locusts cleared up any food they could lay their hands on, then formed groups around, killing time. Among them were several small children who tore up all the paper they could find, so that the camp looked like the day after Carnival in São Paulo. Roberto and José left with two of the 'visitors', rowing over to an island to collect a canoe. He was not expected to return before nightfall, so I prepared myself to suffer the remaining hordes until his return. They stayed all night and I could not sleep for the eating, shouting, crying of babies, and coming and going all night long. Then, during a moment of oblivion, an opossum crunching loudly in a tree awakened me. It occurred to me that he was devouring the last of our fish, and I jumped out of my hammock and, torch in hand, ran to the trees from whence the sound came. I flashed the light on the creature, hoping to scare it, but it ignored my efforts and, bold as brass, crunched all the louder. The last remnants of our fish littered the ground.

Billbergia porteana

An opossum raided our supplies

Tabebuia sp.

There was no doubt by now that Roberto had malaria. He returned from fetching the canoe in bad shape, though I wondered if he was exaggerating his ills to avoid routine camp work. Anyway, he was a bad invalid, and I prayed for the arrival of the rubber tappers' launch to get me out of the camp, where I was marooned and felt unable to do any work, collecting or painting. And food was very scarce.

Next José developed malaria and lay in his hammock with a high fever. It appeared that the island where the two men went to collect the canoe was the source of the trouble, for it was after the journey there that they both developed malaria. To make matters worse, there were hardly any remedies left. I walked over to the *maloca* one afternoon, only to find that Tapiama had malaria too: not so very serious, as I suppose he had a certain immunity, being an Indian of the region.

Inside the *maloca* it was dark and peaceful. I sat on the floor with the beautiful Indian girl Sheba and her baby. Sheba was peeling sweet potatoes which she mashed in a mortar, put into a pot with water and then added fish tripe. I tasted the wild honey which Tapiama got from a tree – it was delicious.

A sequel to Roberto's urticaria rash was the cure by Radiokubi with his knowledge of herbal remedies. He emerged from the forest with rolled leaves under his arm (I could not identify them), roasted them over the fire until the sap flowed, then dabbed this on the affected parts of Roberto's skin. In a short time his weals had disappeared. But he then succumbed to malaria and staggered back from the woods where he had gone hunting with Barari and fell into his hammock where he spent most of the day in pain and delirium. I felt desperate, and asked Radiokubi and José to paddle for help.

Night came. With nothing to do I could have enjoyed the marvellous stillness, the wide river before me, the star-filled sky, the cries of nocturnal birds and droning of insects to break the silence. Along the river bank hundreds of little phosphorescent eyes looked at me. I thought that one pair might be those of the coral snake – I saw him close on one occasion, a metre long, black white, black red, yellow bands, sliding along the river bed. Instead I decided to try and sleep, put on my pyjamas and got into my hammock with the revolver at my side.

A little while later I heard a splashing of oars. In response to our plight Raimundo, a kind rubber tapper from Ceará, had arrived with José and Radiokubi. Raimundo took things in hand immediately and, by the fitful light of a kerosene burner and the help of my torch to see the syringe needles, he gave Roberto two injections. He made an offer to move us, lock, stock and barrel to his *maloca*, and I would have gratefully accepted, but Roberto was insistent on remaining in the camp as we had to make sure Barari and his family stayed in case John returned. But I had a strong suspicion that the Indians were preparing to return to their *maloca* in the forest, fed up with the flies and the lack of fresh food. All they had been getting at our camp was rice, manioc, the fish caught and a few nuts. My hunch proved correct, for a little while later José came to me and said that the Indians were leaving. Their chief Barari confirmed this, explaining that the blood-sucking flies were insupportable in Aripuana. In his region there were none. He was going back to plant maize, sweet potato and banana and to live well. Of course, I agreed, it was the only reasonable thing to do, but he said that he would wait until the rubber tappers' launch arrived and Roberto and I were able to leave.

Coral snake (*Micrurus narducci*)

The rubber tapper Raimundo was a fine character, kind hearted and truly concerned about our difficult situation. Without help, he said, we could die here. He spoke from experience, for he once had malaria and was alone for eight days without food, when a rubber tapper found him and took him to Gleba. The more I saw of Raimundo, the more I admired him for his calm stoicism and courtesy, characteristics quite out of keeping among most of the rubber tappers I had come across. In appearance he reminded me of a Renaissance sculpture of John the Baptist wearing the traditional headcover as a protection against the ubiquitous flies. The next time he came to give Roberto an injection, he renewed his offer to take us upstream to his *maloca*.

Finally, things reached a climax when Roberto cracked up both in health and spirit. The fever raged. He vomited and cried for home and set me running to get water and a hundred other things. I was desperate, and vowed that, at the next opportunity, we would accept Raimundo's hospitality. However, instead of Raimundo, our next visitors were a member of José's family and a friend who turned up in a couple of canoes. They were so kind that I forgave the frequent spitting and the stacks of dirty cups and plates they produced. Then came their inevitable leave taking next morning, and again the invalid, José and I were alone in the wilderness.

Roberto improved after the injections but remained very weak and complaining. I told him firmly that I was in command and that we would accept Raimundo's offer come what may, even if I had to row to his *maloca* myself. At last Roberto, completely demoralised, but in one of his more lucid moments, agreed, and I asked Radiokubi to row with José to Raimundo to ask him to come and take us away. But Radiokubi fled to the forest with a gun to hunt monkeys, and all the other Indians were occupied with a *festa*. So I decided to paddle to Raimundo's *maloca* myself, taking José to help and navigate, since he knew more of the river than I, having been on it with his father.

Soon after noon, José and I set out in the heavy canoe. I wore my thick leather collecting gloves and black mosquito veil. We paddled hard for four hours or more, stopping once at Paraíba Doido's hut, where we accepted coffee with some misgivings in view of his reputation for violence. There we exchanged our heavy canoe for Doido's light one, which was so unbalanced that a sneeze would have tipped it over. Had there been no urgency, the journey would have been a pleasure, for the woods, plants and birds were enchanting. We passed groups of smooth stones enclosing lakes and forested islands, and many rapids. Twice José became confused and we struck rock, but managed to keep an even keel. Then we had to push ourselves clear of a tree lying just below the water surface in whose branches we became trapped. José, completely exhausted and near to tears, almost lost his paddle, declaring that he could go no further. I pointed out that if he did this he would never see his mother again and we could both expect a watery grave if we did not reach Raimundo's hut before nightfall. I tried to cheer him up, telling him to take courage, and he soon responded with spirit and, repeating 'courage, courage', paddled with all his might. Just as the great red sun dipped below the horizon we came in sight of Raimundo's distant palm thatched *maloca* at the tip of a long narrow island dividing the river into two arms. At this point the river was seething with rapids, and it was with great courage and concentration that the boy followed the channel which his father had shown him, through the turbulent waters. We fell exhausted on a white sandy beach just as the sun went down behind the forests.

Raimundo, who had seen us approaching, came down to the beach. He was amazed at our feat, and decided to paddle us back to our camp in his large canoe. Night had already fallen when we started our journey. There was a brilliant half moon and a star-filled sky lighting the swiftly flowing river. A heavenly night. Only bird cries and the plashing of the paddles on the water broke the silence. We grounded on a rock but, with careful

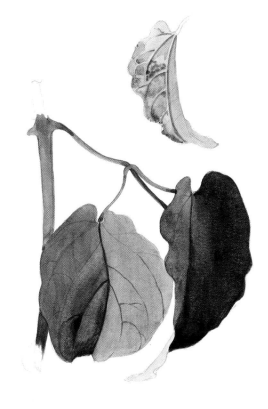

Lundia sp.

Aechmea bromeliifolia

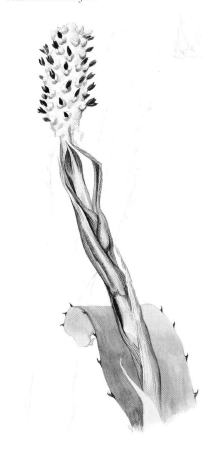

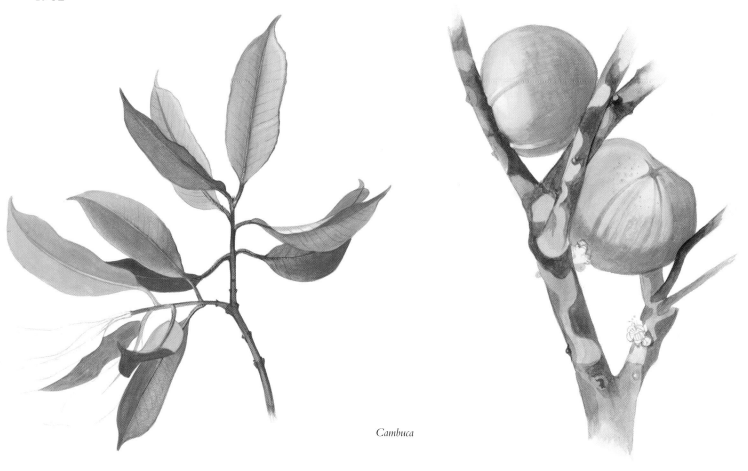

Cambuca

manoeuvring, Raimundo freed the canoe, but nevertheless water came rushing in, and I bailed out until my arm ached, but to no avail. Then we all three bailed and managed to clear most of the water, but when we reached a convenient stopping point the canoe was on the verge of sinking. Raimundo hung his hammock for the night, and I went off and had a bathe by moonlight.

Early next morning we repaired the canoe as best we could and finally reached our camp where we loaded two canoes with my plants and other baggage. Raimundo would go back to fetch Roberto later. After an exhausting journey in the heat of the morning sun, we reached Raimundo's *maloca*. On the way I was thrilled to see a jaguar sunbathing on one of the islets.

Raimundo's *maloca* was typical of the region, lightly built and covered with the leaves of *babaçu* palms. It was spotlessly clean, and the pans hanging in the kitchen shone like silver. He had cultivated papaya and watermelon and a few native vegetables in his little garden which was constantly raided by cutting ants. As usual, he had some 'guests' – not very welcome I felt – who sprawled around – two men and two women with three children, eating enormous portions of turtle. I told Raimundo that I preferred to sleep in the open, as I should feel too crowded sleeping inside the hut with the women and children. So once again I slept under the trees. And my plants were well looked after, for Raimundo made a rack in the forest, where I hoped they would be safe from the attacks of the particularly vicious ants which were a menace. Every time I visited the plants an enormous lizard bounded across my path.

Raimundo and two rubber tappers returned to the camp at Aripuana to fetch Roberto, still an invalid and complaining incessantly. Later the men went back to the camp again to collect the rest of the baggage and John's equipment from an abandoned *maloca* where it had been hidden. The equipment would remain stored away under the careful eye of Raimundo, the most respected rubber tapper in the area. Once all this had been successfully accomplished and we were reunited our plan was to await the rubber tappers' launch to take us to Gleba Arinos. There then followed weeks of peace and tranquillity, when hunger and fear completely disappeared. Each evening the sun went down in a golden blaze over one arm of the river, and the white moon rose over the other. As night drew on the landscape was bathed in silver light, and we sat in front of the hut, Raimundo telling us tales.

But the day came when I had to leave this haven of peace. The sound of a distant outboard motor gave rise to much speculation as to who could be coming this way. At last, it was Geraldo with the rubber tappers' launch. The boat moored outside Raimundo's *maloca*, and we all greeted each other, three of the new arrivals speaking English! Along with Geraldo and the crew, there were two students studying the local tongue, a Swiss traveller and a man named Fritz, a remarkable man and an old friend of Roberto. The students and Fritz set up camp with Roberto who had cheered up considerably on meeting Fritz. That night, a tall rubber tapper visited us and spun stories of the forests. Others appeared, including Paraíba Doido, and we had quite a feast which I helped prepare. With the launch came a letter from Greville, so long awaited, as well as much needed malaria remedies.

The next day the rubber tappers' boat and its passengers left for the *Posto Indigena*. When it returned in a few days Roberto and I would join it for the journey to Gleba. In the meantime, I went collecting with Raimundo who, tired of endlessly collecting raw rubber, offered to take me to a little rocky islet by canoe which was impossible to reach by other means. It was gloriously peaceful paddling along the river to the island, which

The jaguar is a big cat, and likes to play

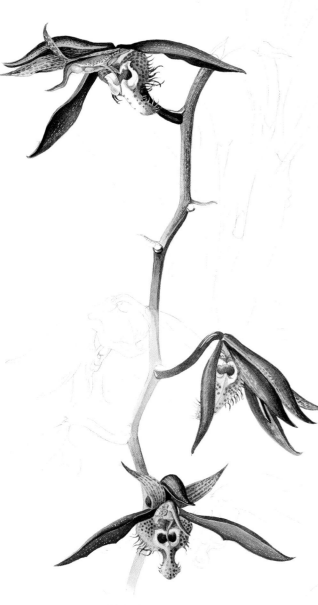

Catasetum saccatum

was a veritable paradise for plants. There I found a remarkable orchid, *Catasetum saccatum*. Over the gnarled trees, which resembled guavas, and were certainly of the Myrtaceae family, were the massed silver roots and large pseudo-bulbs of the orchid, some even with dried feminine flowers. On the lichened bark, clinging to the very roots, were groups of wasp nests – neatly-lidded papery cups made of a substance like papier maché. The wasps (or bees), whose homes they had been, had left when the orchid flowers had faded. Dried water plants festooned the twigs and branches of these trees and bushes and the waterline on the smooth stones showed that the Catasetums could only have been about half a metre above the river's surface during the rainy season.

In company with this orchid two species of bromeliads grew in the trees, *Tillandsia paraensis*, with its pink and silver foliage and cyclamen flowers, and a magnificent *Billbergia* whose leaves formed a tube protected by cruel black thorns. From this tube hung a lovely inflorescence, below a collar of magenta bracts, and above a complex spike of green calices crowned with yellow flowers.

Later I went down to the rack in the forest to prepare my plants for the journey to Gleba. But I did not get very far before I saw a jaguar's tail waving behind some bushes. Remembering Raimundo's warnings not to run away, for the jaguar is a big cat, and likes to play, I walked away at a smart pace, looking behind me from time to time, until I felt the distance between us was great enough, then took to my heels and ran like the wind. Raimundo, aware it was around, appeared, rifle in hand, but fortunately the beast had moved away and was safely hidden in the forest.

There are rumours that John has not been suffering from malaria for some time and so has decided to return soon. He will get a shock to find the camp dismantled, the Indians, his henchman and me gone. We also had reports that the rubber gatherers' launch was now returning via Ceará on its way to Gleba. The news arrived with the German pastor, who had left the *Posto Indigena*, and about whom we had heard so many rumours. He was at the helm of his launch, and aboard were the three English speakers. They stopped awhile to prepare a wild boar which they had shot on the river, and to give Raimundo a portion as custom dictated. The pastor was a dour, humourless German, who spoke very poor Portuguese. As it departed, their launch, which had a heavy list to portside, nearly took away two trees from the river bank.

Aechmea tocantina

There were turtles on these islets

We returned to the *maloca* and I got my plants and other belongings ready just in time to see the rubber collectors' launch arrive. Geraldo was in a hurry to leave and did not want to linger.

I left Raimundo with many regrets. He had been so kind and generous, his *maloca* had been so pleasant and peaceful, and the collecting trips with him so rewarding. There had been wonderful moonlit nights when we and his companions had talked far into the night under the trees. I had been able to bathe in the Alto Juruena by moonlight, after the heat of the days. And now I faced a difficult journey.

We had passed two rubber plantations when we saw the pastor's launch moored. The crank shaft had broken, so the complete crew with baggage boarded our launch, already overladen with passengers and rubber stinking to high heaven. After more than an hour spent with the pastor retrieving usable parts of his engine, we left and soon were within sight of the Baiano's plantation. Jeronimo shouted a greeting to Geraldo to stop, but Geraldo turned a deaf ear and sped on in spite of the Baiano's insistence that I should disembark for the plants he had collected specially for me, as promised. So, followed by curses from the angry fellow, we sailed on, leaving him with a scowl on his face. I wondered what lay behind this, but Geraldo was reticent and I never found out.

To lighten the load, we had to land four or five men when we came to one of the most dangerous of the rapids. A great barrier of rocks over which foamed gushing waters confronted us. How Geraldo found a channel, I could not imagine, and we were stationary at times, the currents were so powerful. On the rocks under the water, a pink aquatic flower grew in profusion. We picked up the men in calmer waters, but even then they had to wade out waist high to embark.

All the way the forests were lighted with the golden flowers of Ipés (Bignoniaceae) in full bloom, and bombaxes sprouting new leaves from recently bare branches. It seemed as though it was springtime in this part of the river!

At the approach of night we moored off a small island, and hung our hammocks in the trees. The isle was one large rock, full of inland pools and forested on two sides. The men loaded their guns before retiring to their hammocks, as they assured me that this was a haunt of jaguars. After supping by the light of a big fire and a full moon I had a dip in the cool waters. The night thrilled with bird cries and the humming of myriads of insects.

I could not sleep for thinking and remembering what I had seen during the day along the Alto Juruena: the strong dangerous currents which only experienced men could handle in a canoe; herons on the numerous little islands in the river; on the sandy shore, minute purple and yellow flowers; shrubs full of berries and lichens amongst which grew orchids and tillandsias, and the aggressive *Aechmea tocantina,* armed with large black thorns. Apart from the beautiful birds which we saw on these islets, there were tiny bats, turtles and the much feared constrictor, the anaconda.

At Baracão I did a ridiculous thing. Stepping into the launch from the canoe (the waters were too shallow for the launch to land there), the canoe not being secured, I fell backwards, knocked the back of my head and was totally immersed. My first thought was for the camera and sketchbooks, but Paul (one of the student linguists) was quick witted enough to rescue these, whilst Geraldo hauled me up, a groaning, dripping mess until I could stagger into a *maloca* to change. My head ached the next day with the slight concussion and large lump on the back of my head.

One morning, the sun shone on an imposing barrier of rock across the wide expanse of river – the Cachóeira dos Indios. There we proceeded to unload some of the cargo as the waters are shallow and the currents furious. Fortunately it was only a short distance on foot through the forest, over the

rocks which are totally submerged after the rains. From the shore we watched the launch struggling to cross the rapids, but three times she failed to make it. So the remaining cargo of raw rubber was unloaded and the petrol cans shifted to the front of the boat. At last the rapids lay behind, the cargo was reloaded, the passengers re-embarked and we sailed on in calm waters. But the calm was shortlived, and a few hours later our pilot was struggling with more rapids. There we made no headway over the surging river. So all the male passengers left to lighten the boat, and eventually we struggled through.

There was no end to our adventures that day on Rio Arinos, for soon after passing the mouth of Rio dos Peixes we struck rock with tremendous force. The crash tilted the craft to the left, and while Geraldo tried to right the boat the other side hit the water so fiercely that we were drenched, the canvas awning unfurled and some of the cargo and passengers' belongings shot off the roof of the launch into the river. I saw with dismay my precious plant tins and sacks careering downstream with assorted boxes and a big petrol drum following. The rescue team – crew and passengers – dived into the water like a pack of otters, fishing out the cargo. There was a desperate race to stop the petrol drum from reaching the rapids, the stronger swimmers managing to head it off. All the floating objects having been retrieved, the divers got busy salvaging torches, tin mugs and plates from the depths. It took some expert manoeuvring on Geraldo's part to reach groups of men on the rocks with their rescued items. I hardly dared look at my plants, though the tins floated beautifully. I think most of my food supplies went down, including my precious packets of soup.

The next day proved eventful, too. We saw seven tapirs on our way up Rio Arinos, two of them young, lovely creatures. The men shot at them, but missed every time – happily. So they decided to disembark and hunt the next tapir they saw. Soon a large animal came in sight, bathing in the river. The men took their guns and Paul his camera to photograph the 'kill'. But the wily tapir, facing a row of rifles, charged into the midst of them, scattering the 'brave hunters' on the forest floor and knocking the cameraman and his machine flying. I laughed with delight when they returned empty handed and dishevelled with glum faces.

Cinco Bocas, the last rapids of the voyage, were spectacular. A complicated meeting place of five streams, full of treacherous rocks and fast flowing currents, it was one of the most difficult to pass at that time of year (August) when the water was low So I was thankful when the overcrowded boat finally arrived in Gleba Arinos. There Geraldo put my plants and baggage in his truck, and through clouds of red dust drove me to the so-called 'hotel'. When I reached the doorway of this large *maloca* on stilts, I ran straight into Susan and John. Had they seen a ghost they could not have paled more, nor looked more incredulous. Apparently they were convinced that I had died in the forests of Alto Juruena, either of malaria or starvation. I reproached them for not having sent anyone to rescue those of us they had left behind in the camp, and was embarrassed by the lame excuses they gave – short of petrol, their pilot ill, etc. I did not pursue the matter any further, but I knew I would never forget their thoughtlessness.

I recovered my calm somewhat, when on the journey to Cuiabá in the truck of some prospectors from Gleba, I was rewarded by the unforgettable sight of the superb tree, *Qualea suprema (Erisma calcaratum)*. There, in the gallery forest, gleamed this blazing blue canopy, the colour of gentians. I saw this spectacle again in the Corrego do Rio Mutum. I decided that one day I would go in quest of the blue Qualea.

Two years after that journey the billbergia I collected with José's help flowered for the first time. The long pendent inflorescence was encased in pale green bracts from which gradually emerged olive green flowers, long petals gleaming like satin, which rolled up into little scrolls above the furry white calices. As I painted the exotic bromeliad I had

Seeds of Billbergia

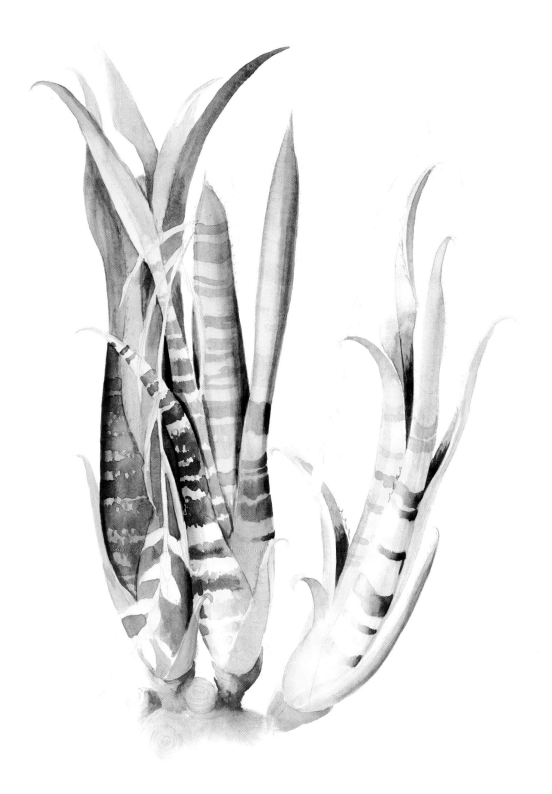

Billbergia decora

found, my mind went back to that primeval forest in the Alto Juruena as I had seen it last, golden with the flowers of the Ipé trees and the magnificent river flowing swiftly over its rocky bed.

The catasetums I found with Raimundo in August, when the heat was overwhelming, were so full of tropical vigour that the most mature plants flowered in the temperate February climate in my garden in São Paulo. A spray of seventeen dark red blooms developed. They were bat-like in form, and below their spreading petals hung the fringed spotted labellum. Later I was able to paint the feminine form, with its three large flowers, which had originated on that same rocky islet far off in Rio Alto Juruena.

1964/5

UAUPÉS AND BEYOND

KINDLY NUNS, DRUNKEN GOLDWASHERS AND A SPEED-BOAT

Clusia (taracuá)

The camp in Aripuana (Mato Grosso) had been within two days' paddling by canoe of the Rio Tapajós which in turn flows into the Amazon. The thought that I had been so near direct access to that great waterway determined me that my next journey would be to the heart of Amazonas. In discussion with scientists who had explored that region, and after poring over maps, I decided to make my next goal Rio Uaupés, in the far north-west corner of Brazil.

The Brazilian Air Force plane left Congonhas Airport, São Paulo, on a cold, grey November day with a chill wind blowing. The plane's interior was spartan – wooden benches and no comfort of any kind – but the aircrew were pleasant and friendly. I was the last passenger to embark, after a Uruguayan journalist, an old Indian on his way home to Manaus and a friendly young man, Claudio, a gold prospector on his way to a mining camp on the Rio Tapajós.

We refuelled twice before landing for the night in the village of Aragarças on the edge of the Mato Grosso, where the only hotel, though very picturesque outside, was far from clean or convenient and had no washing facilities. However, it was Hobson's choice, and at least it had the advantage of a restaurant where even the stodgy food was welcome after the long flight. Claudio, the prospector, and I dined there together, and before parting for the night strolled to the bridge which spans the broad Rio Araguaia, the boundary between the Brazilian states of Goiaz and Mato Grosso. The Mato Grosso side was superbly forested and untamed.

My room in the hotel was minute, almost filled by a bed with a messy mattress which I covered carefully with my indispensable hammock. The dreary mottled walls, recording the deaths of legions of mosquitoes, were darkened by the shadows cast by the flickering flame of the kerosene lamp. Through the thin partition dividing the quarters, I could hear two women discussing their adjoining room. One of them shudderingly suspected that it must be alive with *chagas* beetles, so I took the hint and let my lamp burn all night, to keep the creatures at bay. The thought of this beetle which, if it bites, can transmit an incurable disease was not conducive to sleep, and added to these disturbing thoughts were the cries of a baby and constant attacks by hordes of mosquitoes.

It was a relief when day dawned to roll up my hammock and make my way to the airstrip. The baggage and cargo stowed in the aircraft included the gruesome and bloody carcass of an ox, the hoofs sticking out stiffly from the torn corpse. Later it became fly-ridden and the passengers crowded as far away as possible from the sickening sight and smell. The meat was destined for Indian villages along our route and at each stop chunks were thrown out on to the airstrips.

As the journey proceeded the country became more beautiful – forest, forest and more forest, varied occasionally with *cerrado*, and escarpments of red stone, whose sheer walls had been scored deeply in prehistoric times. Vast rivers meandered through endless jungle, the sun transforming them to liquid gold. The plane flew low and the colossal emergent trees of the forest could be seen in detail. For ten hours we flew over this paradise, then landed in Xavantina. On the airstrip a group of Xavante Indians were waiting to see the plane land. Survivors of a warlike tribe, they were handsome men, powerfully built and tall, but wearing the tatty clothes cast off by the 'civilizados'. They posed for their

Opposite. Streptocalyx poeppigii

Xavante Indians, handsome men,
powerfully built and tall

photographs, for which they demanded payment, against a bizarre background of ceramic lavatory bowls.

At the next landing stage, Reserva Villas Boas, the Uruguayan journalist left us, telling me that he would be collecting and studying for some months on the reserve.

Later, we landed in a small clearing in Xingu, where an Indian woman wanted my moss-agate necklace and I had to try to explain to her that my mother left it to me; I think she understood, because she prevented a young boy from tearing the necklace off my neck. When we arrived the Indians had just caught an enormous fish – like a bewhiskered cat-fish it had a white belly and orange tail and fins.

By the time we landed in Manaus I was truly weary, for it was 5 o'clock on the second day of the flight. Luckily, Claudio had recommended a modest hotel, where I was able to have a refreshing shower and lie flat on a clean bed.

The next day I moved into the student quarters of Instituto Nacional de Pesquisas de Amazonia (INPA, National Institute of Amazon Research), and from there made various visits to the Reserva Ducke, a beautiful area of forest named in honour of the Brazilian botanist Adolpho Ducke, who lived in the Amazon forests for long periods, studying the flora throughout the seasons.

I painted enthusiastically for there was plenty of material both in the Reserve and its environs: *Heliconia acuminata,* with pale yellow bracts, in a large colony under forest trees; *Streptocalyx longifolius,* whose flowers are pollinated by bats at night; *Streptocalyx poeppigii* with long red and purple inflorescences; all these and many other wonderful plants.

The journey from Manaus to Uaupés was exciting. I left Manaus in a Catalina, an amphibious plane, flying over jungle traversed by sinuous rivers and densely forested archipelagoes, finally coming down on the river in a cloud of spray at the little settlement of Mercés which consisted of two or three wattled huts to which we were ferried by

An enormous fish – like a bewhiskered cat-fish

Heliconia acuminata
Proc: Amazonas, near
Manaus, Nov 1964
Margaret Mee

Heliconia acuminata

The white tower and monastery of the Salesian Mission on the outskirts of Uaupés

canoe. In Uaupés I was to enjoy the hospitality of the Salesian Mission, and in Mercés a padre and two nuns from the Mission were there to welcome me. We embarked on the mail boat bound for Uaupés and were seen off by a small group of Tucano Indians.

We had scarcely left our mooring before driving rain forced us to close all shutters, and as we sailed on, Tucumã, our pilot, peering through a small opening, had to battle with numerous rapids. When the storm had passed, the distant Serra da Curicuriari was visible on the horizon. Due to the shape of its contours, the local name for this mountain range is Bela Dormecida (Sleeping Beauty); it dominated the landscape for many kilometres, forming a seductive background to the groups of granite islands in the great expanse of Rio Uaupés. Tumultuous cataracts stormed over these rocky barriers of stone which stretched from shore to shore, masking all other sounds with roaring waters.

Some hours of sailing brought us within sight of the white tower and monastery of the Salesian Mission, which lies on the outskirts of the little town of Uaupés (São Gabriel da Cachóeira). We coasted on to the beach where our party and its baggage was picked up by a lorry and driven to the Mission. There I met the kind and friendly Sister in Charge, Elza Ramos, who showed me my little room — secluded and light enough for painting — and then gave me lemonade to quench a raging thirst.

My next move was to explore the country around the mission and to wander beside the spectacular falls of São Gabriel, where from every angle there were superb vistas, while the nearby swamp was teeming with flowers new to me. Down on the sandy shore hordes of pale green and yellow butterflies rose like petals in the wind and then vanished. I later learned that these butterflies suck saltpetre from the wet mud on the river verge. In this region I hoped to meet Tucano and Maku Indians, the latter living in the more remote areas where they make curare, a poison used to paralyse when hunting prey — and sometimes their human enemies.

Rio Uaupés

Rio Negro, with Serra Curicuriari in the distance

Opposite. *Heliconia chartacea* var. *meeana*

People from the Salesian mission

Four of the Tucano girls from the mission borrowed a canoe and took me with them to collect plants, paddling past the rapids and landing in a *caatinga* forest. As I wandered through the strange dry growth, examining the enormous Anthuriums with dark cushiony leaves and the small red-leafed bromeliads (*Neoregelias*), I chanced upon a primitive shelter beneath which a wrinkled old Maku Indian and a young boy were making curare in an earthen pot. They were shy and found it difficult to communicate.

We came out of the *caatinga* forest into a dark jungle of giant trees where scarlet heliconias grew shoulder high and the ground was carpeted with moss and selaginellas. Then we lost our way and wandered around until eventually we reached the river bank where our canoe had been moored. The canoe was no longer there; in our absence someone had exchanged it for a smaller one which would only hold three, obliging one of the girls and me to make our way through the forest on foot. We struggled through the dense woods, always careful to keep within sight and sound of the river. The petals of a blue *Qualea* flower (*Erisma calcarata*), for which I was always searching since my journey in Mato Grosso, lay strewn on the ground around me, but I was too exhausted to investigate, and voices from the now distant canoe were urging us on for the forest was darkening rapidly. At last we reached the mission, sweating and weary.

That night at 'lights out', an Indian girl, Ceci, came to collect my lantern and brought the news that the padres' launch would be sailing for Curicuriari early next morning, and as I was planning to go she would waken me at 5 o'clock. Aware that there would be no light at that hour I did some hasty packing, then snatched an hour of two of sleep. I was awake before the appointed hour as the night air was sultry, and a full moon shone in through my open window, floating in a lightly clouded sky. A vampire bat flew in and out of of my room and the sound of his beating wings was like the sound of muffled drums. As I arose in the semi-darkness, in a streak of moonlight I saw a large black spider advancing towards me, but a light kick sent him scurrying away. I drank coffee in a hushed refectory, where a few white-habited nuns, being on retreat, flitted around silently. One of them handed me a box of food, whispering that there was nothing to eat in Curicuriari.

Dawn was breaking over the silver Rio Uaupés, as three Tucano girls and I wended our way to the 'port' where the padres' launch was moored. As I embarked on *Pope Pius XII*, I saw Tucumã, the same old Tucano pilot who had brought me on the mail boat from Mercés. He greeted me warmly and introduced me to another Tucano, João Firma, whom he explained would take me to Curicuriari, for he himself had to return to Mercés. When Tucumã told João that my objective was to collect plants in the Serra do Curicuriari, João looked at me with obvious doubt, saying that I did not appear strong enough for a trek in that mountainous region. I felt slighted by his remark and assured him quickly that I had experience of walking in forested mountains. Tucumã seeing my disappointment added his assurances, but I was slightly disconcerted at being left in the sole charge of João, for on my arrival in Uaupés I had seen him in the company of a very disreputable looking fellow well soaked in rum. Later, however, I realised that João was a highly intelligent and reliable man and, I suspect, related to the his tribal chieftain.

As day dawned we sailed through a succession of foaming, raging rapids to the foothills of Bela Dormecida, passing glorious vistas all the way. On the isles in the river the trees were white with orchids and the air full of their perfume. After about three hours of sailing, we reached a settlement where we did not land. Instead, some of the cargo was thrown ashore beside the tangled roots of an old tree which resembled Medusa's snake-like locks hanging down into the dark waters of the river. Some Tucano women shouted greetings from the small group of huts which

Heliconia naupensis E.M.
Amazonas, Rio Naupés

Margaret Mee

With Tucumâ on the Uaupés

João swinging across to a neighbouring tree

crowned the steep and rocky banks as the launch moved on towards Curicuriari.

We reached the 'port' at Curicuriari, marked by a fallen giant of the forest which hung over the river bank like some writhing primeval creature, and clambered up the steep rocky path to the village. This consisted of a small number of huts, all set some distance apart one from another and well hidden by trees. One large hut, the original spacious *maloca,* was only used for ceremonies and celebrations.

The hut in which I slept during my time in Curicuriari belonged to João's brother who was away at the time. It was a wattle construction with a thatch of buriti palm, and though the walls were full of chinks it appeared weather proof. I hung my hammock from wall to wall in the centre of the room, but even though the doors and windows had beautifully made shutters of assai palm on bamboo frames, there was no way of closing them, and when the wind blew they danced around like kites in a gale and the rain poured in on me. The floor was clean-swept earth and the furniture consisted of a rough table and a box for a seat. The only ornaments were a rosary and a white toucan feather hanging on a wall. Four wooden steps led to the doorway. Outside the black Rio Curicuriari flowed silently, copper-red in the shallows, the falls rumbling dimly in the distance.

The people of the village paid me frequent visits. Every day, before daybreak, as I lay in my hammock, women would enter the hut silently and sit on the floor, waiting for me to get up. Dressing in front of curious eyes was an ordeal which I accepted with resignation.

We were to spend one night in the village before beginning our two-day journey to the *serra.* It meant that we would need to spend one night in the forest and João told me in detail what I should need to carry: a hammock, and as little as possible besides. As for food, I should take what I liked – they would eat birds. When I told him I did not want to see dead birds he laughed long and heartily.

At dawn the next day, João, another Indian and I met ready to set off, but as it had stormed during the night, João decided that the weather was not settled enough for a long journey. However, he offered to take me by canoe to collect along the river, but there again I was to be disappointed, as a trader from Manaus turned up with a cargo of rum and bullets, and everyone, including João, disappeared to inspect this. When João returned, to pacify me, he climbed a rotten tree for a catasetum that I had had my eye on since arriving. But to my horror, when he reached the plant, the tree collapsed and João fell about twenty feet, landing neatly on his feet amongst dead branches and thorns. With contempt he brushed aside my suggestion that he might be hurt, and climbing a neighbouring tree swung across on a liana and threw me a *Catasetum barbatum* clone. But at least the weather had improved and we decided to set off on our trek next day.

At 5 o'clock João arrived, and though it had been raining all night, told me that he had found a companion for that day's journey. Octavio, also a Tucano, was a strong, fine looking fellow who had not been in touch with the 'civilizados' and thus spoke not a word of Portuguese.

We paddled upstream for about an hour with no rapids to hinder us, I keeping my gaze riveted on the river banks where I was rewarded by finding *Aechmea chantinii* and a fine *Galeandra.* Our canoe was moored in a shadowy spot at the mouth of one of the many streams which flow into Rio Curicuriari. The two Indians led the way and we entered the forest by way of an *igarapé,* dry as they all were at the end of the year. I was still elated by the collection of rare plants I had found on the banks of the river and which I had left beside the canoe. As we proceeded, the forest of enormous trees, many supported by buttressed roots, grew denser and the light dimmer, and in the soft green light I saw a colony of Rapateceae, strange aquatic plants. From their large leaves, deep pink at the centre, rose slender stems crowned by two triangular, rose-coloured bracts, between which clusters of pale yellow petals emerged from massed dark burgundy calices. The petals were

Near Mercés

as delicate as gossamer and would fade during the journey, so I decided to leave them till our return. Soon we had left them far behind, and found ourselves entering forest as dark and resonant as a great cathedral.

From this we suddenly emerged into a brilliantly green *caatinga* forest. The trees, no longer of impressive size and grandeur, were festooned with epiphytes growing down their ribbed trunks and over the arched roots to the fern-covered ground. Leaving this

João Firma's canoe

Catasetum barbatum
Lindl.
Amazonas, Rio Unini

Margaret Mee
1946

green illuminated forest we found ourselves again in sombre jungle, relieved only in colour by the amethyst flowers of *Heterostemon ellipticus* growing high in the canopies.

I was to see many new sights and hear many strange sounds on that eventful two-day walk towards the sombre *serra*. The dark forests resounded with the ringing cries of flocks of birds which seemed to dominate such areas. Once, after an exhausting struggle at the hottest time of the day, I asked my guides whether there was any water in the area. They looked around a little, then began to slash at a giant liana with a knife, and a stream of refreshing water gushed from the stem. We all drank gratefully.

A drizzle had set in as soon as we left the canoe. It continued throughout the day and the light began to fade rapidly. João announced that it would not be possible to reach the *serra* before nightfall, for though it was only four o'clock, it was already dark in the forest.

The Tucanos chose a camp site beside an *igarapé* and started to build two shelters, working together in complete silence and with amazing rapidity. Great Patoa palm leaves were dragged rustling over the dead leaves for the roof, saplings became posts and liana was used to bind the joints. Eventually, I hung my hammock in a beautiful green-roofed shelter. Then João lit a fire and I cooked packet soup over the flames.

The night was very dark and stormy. I slept fitfully, tossing and turning restlessly in my hammock, cold in spite of my slacks and long-sleeved shirt, and plagued by minute ticks which had collected in my clothes during the day. I was only calmed by the strange notes of nocturnal birds and the chorus of tree frogs. But there were other disturbing sounds of movement in the undergrowth nearby. Dozing lightly, I realised that João and Octavio had heard it too, and through half-closed eyes I saw them rush out of their hut, cocking their antique rifles, and run towards a dark mass of trees into which they peered cautiously, only returning when they were happy all danger had passed.

Next morning after the last embers of the fire were quenched we started our climb to Serra do Curicuriari, the *serra* that Richard Spruce the botanist had explored in 1852. Well over a hundred years had elapsed since his journey, but it is doubtful that the region had changed since then, for a century is but a moment in the life of an ancient mountain.

Climbing steeply over the wet slopes, rocks and roots of trees, we passed deeply-fluted

Catasetum

Opposite. *Catasetum barbatum*

columns of granite, green with lichens, guarding the way to the summit. Raging storms had brought down branches and tree trunks across all the paths; trees were smaller; plants fewer, ants swarmed over everything. At the summit the view which I had hoped to see was obscured by the dense foliage of trees.

The ascent had been a struggle, but the descent was more difficult as the danger of slipping and falling was greater, but we reached our camp in the forest without mishap.

As we returned to the forested plains a brilliant orange bird with a flaming crest (Galo da Serra) followed us, darting from tree to tree, watching with curiosity from on high. I was afraid the Indians might kill it, since it was apparently completely unaware of the treachery of men, but João exclaimed that he would not think of killing a Galo da Serra. But he did kill a paca, and a guan that he tried to shoot made off in a hurry, to my great relief.

I gathered some of the Rapateceae plants I had seen earlier, but by this time my boots were heavy with mud and water, and the last few kilometres had exhausted me so I abandoned any further serious collecting. It was a welcome sight when, at midday, we saw the river and the canoe moored beside the bank. I climbed in and sank down wearily. How soothing the sound of dipping paddles can be!

The next day, as usual, shortly after dawn, the village of Curicuriari was deserted and silent, for the Indians had paddled away to look after their plantations – clearings in the forest which were planted with manioc, yams, pineapples and fruit trees. The villagers spent the day working these, returning only at dusk. João and Amelia had departed taking their two children with them, but leaving Marciana, a girl of twelve to look after the house. We two were alone in the village.

Fresh from the Serra do Curicuriari, I arranged the plants I had collected on the journey, painted the Rapateceae, and was sitting in my hut sketching when, to my astonishment I

Galo de Serra (Cock-of-the-Rock)

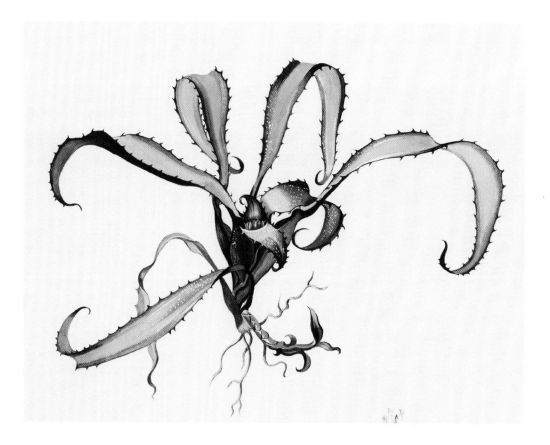

Neoregelia sp.

heard a motor-canoe coming upriver. I listened intently, wondering who could be paying a visit when at this hour all the villagers would be away. The motor shut off in front of João's house and I hurried to the door of my hut to see who had disembarked. Led by a burly figure wearing a big black sombrero, a crowd of rough looking fellows came swaggering up to my cabin. I was more than alarmed by the aspect of these men and wished João was here or would return soon, which was unlikely. The leader came up to me exclaiming that he had not expected to find a woman like me in Curicuriari, and where was my husband? His familiarity was most disturbing, but I realised that, above all, I must show no fear, so answered that I was working here and my husband was in São Paulo. The fellow informed me that he was a gold prospector, going upriver with his team of goldwashers to look for gold and wood. Had I any whisky? No. Rum? No. Well then, alcohol? To which I replied that I had a little alcohol for my stove. What else had I for him? he inquired insolently, moving towards me in the doorway. He wanted to converse with me, he said, but that could wait until he returned.

The gang left, and with intense relief I heard the motor canoe's engine getting fainter and fainter but, oddly I thought, going down stream. I was alone again, thank heaven! And before his return, which might be in many days, I should have left Curicuriari.

But I was not alone, for when I looked through a crack in the wall of my hut I saw three of the gang circling my hut. Hoping they would not see me, I ran to Marciana with the little money I had to hide it in João's house. Then I hid my camera under an old cloth, my diamond ring in a chink in the wall, and my bullets in an old shoe, loaded my revolver putting it under my box seat, then sat and waited for what seemed an eternity.

Rio Negro, 1964

My hut in Curicuriari, where a drunken gold prospector tried to assault me

My heart beating furiously, I heard the motor-canoe returning, coasting and mooring in front of João's hut, and a few minutes later the goldwashers were coming up the path again, and the leader was at my door, swaying and as drunk as a lord. He made no bones about entering my cabin, and started to come up the steps, but I was ready, revolver in hand. Taken aback his dark face paled and he held up his hands, backing away as he did so. Suddenly I felt calm and in control of the situation, and seeing the humorous side laughed aloud as I followed him down the steps into the open.

Disconcerted by my unexpected reaction to his attempted assault, the leader began to talk in a pacific vein. Then, recovering his bravado, sprang to disarm me but failed. The others were watching at a safe distance, wisely out of range of my revolver. After a few minutes' hesitation, they all left. Marciana, who had been a witness from afar, ran to me, and flung her arms around me, weeping with relief. The tension over, I too, burst into tears

Like a miracle, João and Amelia returned within the hour, bringing reinforcements, including a tall, powerful looking Indian. They knew the story as did the whole neighbourhood, for the ill-fame of these so-called 'prospectors' was common knowledge, not only in the village but also from the source to the mouth of the river.

This incident changed the attitude of the villagers towards me. Hitherto there had been a suspicion that I was a spy – a rumour started by the trader from Manaus who had managed to convince them with some story, helped by draughts of rum. As a result, they had refused to sell me any food, and I had been living on packets of dried soups and the few rations which the sisters had insisted on giving me. But the unexpected event that day altered things completely and suspicion changed to warm friendliness. Realising that I was an ally, the Tucanos treated me like a queen, bringing me plentiful supplies of fruit and fish.

However, the unexpected and frightening visit had unsettled me and my collecting suffered as a result. I was in a continual state of alert and did not wander far, always expecting the return of the gang. It was lonely in the village when the Indians left for their plantations at dawn and returned at nightfall. Nevertheless, without going far afield there was plenty of wildlife to be seen around the village. When the sun rose, a slender iguana (one which can attain two metres when fully grown) basked on the stones, and three small toucans, black- and yellow-billed, disputed territory with alarming cries.

A slender iguana basked on the stones

Margaret Mee
1976

Urospatha sagittifolia

Amazonas

(Rudksch) Schott.

Tucumã, the best pilot on Rio Negro

Robin Hanbury-Tenison and Sebastian Snow in Uaupés

The night before my departure from Curicuriari, I sat in the gloaming talking with João and Amelia outside their hut by the light of a dim lamp. They told me about the *serra*, its animals and birds, the trees and plants of the forests. When they left me, they paddled downstream in their canoe to their hut, and the paddle's faint splash in the river seemed to mark the end of this journey.

Morning came, but no Tucumã to fetch me as we had arranged, and I became rather agitated at the thought of staying another week in the village, so João went down to the 'port' to make inquiries and returned with the news that Tucumã would arrive the next day. By way of consolation, he brought me fish and manioc meal cooked by Amelia.

I left the village the following day in the padres' launch. The sky was magnificent with storm clouds and we encountered rapid after rapid. When we landed in Uaupés, I was astonished to see, moored in the bay, a rubber speed-boat with two powerful outboard motors. On further examination I noted a couple of crash helmets, a British and a Brazilian flag and a Paisley scarf. A tall, blond, suntanned young man came up to greet me as 'the English woman they have been telling me about'. Who was he, and where was he going? I wanted to know. He and his companion were representing the *Daily Telegraph*, reporting on the longest river journey on record. Robin Hanbury-Tenison and Sebastian Snow had come to Amazonas by way of the Orinoco from Venezuela, and were heading for Manaus and Rio Madeira in their speed-boat. There was some excitement on my return at the mission and the nuns embraced me and asked if I knew of the arrival of two Englishmen: 'What courage!' That evening the two adventurers and I dined together at the invitation of Sister Elza and talked late into the night.

The next day Robin confided to me that he and Sebastian were worried about the weight and bulk of their pilot, Salvador, fearing that he would slow down their journey to Manaus. So I suggested Tucumã as the ideal pilot, being very small and light and, by repute, the best pilot on Rio Negro. So Tucumã, carrying an umbrella bigger than himself, went to the church to persuade the heavy Salvador, who was celebrating mass before his journey, to relinquish his place on the voyage to Manaus. There seemed to be no problem with Salvador, for Tucumã returned with a smile of almost delirious delight – he would meet his son in Manaus whom he had not seen for twenty years

The departure of the speed-boat and crew caused a sensation and the whole village turned out to witness the event. As she took off the craft appeared to be airborne, followed by a shining trail of spray like the tail of a comet.

That night we saw the warning signs of an approaching storm, when white aquatic birds were seen circling against a black sky streaked with red flashes of lightning. The following morning, the storm broke with tremendous force and fury. When the tempest was at its height a stream of water gushed through the ceiling of my room and I had to tear around to save my belongings from a drenching. My mosquito net, bed and clothes were already wet through and a lake appeared in the middle of the room. Fortunately repairs were done quickly, for another storm threatened. A benefit of the storms was that the shower and toilet, which had been giving trouble, started to function!

At 5 o'clock one morning I was up and ready for my next river journey – to Taracuá (Giant Ant) upriver on Rio Uaupés. To get there I had to go by motor launch to Mercés, and then by amphibious plane to Taracuá. It was an exciting journey in the plane: below, meandering rivers threaded their way through high

forest varied with scrub land; from low lying swampy ground an isolated group of densely forested hills rose. The tremendous rock on which Taracuá lies is said to be imprinted with the footprints of *Jurupari* – the Devil. We could see the long building of the Salesian mission as the plane approached, for it was situated on the crest of the stony hill. I was assigned to the Santa Casa of the mission and, after various introductions, I escaped the clouds of mosquitoes which were besieging me by diving under my net where I lay in peace.

The Salesian mission at Taracuá

Distictella

A *teju* (lizard) kept as a pet in our garden in São Paulo. These can grow to over three feet long

But not for long, for I was eager to explore my surroundings, and on the first excursion to the nearby countryside I found many interesting plants – a beautiful white and yellow bignone, *Distictella magnolifolia*, which was first found by Humboldt on his journey to the Orinoco in 1800, and only found again in the same area by Koch in 1905. There were clusias and a variety of orchids and an extraordinary swamp plant, *Rapatea paludosa*.

I celebrated Greville's birthday by a trip into the forest, led by Vincente, a very mercenary-minded Indian. The *caatinga* of Taracuá was one of the most beautiful I have seen. Epiphytes clung to the trees, half enveloped in wet mosses, and in the middle of a lake surrounded by swamp grew a clusia tree bearing panicles of white flowers, red at the centres, pendent between large oval leaves. These were just possible to reach by walking along a fallen tree-trunk, so Vincente was able to get me a few clusters of flowers and leaves. The whole area was a paradise of plants; there grew three species of *Rapatea*, anthuriums and a charming orchid with feathery spikes of greenish flowers. When I tried to move one of these plants embedded in moss, an unseen creature stung me so viciously that I cried out with pain. As I was accustomed to find ants in every plant, I imagined this must be an ant's sting, but the pain was so acute and persistent that I asked Vincente if it could have been something more violent. He suggested a small red scorpion, and hurried on towards the river, since it was raining heavily. By this time I was feeling dizzy, my head was aching, and I was stumbling as I went, so had difficulty in keeping up. But in spite of my condition, Vincente increased his speed and was almost running when he reached the boat. I was so angered by his behaviour and lack of concern that I decided then and there that I would never ask him to collect with me again.

One day, wandering alone and tranquil through the partially cleared land behind the mission, a spectacular clusia tree came in sight. Covered with deep rose-coloured flowers, and hung with fruit which looked like Chinese lanterns, it was the feminine form of *Clusia viscida*. Not far away, the following day, I was able to collect the masculine form of the species growing on a slender tree nearby, its white flowers with a tinge of yellow.

One rainy day, having finished the painting I had in hand, I took advantage of the rain to visit Padre Martins who had a impressive collection of butterflies and beetles. His knowledge was extensive, and he was interested to hear about the miniature lizard which fell out of a piece of rotten wood on the roots of a bromeliad I collected. I could only see it in detail through a magnifying glass, and explained it to the Padre who told me that these creatures are extremely rare and that he had seen a blue and a green one but never one mottled brown like the one I had found. When I got back to the mission, the lizard

Rapatea paludosa

was still in his wood dust home, and I found a safe and suitable place outside where he could live in peace.

My stay in Taracuá came to and end when the launch bound for Uaupés arrived late one night, and I embarked the following morning. I spent the day seated in the prow of the *Dom Savio*, watching the river banks slip by. We moved on steadily without stopping until 8 o'clock at night, when we coasted for a brief moment at Ilha de Paacu and Trovão, two tiny settlements, then continued our journey until we reached Bela Vista where we moored for the night. I stood at a window, watching the jungle come to life after the heat of the day, hearing the splashing and sighing of the dolphins playing beside the launch, until sleep overcame me and I dived into my hammock, thankful for my netting, for the mosquitoes were ravenous. Though I loved listening to the deep voices of the Indians talking into the night, prolonged conversations in the Tucano language, a rather gutteral one, were not conducive to sleep!

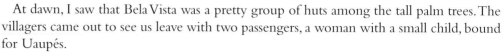

Clusia viscida

Bela Vista

At dawn, I saw that Bela Vista was a pretty group of huts among the tall palm trees. The villagers came out to see us leave with two passengers, a woman with a small child, bound for Uaupés.

We passed forests that were full of flowers, the most spectacular being Rabo de Arara – *Norantea amazonica* – a true parasite, whose long scarlet plumes crowned the tallest of trees. Beaches and sandbanks started to appear, for the level of the river had fallen considerably since August and by this time was very low. The temperature too had fallen and it was almost cold, quite a relief for my sunburnt skin. The few and isolated huts along the river were perched on rocks beside eddying falls and amidst groups of palm trees. Most of the mountain ranges were some way off, though I learned that the nearer ones could be reached by canoe without difficulty.

One of the passengers, a little man who had been my neighbour at the mission Taracuá, was a source of information about the names of the villages, trees and plants, He was an excellent companion for the long journey, though very ugly. By contrast, the crew of Tucano Indians were handsome and friendly, and gave us lunch consisting of an enormous plateful of rice and sausages, washed down with plenty of coffee.

As we approached Uaupés, the small canoe, usually in tow, was lashed to the launch, for between that point and Uaupés there was a series of turbulent rapids.

Shortly after passing the junction of Rio Uaupés with Rio Negro, we reached Ilha das Flores, which belied its name. I had expected to find *Aechmea chantinii* there in great

Rio Negro, 1964

quantity with other interesting plants, but instead found that most of the natural vegetation had been destroyed leaving it disappointingly dull. Beyond this little isle lies a region of enchanting beauty which I hoped to explore one day, unless, like the Ilha das Flores, the natural beauty has been senselessly destroyed by then.

On arriving in Uaupés, I hurried to examine my plants in the mission garden, and found them fresh and green thanks to frequent rain and the conscientious care of Ceci who had been in charge of them. From Ceci I learned something of the gang which confronted me in Curicuriari. The leader was the son of a pastor in Manaus and one of five brothers, each one worse than the other. It appeared that no woman was safe if they were in the region, and anyone who dared denounce them would be threatened. As a result no one complained about them and the villages continued to be terrorised. It seems that as I had had a firearm I was the first woman to confront one of the villains successfully.

I had been hoping to make a journey in a Brazilian airplane to Içana, a small village on Rio Içana. But the day of departure had been one of uncertainty since the small hours, when I had awakened and heard what I took to be a mass for the departing aircrew. Thinking that they must have arrived the previous night and would leave at dawn, I dressed and packed in record time, only to find that I was mistaken, and that the plane would only arrive at midday. So I filled in the time by conversing in the little mission shop about future journeys, learning that Rio Cauaburi (a river I longed to explore) flows into Rio Negro about halfway between Uaupés and Tapurucuará, and is virtually unexplored according to the well-known botanists Froes and Ducke.

At one point I heard the plane overhead and the waiting passengers rushed outside despite the pouring rain – but no plane was visible. Then the mission truck, Sister Elza sitting beside the driver, came tearing towards us. We got in and sped towards the place where the plane had landed. The truck journey was forty-five minutes of jolting and splashing through mud and water; at one especially rough

Clusia viscida

95

Padre Alfonso, a fine musician

jolt Sister Elza would have fallen out had I not clutched her flowing habit and dragged her back. On the way we had to stop and wait impatiently whilst the overheated radiator was filled with muddy water from a nearby *igarapé*. Eventually we reached the field which served as an airstrip. It looked more like a lake and the aircrew were drenched, standing disconsolate on the soggy ground. My rucksack was running with water and my shoes squishing, but my main preoccupation was for my sketchbooks packed in my dripping baggage.

Finally the plane took off with visibility nil, though, as we rose in the air, we entered patches of clear sky from which I could see the magnificent indigo *serra* and peaks of Içana above a bank of solid white cloud.

We had flown some considerable distance when I noticed extreme tension amongst the crew who were peering down at the undercarriage, signalling to each other, running backwards and forwards to the pilot. The young Salesian sister was praying, pale with fear as she fingered her beads. The only other passenger, an Indian, sat silent and mystified, his eyes as big as an owl's.

Within half an hour from Içana the pilot decided to return to Uaupés. He sent a message to keep calm, that he would do everything possible to make a safe landing, a difficult feat, as only one of the wheels had retracted. He had hoped it would be possible for the amphibious plane to make a water landing on the narrow channel of Rio Içana, but because of the faulty undercarriage the floats would not descend. Return to the 'airstrip' at Uaupés was the only answer. Our anxiety was over when we landed safely on the swamped airfield amid cheers of relief and triumph from crew and passengers. So ended my first attempt to reach Içana.

But I did not have to wait for too long to get there, this time by the padres' launch, for one of the padres, named Padre Içana, was to visit the mission at Içana.

Benediction having been said, the little launch left Uaupés. We were five passengers besides the crew: myself, two padres, a sister with a face like Queen Nefertiti and my old friend the pilot Tucumã.

We travelled for two days without stopping – even braving the dangerous and frequent rapids after dark in spite of the pilot Tucumã's protests. But Padre Içana and Padre Alfonso, a fine musician, insisted on keeping to schedule, for they had promised to celebrate mass in the unfinished chapel on the Ilha das Flores, and their word was law.

The sunsets were unbelievably beautiful. The sun went down in fiery splendour, gilding trees, rocks and river. Then the hot brilliance gave way to silver and deep blue, as night swiftly enfolded the river in darkness.

Old Padre Içana, heavy with years, dozed beside the pilot. I slung my hammock beside that of Sister Antonia, but slept little and uneasily, for the hammocks swayed as the launch swerved to avoid rocks, hurling us against boxes of cargo which were also moving from side to side. Above me, in my straw hat a little *Catasetum* which I had found near São Felipe was showing signs of bursting into flower.

It was nearly midnight when we reached the Ilha das Flores, where I could vaguely see the dark chapel against the sky. I stumbled out of the launch sleepily and, as I was wearing slacks, dreamily watched the ceremony from the doorway of the chapel. Inside it was dimly lit by a few flickering candles. The unaccompanied singing merged with the music of the river and forests.

Then we continued on our way, only resting for an hour or two moored by the river bank. Towards the evening of the second day, the river became more tranquil and, as there were few rapids to pass before Içana, we moved on through the night. Before day dawned I was awakened from a deep sleep as we were about to disembark. Lights moved towards

The sunsets were unbelievably beautiful

97

Heterostemon mimosoides

us through the darkness. Three nuns, white robed and carrying hurricane lamps, had come to meet us and led us up the slope leading to the primitive Santa Casa of the Içana Mission, where Mother Superior saw me installed in a large unoccupied room. Next door a rough wooden door opened into a large barn-like room where, to my dazed eyes, there seemed to be a forest of hammocks. The room teemed with children – all curious – and adults, all singing, talking or coughing (there was an epidemic of whooping cough). As she closed the door, Mother Superior remarked that the Indians liked to sleep together in the same room. But despite the noise I slept soundly for what remained of the night.

Eager to explore this inviting region, I waited impatiently for the promised guide to appear, but, losing patience, set off alone. I had not gone far when I heard shouts behind me from a girl who had been sent to see that I did not lose my way. Two other Indian girls, joined us. They had warned me of the danger of going alone into the forest as *Jurupari* – the Devil – might be lurking there to attack wanderers. He had the unpleasant habit of pulling off the head of his victim and devouring the brains. The only way to kill this Devil was to stick a knife or sharp bamboo into his navel, but that would be difficult for he was a giant and very agile although he had only one eye and his feet were set backwards. These two had watched me going off alone with misgivings and were pleased when the mission had sent someone to accompany me. With the three girls I entered one of the most beautiful *caatinga* forests I had ever been in. The humidity was extreme and all the twigs and branches of the trees were covered with ferns and mosses. The swampy ground was covered with aroids whose long spiralling spathes, rising high above the leaf canopy, were like olive-green and chestnut-coloured velvet. Colonies of swamp plants with coral-coloured hearts, and leaves which fanned from a glowing centre, grew beside them. I had collected these plants – Rapateceae – in the swamps of Curicuriari. As we left this forest I noticed a group of small catasetums on a rotting tree. With great care I lifted them from the bark.

It was in this awe-inspiring forest that I found a tree of *Heterostemon ellipticus*, with a wealth of amethyst flowers. It is often known as the Orchid Tree as its flowers superficially resemble laelias and cattleyas. Luckily, I was able to collect some flowers and sprays of leaves, as the tall *Heterostemon* had fallen in a storm and was lodged in some branches within easy reach. I had been longing to paint this legume ever since seeing it in Curicuriari.

Another day, this time with a guide, we had been walking all morning in the forests bordering Rio Uaupés. Herculano, my guide, had known these forests since childhood, and was tireless in his efforts to find plants for me. He led me over swamps and across streams where we quenched our thirst, drinking the dark water in deep draughts from cups made of large heliconia leaves. The dark waters appeared red-gold where the light played on shallow pools, and had a jewel-like quality in their deep green setting.

Beside a waterfall we rested and had a bite, all the time scanning the thick forest on the other side of the river for flowers. Then we continued our search through the high jungle, and over black, swampy ground. Once I slipped into this mire from the fallen tree along which I was balancing and nearly lost one boot as I pulled my leg out with tremendous effort from the bog.

I found *Gongora quinquenervis* in this forest, growing head-high on a large tree. It was the only one of its kind which I was able to find during that journey. The jungle in which I found it had little undergrowth, apart from a tall type of aroid, known as *Aninga montrichardia*. But in the trees there were many epiphytes: bromeliads, orchids and aroids. The flowers of the Cannonball Tree (*Couroupita guianensis*) sprinkled the ground with their cream and bronze petals; the black-red bells of a bignonia lay beside them, having probably

Opposite. *Clusia nemorosa*

98

fallen from one of the giant lianas which wreathed themselves amongst the enormous trees.

Laden with plants we made our way back to the mission. The shadows lengthened; peace enveloped the forests, only stirred by the late songs of birds and the rustle of animals seeking shelter for the night and the roaring of howler monkeys.

Christmas Eve came, and with it an invitation from Mother Superior to attend Midnight Mass. I was curious to see how it would be celebrated by the Indians in this isolated village. Before leaving, I locked my room as I was somewhat doubtful about the occupants of the quarters near mine. They were strangers in Içana, and were drinking heavily, whistling and screaming late into the night.

The mass was impressive. It was held in the church which was still under construction and where the lighting consisted of candles and one or two lamps. The Tucano women wore full skirts and brightly-coloured dresses, their heads covered in white veils, but barefoot and walking with the freedom that they had learned in the forest. The nuns were in spotless white and the painted Madonna wore a halo of tiny lights. More than half the service was sung and spoken in the Tucano tongue, and while it was in progress I was able to observe the fine faces of these people, reminiscent of Gauguin's paintings of South Sea Islanders.

The celebration over, another, very different invitation came my way – a visit to the Serra de Içana, which I accepted eagerly. The early morning mist lay white and thick over Rio Içana when, together with several sisters and six Tucanos, I boarded the launch, but the sun soon dispersed it, and by the time we had reached the *igarapé* which flows from the Serra de Içana, the heat was intense. However, on entering the shade of the trees the temperature fell by degrees, which was fortunate, as we had to make the journey by foot, the *igarapé* being blocked by fallen trees and anyway, as it was dry, not navigable. First we passed through a small *caatinga,* and from then on were surrounded by high trees. The ground was swampy and in no time my shoes were completely saturated, and the sisters' white habits were drenched and thick with mud at the hems. Whilst collecting, I was stung by an ant and continued in pain all day. We crossed many streams, stopping eventually beside an *igarapé* for lunch. It was an idyllic spot, remote, and silent but for the faint trickling of a nearby stream and bird cries.

The sisters lit a fire with amazing speed in spite of everything around being saturated, and we shared our lunch with thousands of ants and bees – bees which got into the mouth and eyes and proved very acid and bitter.

The Tucanos in the party were going to climb the *serra*, and I decided to join them, but they moved at such speed that I had trouble in keeping up. After following them for some time, I stopped to collect plants and found myself alone in the forest. I was reminded of a similar experience when, in the forest of Alto Juruena, the Indian guides had run ahead and left John, Susan and me to find our own way back to camp. But on that occasion I was with two companions; this time I was alone and utterly helpless. I walked back a little, but seeing two divergent tracks could not decide which to take, so I shouted and called, but my voice, muffled by the trees, sounded so weak that I despaired of being heard. Teasingly, birds answered my calls. Then I tried to follow a stream which I thought might lead back to where the nuns had picnicked, but in that spot it was just a trickle and I could not tell which way it was flowing. Despairing, I decided to stay where I was, hoping the Tucanos would pass me on their return. Hope had almost ebbed away, when I saw with tremendous relief, in the distance, one of the Tucanos coming towards me. She showed no surprise to see me in that isolated situation, and, as she could speak no Portuguese, we communicated by signs. It seemed she knew where the sisters were, so we returned together to the bank of the *igarapé* where they were still picnicking.

On the return journey I was curious to see a group of rocks, strangely inscribed with symbols, so we moored and climbed to a little hut on the summit of the rocks where we

had to drive off six snarling dogs. No sooner had the surly pack been driven off when I turned to see two of the Tucano girls run shrieking to the river, pursued by a snorting and enraged pig. As they reached the launch, the animal caught sight of and came charging towards the group I was with. Like lightning one of the girls was up a tree, and I scrambled on to a tree stump, somewhat impeded by the heavy camera hanging round my neck. As soon as the pig disappeared behind the hut we dashed to the boat just before the infuriated animal charged again. I never discovered the meaning of the rock symbols.

The little *Catasetum* from São Felipe came into full flower, a charming creature with a fringed labellum, in fact pretty well only fringe – a fascinating construction which was quite complicated to paint. Having finished the painting I cleaned up my plants and packed them provisionally, having heard that Salvador was leaving in the launch for Uaupés.

My return journey to Uaupés was involved. Salvador would take me there in his motor-canoe, but stop *en route* for a day or two on the way at his home in São Felipe. There he would arrange a canoe to take me into the *igapó*, or rain forest, to collect. I left Içana with adieus to the sisters and padres who had been so kind and hospitable.

New Year's Day passed almost unnoticed as we journeyed along Rio Içana towards Uaupés. The motor-canoe was laden to full capacity and was really too small to accommodate Salvador (as we have seen, a heavy man), his daughter Maria, Tio his uncle, three small boys, me, and Arminda, Salvador's tiny Baniwá wife, a pleasant companion who spoke good Portuguese, though naturally she preferred to speak Baniwá whenever possible. As a guide she was excellent, for she knew all the names and locations of rivers and *igarapés*, as well as birds, animals, trees and plants.

The sisters, so kind and hospitable

Velloziaceae

The Penta engine ran well, but in the early stages of the journey we were caught in a heavy rainstorm and everyone and everything was drenched, for our only protection from the stormy skies was a half awning of ageing straw. We stopped at many places, for it seemed that Salvador was a trader in a small way. His intention was to reach São Felipe at night, but a storm was blowing towards us, and he was afraid of sailing up the wide and exposed expanse of water where Rio Içana flows into Rio Negro. So it was decided that we should spend the night in Vila Içana in the traveller's shelter. We had just reached this refuge when the storm broke with tropical fury. The wind made it impossible to secure the motor-canoe, so one of the boys stayed with it to prevent it breaking loose from its moorings.

In the shelter we piled our possessions as far away from the walls as possible, for these were constructed of widely-spaced boughs and the rain, driven by the raging wind, came through in gusty torrents. My hammock was drenched at one end, but this hardly mattered as my shoes were already full of water and, with the exception of my work and camera in a palm fibre bag, my baggage saturated .

We ate a frugal meal by the dim light of a kerosene lamp, which cast changing shadowy shapes in the gloom. After they had retired to their hammocks, the family talked and talked, then talked again in their sleep, alternating with coughs and snores, so with that and the frantic itching of mosquito bites I dozed fitfully to be woken at 5 o'clock by the loud voice of Salvador calling that it was time to be on our way.

Stirrings of life began and the howler monkeys were roaring in chorus, as they do at dawn of day. It was still completely dark and I packed and rolled up my wet hammock with difficulty, had a miserable dry-clean in the dark and, after drinking watery coffee, embarked. I shook with cold as the mist lay thick around us and everything was dripping wet. It never failed to surprise me how rapidly dawn became day on the Equator, the sky turning rosy, lighting the mist hanging over the river. Soon the sun had burnt off the last of the mist and was beating down on us mercilessly.

The river was unbelievably beautiful. I had passed this stretch by night with the padres

Pitcairnia caricifolia

Salvador's motor canoe with a half awning of ageing straw

on the journey to Içana. Now I was able to see the *igarapé* forest where trees stand in water all the year round. The heat was intense and steamy, the river surface so calm that the dividing line between reality and reflection was almost indefinable. The forest in this region was not very high but extremely dense, cut by dark waterways which penetrated deep into the jungle. Tree roots stood above the water, forming arches under which a canoe could pass. Plants grew in rich profusion, rooted in treetops and branches and festooning the canopy of the forest. In the transition from *igapó* to high jungle, epiphytes hung from the boughs and clustered in the forks of branches; brilliant spikes of Arara blazed like fiery plumes in the treetops; aroids crowned the giants of the jungle or hung from palms which fringed the water's edge; white clusia flowers shone like stars in a dark firmament.

Salvador stopped for some time at one or two huts on our way, including that of Tia Surda (Deaf Aunt), as she was popularly known. The poor old woman was only half there and had become stone deaf after taking a remedy for worms – unable to read the instructions on the packet she had swallowed at one go the contents which were intended to be taken over a period of time.

In the morning we reached São Felipe, where the three boys, Armindo, Joachim and Ademar, paddled me by canoe to collect in the *igapó*. At one point, Armindo was crawling along the branch of a tree when he disturbed a lizard which fell into the canoe. Its expression of astonishment was delightful to see. It took some time to regain its equilibrium, then dashed over the side of the canoe, swam across the water and scurried up the same tree from which it had fallen. Up it climbed, but as Armindo came sliding down it got another shock, jumped back into the river and disappeared. It is all very well

Through the igarapé forest where trees stand in water all the year round – Rio Içana, 1964

A fascinating trumpeter bird followed me into the woods

Catasetum

relying on boys to collect, but they soon weary of it and want to go home, so at the first signs of a storm we started to paddle back. On the way back to São Felipe the canoe nearly capsized twice, due to quarrels in the rear.

It was more tranquil to explore the forest behind Salvador's house, and more interesting, for there grew ancient trees fringing the endless forest and towering to the skies, including three enormous clusias, two of which bore the most glorious flowers, deep purple-bronze petals with a lemon fringed centre. They were scattered over the ground below, while the trees were so tall that the flowers growing in the canopy were hardly visible. I realised it was most unlikely that anyone would climb to get them for me, as between the roots of the strangler, which formed a basket work around the rotten trunk of the victim, there were dark hollows, homes of the dangerous *jararacussu*, which is particularly venomous, and one of the few Brazilian snakes which is aggressive. Its poison is often fatal.

So it was no wonder that Maria, listening intently at the foot of this giant clusia, turned pale at the sound of the snake rustling through the undergrowth. We fled rapidly, climbing over and under fallen trees and branches, through scrub and underbrush until we reached a lighter part of the forest. There I was fortunate to see, as we paused for breath, a bromeliad in the fork of a large tree, one of a group of plants all of which were swarming with ferocious ants. They were without flowers, but of a very different aspect from any other I had seen in the region.

In Salvador's house I was honoured with a room to myself – what a relief it was to be alone for a little! Not quite alone, for the voices in the other room never ceased – an Indian language which might have been Baniwá or *Lingua geral*. And in spite of a refreshing bath in the river under cover of darkness, my mosquito bites were driving me mad, keeping me awake though my eyes were closing with sleep.

When morning came, Salvador, his son Eduardo and I left São Felipe in the motor-

Lundia sp.

canoe. It looked as though we were not going to reach our destination that day, for Salvador was hanging about at one of the villages with his merchandise. And it was raining, cold and miserable in the boat where I was waiting, shrouded in plastic. It was the smelliest spot that we had stopped, with very dirty looking people. But there was a brighter side to the picture, for a fascinating trumpeter bird followed me into the woods where I had gone to stretch my legs. I gave him a piece of pancake in the hopes of getting a photograph, though the light was bad and he kept moving all the time. It began raining hard whilst Salvador was still drinking rum and driving a bargain, so I went down to the boat again and passed away the time, eating my greasy, unappetising lunch. The rain was steady, having set in for the day. I fidgeted about, then remarked to Eduardo that his father was staying too long and that I needed to get to Uaupés urgently. So very hesitantly Eduardo went to the hut where Salvador was negotiating and soon they both came rushing out, Salvador full of excuses.

As our journey continued the rapids became more and more turbulent and difficult to navigate, the river wider and the *serra* closer to the shore, but at least the rain petered out. At the most tremendous falls we encountered two fisherman stranded on rocks surrounded by swirling eddies, one using his white shirt as a signal, calling for help. Poor wretches, their canoe was half under water and they were still searching for their possessions among the raging rapids. Though not overkeen attempting a rescue in those turbulent waters, but feeling that at least we should make an attempt to save them, I anxiously asked Salvador if the men were in imminent danger of drowning and could we not give any help: 'They are accustomed to this', he said callously and sped on.

As we neared Uaupés we narrowly missed grounding on rocks, although Eduardo was signalling frantically to keep clear. Eventually, Salvador decided to land as soon as possible and moored at some distance from the mission. So I had to go down a long slippery track

Cacaué

Neoregelia sp nov.

Neoregelia concentrica

to get helpers to fetch my belongings which were heavy and cumbersome.

Everyone at the mission was glad to see me back safe and sound and invited me to stay until I was able to get a flight back to Manaus, and thence home. During my absence someone had abandoned a little Brazilian nightingale in a tiny cage. Its feet were curling up through lack of space and the right food, but I managed to acquire a larger cage and fed it every day on fruit and grasshoppers which young Indian boys found for me in quantities. Whenever it saw me the little bird went crazy and held my finger in its beak. After I had left the mission, I often wondered if the sister who regularly released captive birds would free the little nightingale when it was stronger.

Two months after my return and more than two thousand miles distant from its native forests of northern Amazonas, the *Gongora quinquenervis* flowered in my garden in São Paulo. When the pale buds opened they revealed inflorescences of soft shades of purple and apricot with a peculiar musky scent. The long flower stem was fine and pendent, so that the delicate blooms seemed to float and dance on outstretched wings, and I imagined them in my mind's eye against the dim leafy background of those distant jungles.

The catasetums I found in the forest where the Devil was thought to live also flowered a few months later in São Paulo. The outside of the petals were the palest silver-green, and inside a deep burgundy-red. It appeared to be a new species.

Some months after my return to São Paulo I noticed that the centre of the bromeliad I had found with Maria behind Salvador's home was tinged with crimson, a sure sign of flowering. Day by day the red area grew larger and more intense in colour. Then, in the heart of the rosette, opening in the pool of water which collects there, appeared a colony of small white flowers, faintly tinged with pink. A few weeks later the offshoot bloomed too. The fruit was a brilliant metallic blue. It was later named as a new species, *Neoregelia margaretae*. During the months of heavy rainfall, those distant forests would be studded with these magenta jewels.

Opposite. *Neoregelia margaretae*

cattleya violacea
rio burni, Amazonas

1967
PICO DA NEBLINA:
DEFEATED BY THE RAIN

Clusia grandifolia sketches

The results from the tributaries of the Alto Rio Negro yielded the most unusual plants: a trumpet vine (*Distictella magnolifolia*), a most extraordinary swamp plant (*Rapatea paludosa*), a number of lovely flowers from strangler trees (Clusias), and an orchid – *Gongora quinquenervis*. In fact I had material for sketches and paintings which would keep me busy for many months. One of the Rapateceae plants I had collected on the Serra de Curicuriari survived and thrived in my home in São Paulo for many years.

On my return from Rio Uaupés, I had seen from the Brazilian Air Force plane the distant Serra de Imeri. The highest peak of this range of mountains in Brazil, the Serra da Neblina (Mountain of the Mist), is known as Pico da Neblina. True to its name the peak was capped in cloud. The sight of this beautiful and mysterious *serra* excited me and I vowed that one day I would return to explore the wonders of the mountain.

An opportunity came when my project to collect and paint plants of the region was accepted and sponsored by the National Geographic Society. I left São Paulo for Manaus in the middle of July, accompanied by a young Brazilian, Paulo Cardone, who was to assist me. He was the ideal choice for he enjoyed learning about plants, and loved and understood animals. The society also arranged for me to have an experienced photographer, Otis Imboden, and we met up with him in Manaus. There I hired a boat – later to prove a great liability – and a canoe in tow.

Having purchased the necessary provisions, we left the hot and busy town by back streets, picking our way through black mud down to the small launch we had hired to take us up Rio Negro to the Serra da Neblina. The launch was moored in an *igarapé* overlooked by shanty town houses, the remains of the older part of the town. The massed green of aquatic plants and the banana palms on the banks gave the *igarapé* a tropical aspect, intensified by the sultry air. Our launch was typical of those found on Rio Negro, with a small deck fore and aft and a wooden cabin of rough construction sheltering a noisy, oily inboard motor. A small canoe with an outboard motor and a crew of two came with the launch: the 'captain', Santino, an Amazonense, and João, a Tariana Indian, very deaf since doing his military service – gunfire he explained. He was a pleasant, good-humoured fellow who bore patiently the gibes of Santino.

We had scarcely passed Ponta Negra, where the port of Manaus almost disappears from view, when Santino discovered that he had left behind a suitcase containing all his possessions and decided to go back for it in the canoe. While we waited for him to return we bathed in the cool, dark waters of Rio Negro. It was already nightfall when we saw the small light of the canoe approaching and Santino came aboard with his suitcase and some embarrassment. During the night we sailed on until weariness overcame the crew and we moored in an enchanted spot beneath a great tree, which, by morning light I recognised as Swartzia – full of white flowers.

During the night it had rained heavily and to our consternation the canoe had filled with water. The motor was submerged and showed not a spark of life. The men baled out hastily before the petrol drum and other contents of the canoe sank to the bottom of Rio

Cattleya grows on trunks

Negro. It was the first day of the journey, and I had begun to lose confidence in the efficiency of the crew.

The floods were still high and the trees stood deep in water bringing me nearer to the flowers in their canopies, including massive philodendrons which crowned most of the older trees and whose roots, mingling with those of clusias, hung in curtains seeking sustenance from the soil. Parrots and toucans played and fed in the spreading branches. Delicate violet mimosa flowers fringed the river banks merging into yellow aquatic blossoms.

Isolated shacks drifted by, most abandoned, some completely flooded, their tattered straw roofs floating among the remains of plantations of bananas and sugar cane. For mile after mile there was no terra firma. Soon after passing this rather depressing area we came across a spectacular sight of giant trees clustered with epiphytes and entwined with clusias. On the verges of the river was a fine *Bombax munguba* (kapok tree) amongst whose branches large white flowers bloomed and fruit hung in scarlet pods. As the pods burst they loosed silken parachutes, covering the deck as they drifted in with the wind.

A band of small yellow-limbed monkeys followed the boat, whistling with excitement as they peeped between the foliage of the trees at the water's edge. Soon they were followed by small chestnut-coloured monkeys springing from branch to branch, chattering loudly.

As the night was calm and starry, I decided to sleep under the sky and the brilliant moon. From deep sleep I awoke with a start on hearing a commotion on board, and at the same time felt heavy drops of rain. I hurried down to the cabin but not before I had seen our predicament. The launch and canoe had broken loose from their moorings and were tangled in a great floating island of vegetation, the canoe half under water. The men worked frantically to release them, only succeeding at daybreak. Once again, the canoe was baled out, and as its outboard motor had been immersed in water all night it was hopeless then to try to get any life out of it. Various efforts to dry it out were made, and finally, after several hours we were able to continue on our way.

At the mouth to Rio Branco, Rio Negro receives such a tremendous volume of water that it resembles an inland sea. Before crossing this enormous expanse the experienced boatman looks at the sky and takes good note of the weather, for this passage can be dangerous even for large boats. After passing many rocks and rapids, navigated skilfully by our pilot, and as the afternoon appeared tranquil, we sailed on past the mouth of Rio Branco towards the village of Carvoeiro. The gigantic trees which we had been passing became dwarfed in the distance yet still stood out as landmarks. The jungle appeared a faint line on the horizon. Suddenly a wind sprang up and our boat tossed and rolled in

Streptocalyx

Streptocalyx

Spider monkey

the waters which were becoming turbulent as dark masses of clouds gathered. We sped towards the sunset, a golden glow in the west broken by streaks of indigo cloud, forerunners of the storm which broke just as we reached the village.

An awed silence fell as we drew nearer to four towering palms and a church spire dark against the evening sky, which marked Carvoeiro. The primitive landscape of the extensive archipelago lay around us. As our boat was moored, curious villagers came out to gaze at it and us. I rapidly pulled a blouse and slacks over my swimsuit and went out into the dark village to meet the old mayor. We sat and talked with him in the shadow of the church at a table across which came the faintest gleam of light from the open door.

Not realising how impressed Otis and I, at least, were by the wild beauty of the surroundings of the little settlement, and its exquisite setting in this remote, unspoiled corner of the earth, the mayor spoke proudly of the fertility of the soil, how wheat could be cultivated there on a large scale. He had experimented with wheat in a tin, which would have developed had not someone forgotten to water it. Then perhaps he could sell us some eggs? we ventured to ask, but he had none as the hens did not lay for lack of maize. In my mind I contrasted this man with old Antonio Carvalho who had everything he needed in his little farm through observing and respecting nature, without destroying the forest.

Galeandra sp.

Perhaps this rather short-sighted old mayor eventually reached the same conclusion.

Not far west of Carvoeiro a small building had been constructed on the banks of Rio Branco by the American Mission. This was also the headquarters of a scientific expedition and its large boat, the *Alpha Helix*, which – unfortunately, as we had hoped to be able to use it to do some plant collecting and photography – had just left the area. However an amphibious plane was also based there, and Otis piloted it over a lake where we spotted flowering *Victoria regia* (now called *Victoria amazonica*) and flights of parrots.

The launch ran smoothly past inundated isles until we left the open river and were sailing beside a thickly forested region and the mouth of Rio Jarati. As night obscured the landscape I sat on deck until late, watching a great red waning moon reflecting a path of light in our wake, and enjoying the cool air after the heat of the day. When I retired, I hung my hammock in the cabin, where five hammocks were already crowded into the inadequate space, the heaviest one above me and I feared that the ropes might give way. This did not encourage peaceful sleep! Then, in the darkness, our arrival in Barcelos, the first town of any size, was announced. I tried desperately to tidy myself and was not a little embarrassed when the village came out and watched my efforts.

Barcelos in the past was a village of Manaus Indians, named Mariuá. It is now dominated by the Salesian Mission, and the inhabitants are very mixed, Indians (the original inhabitants), *caboclos* and a few of European descent. I did not find the town very prepossessing and was quite glad to leave after we replenished our supplies, which fortunately included eggs and bread.

As we sailed on, the riverscape became more and more fascinating. As before, the region had been flooded and we passed many isolated and abandoned huts under water. On the fibrous stems of the Jará palms, standing deep in the water, groups of perfumed orchids, *Galeandra devoniana*, bloomed profusely. Cerise flowers of *Cattleya violacea* gleamed in the

Victoria amazonica

Margaret Mee
June, 1984

Galeandra devoniana Schomb.
Lago Sapucá, Oriximina,
Pará

trees beside the delicate white blooms of *Brassavola martiana*. Trees of *Gustavia augusta*, with large pink and white flowers, were frequent along the riverbanks.

The day passed pleasantly, and as the sun sank its last rays caught the colourful plumes of macaws, toucans, herons, noisy kingfishers and flights of parrot as they flew homeward. Dangling from the highest trees were colonies of *japims'* nests, their owners protesting loudly at our intrusion on their territory. Dolphins played in the river rippling the surface.

One night I slept peacefully on deck until I was suddenly awakened by a storm wind blowing, and within minutes a tempest was raging. With a struggle I escaped, the wind tearing at my hair and clothes, into the crowded, stuffy cabin where all windows had been closed. Santino managed to moor the boat in a small bay which we had the luck to be near when the storm reached its height, though even there we were tossed and churned about. These violent storms on Rio Negro do not usually last for long, and this one soon abated leaving a rolling swell as it swept on.

The routine of the days and nights was much the same during the rest of the journey. The launch's motor continued to give endless trouble and only Otis could manage to keep it running. Stormy weather was intermixed with tranquil days and nights. Incidents were few, although on one occasion the launch ran into a sandbank and, when free, hit the branches of a large tree breaking the mast and hurricane lamp. I was on the roof of the cabin and emerged from the wreckage with twigs and leaves in my hair.

In the rivers and forests the animals and birds pursued the unchanged patterns of their lives as their predecessors had done before man made his appearance on the planet or in the forests of the Amazon. It was a glorious existence. Time did not seem to exist.

In Tapurucuará (or Santa Isabel as it is often called), Padre João Badelotti from the Salesian Mission came down to the shore to welcome us. Kindly and tolerant, he was a tall, strongly-built man with a thick greying beard. I confessed to him that I was not religious and belonged to no denomination or sect. 'You are religious', he replied, 'for you love and respect nature'.

Gustavia augusta

Padre João introduced us to Irma, the Mother Superior, who asked me after mutual friends when she learned that I had visited the Salesian Mission in Uaupés. Also in Tapurucuará I met Carlos, the pilot who worked for the padres. A Tariana Indian, pleasant and reliable, he would accompany us on our journey up river. He had sailed Rio Cauaburi and the Canal da Maturacá for years, both of which he would have to navigate to reach the Pico da Neblina. It was reassuring to learn Carlos knew both waterways so well, for it would be a difficult voyage as the river was beset with rapids and cataracts, and when the river was low no boat could pass without being poled.

To my relief, Mother Superior allowed me to leave the plants I had already collected in the coconut palms which grew in a sheltered part of the Mission garden. This arrangement also freed my plant baskets for the collection which I hoped to make on Neblina.

We restocked provisions in the village, though only about half of what we needed was available, but we hoped to get fruit and fish on the journey. In the morning of 29 July we left Tapurucuará on our way to the Pico da Neblina, and almost immediately Carlos caught sight of a large bunch of assai fruit and climbed the slender trunk of the palm Indian fashion, his feet in a belt made from the fibre of the tucum palm. Thus we had a store of assai fruit and cucurá, the latter a black fruit resembling grapes.

After leaving Tapurucuará we encountered the first rapids of Rio Cauaburi. These were particularly difficult and dangerous to navigate as the river narrowed considerably and the force of the water was tremendous. The treacherous motor stopped running in the midst of a great eddy, but Otis hurried to the rescue and somehow got it going again, saving us from disaster.

On this stretch of the river we met an Indian paddling his dugout canoe, and invited him to have coffee with us. Before leaving in his canoe, he looked up at me and said. 'I

remember you were in Curicuriari', adding that the Tucanos of his village still talked of
the day when I had threatened their common enemy, a gold washer from Manaus, with
a revolver. So I sent greetings by him to my Tucano friends, particularly Amelia and João
Firma, my next-door neighbours in Curicuriari. I was happy to learn that I had not been
forgotten by the Indians four years after staying in their village.

Padre João Badelotti welcomed us

We wound up the sinuous river, which became increasingly difficult to navigate because
of the many rapids, until late in the afternoon we met the most formidable one,
Destacamento. Without the additional power of the canoe's outboard motor we could
never have overcome those raging torrents, in spite of Carlos and his experience as a pilot.

After this we decided to moor the launch for the night. Nearby, two boatloads of
passengers crowded into a small public riverside shelter, which was nevertheless completely
open to the weather. One of the boats was in the service of the padres from the Salesian
Mission, and we were able to buy from Peixoto, the captain of this boat and friend of
Carlos, three litres of oil of which we were in desperate need, for the inboard motor was
losing oil rapidly. Peixoto was a quiet fellow, but other members of the crew were flinging
bilge water at random, and the loud radio transistor and graveyard coughs so disturbed us
that we decided to move, and found a lovely spot, sheltered by overhanging forest trees.

Next day, Otis managed to put new life into the engine, but only with much difficulty,
as the only wrench had fallen into the river.

We passed the beautiful falls of Jacamin easily, though the Janajos-açu falls which
followed presented a real test of navigating skill. In spite of being slight and small, Carlos
managed to get us through. He ordered us to stamp and rock the boat to free her whilst
he ran the motor at full throttle. The raging waters tried to hold us captive but we always
eventually slipped by. Then another swirling eddy held us, and I anxiously watched a little
tree as a gauge, hoping to see we moved away from it. In spite of the motor working its
hardest it could not move the launch, which was held back by the overwhelming force of
the falls. Then, with a tremendous effort, Carlos instinctively found a channel and we shot
through exultant to calmer waters. After that test, Manajos-mirim and the other falls
which followed proved no obstacle.

In the tense moments of the struggle to pass the rapids I had noticed a noisy flight of brilliant green parrots flying over followed by dozens of delicate scissor birds. Now that there was a lull we noticed more of the animal life around the river. There was a sudden stir aboard and Santino shouted in great excitement that he could see an anaconda on the bank. The enormous creature lay stretched along a fallen tree, a large bulge in its sleek body, for it was digesting a recent meal. It must have been more than four metres long.

Otis was very eager to photograph the reptile, so the crew prepared a lasso on a long pole, hoping to trap it in the noose. Like a streak of lightning, the anaconda disappeared into the river without leaving a ripple on its surface.

Disappointed, Otis determined to get a record of the next animal that might appear, and very soon João shouted that there was a sloth in a nearby tree. A cord hanging over his neck, João climbed the tall smooth tree trunk, not without risk, for the branches overhung the river. The sloth refused to move, and continued sleeping, rolled up in a tight ball. Rather cruelly, João severed the branch with his bush knife, and the sloth, still clinging to the branch, fell with a mass of foliage on my basket of plants. Although unhurt, the poor dazed creature sprawled helplessly on the deck. His long coarse fur was grey-brown, but between his shoulder blades an orange patch marked him as a male. Paulo held him gently by the hands, careful to avoid his long, sharp talons, whilst Otis filmed. Released, the animal struggled to the mast, which he climbed slowly and deliberately, then settled himself comfortably and promptly fell asleep – or was he feigning? For soon, he came down making straight for the river. We moved towards the shore and an overhanging branch, which the sloth clutched eagerly, and, with the strange half-smile on his face, scaled the tree where he doubtless continued his interrupted siesta. I collected an *Acacallis cyanea*, the blue orchid, in full, exquisite flower.

On 2 September we reached Maturacá, our journey having started in Manaus on 15 July.

The black waters of the natural Maturacá canal connect with Rio Cauaburi. It must be one of the most beautiful waterways in Amazonia. Its banks harbour a wealth of plants – the epiphyte *Aechmea chantinii*, with vivid red bracts and silver ringed leaves, scarlet pitcairnia massed on the banks, and a host of other forest plants. Every curve in the river, and they were legion, gave a spectacular view of the forested slopes of the Serra de Imeri. Around one bend of the river a canoe paddled by two young Waika Indians glided towards us, moving swiftly. They were handsome young men, wearing the traditional ornaments of

The Salesian Mission at Maturacá

Acacallis cyanea

their tribe, two scarlet macaw tail feathers bound on their upper arms, bunches of parrot feathers in the lobes of their ears. As the canoe shot past us, its occupants smiled in a friendly way; clearly they had had little contact with the 'civilizados'!

At Maturacá, the Salesian Mission stood high on the river bank from which a large cleared area led down many steps to the 'port' where, no sooner had the boat been moored, dozens of Indian children of all sizes rushed down to the water's edge and crowded into and around the launch, talking excitedly. The Director of the Mission, Padre José Schneider, a tall lean man in a grey habit, came down the steps to meet us, a smile on his face. He wore a small brimmed canvas hat over his white hair. A visiting German, Padre Francisco, accompanied him. We were made very welcome and were invited to have supper with them in an austere room with whitewashed walls. Whilst we conversed, I observed the two men made a complete contrast: Padre Schneider ascetic and saintly in appearance, Padre Francisco, a typical well-fed friar who might have come out of the Middle Ages as depicted by a contemporary artist.

On inspection, the mission building proved large and rambling, lying about ten minutes distant from the Indian village of the Araribo tribe. The Indians here were very primitive people and on the whole handsome. They make fine baskets and feather ornaments, and a few earthenware pots. I met one of the wives of the chief, Joachim, a pretty petite

The most affectionate and natural children one could wish to meet

Paulo with children in the maloca

woman wearing only bunches of red, yellow and green parrot feathers in the lobes of her ears. She could speak no Portuguese, indeed scarcely any of the women could and very few of the men. Unhappily many of the children looked sick and had sore eyes and bad teeth, whilst the adults, on the other hand, seemed healthy and had beautiful white teeth. It seemed that the older generation, living according to their traditions (though they too have been prey to the white man's diseases), fared much better than the children whose lives are influenced by the two cultures. As Joachim had recently visited Manaus with the padres, western influences had inevitably crept in. Indeed, the roofs of some of their village huts were tin, an introduction of the mission.

From Rio Cauaburi I had seen the magnificent Serra do Padre, or Piripira as it is known to the Indians, a wonderful contour against the evening sky . Now it could be seen more clearly as I passed on my way to the Indian village, over a wonderful Indian bridge, constructed entirely of lianas and fine tree trunks, spanning the rapids. A real suspension bridge. It had obviously been there for many years and was now in some need of repair, as I learned when I had to cross and recross it before Otis was satisfied with the filming. Beneath this amazing structure the river flowed over a rock-filled bed, a labyrinth of rapids and falls on its course towards the Upper Rio Negro.

A loud chanting came from the village. The medicine-man, or priest, was dancing and singing in the heat of the midday sun. He was streaming with sweat which had partially washed away his serpentine body painting. He careered through the village obviously fortified with a particular snuff used in religious rites. The powder of the bark of the Virola tree was blown through bamboo tubes into the medicine-man's nostrils and immediately he began to sing and dance wildly. Though consumed with curiosity, I kept my head averted, only surreptitiously glancing from time to time, knowing that women, and above all strange women, were forbidden to witness these rites. Some hours later when I passed, the medicine-man was still dancing and singing with the same energy and fervour.

In the village I was besieged by children who hung on to my hands, hair, and shirtsleeves, smiling and chatting to me in the only language they knew – of which I could not understand a word. I replied in Portuguese, which did not deter them in any way. They were the most affectionate and natural children one could wish to meet. The women were mostly petite, their bronze coloured bodies often painted with coloured dyes. Their clothing consisted of feather earrings of various colours.

Suddenly there was excitement amongst a group of Indians and a little woman ran towards me and threw her arms around my neck, asking if I remembered her. I thought quickly, and recalled that I had met her some years ago in the Mission of Içana. She even knew my name, 'Margalete', though we had only met briefly in 1964. She was married now to an Indian of the Araribo tribe. As I spoke with her, my mind went back to a track beneath the trees in Içana, where I had seen her holding a minute fledgling which was cheeping and struggling with fear. I asked her to release the little bird but she refused. Suddenly tears filled my eyes and, begging me not to cry, she returned the baby bird to its nest.

One of the men took a fancy to my hair, plaiting and unplaiting it, but

I did not protest, for blond hair was a novelty. As he worked, he let flow a running commentary which kept his audience in peals of laughter. Then my straw hat was passed from hand to hand, the Indians trying it on at various angles and eventually returning it to me stained red from the dye on their foreheads.

Besieged by children

Chieftain Joachim arranged for three Indians to lead us to the Pico da Neblina, for without guides familiar with the 'invisible' paths the ascent would be almost impossible. Three strong young men who knew the area were chosen: Placido, Napoleão and Rafael. Placido and Napoleão were handsome young men of approximately thirty and twenty respectively, possibly younger. They had very fine features and their figures were magnificent – broad shoulders and narrow hips. Napoleão had dark green eyes, an uncommon colour among Indians, but I was to hear later that many of his tribe, the Waikas, who lived in the regions between Rio Demini and the Orinoco, were comparatively fair, some even blue-eyed. Rafael, who was sombre and unsmiling, had an unfortunate history which made him behave a little strangely from time to time. Alone and unarmed on the slopes of Neblina he had been attacked by a jaguar, which, after a terrible struggle, he had killed with his bare hands. Torn, bleeding and suffering from shock, he dragged himself back to the mission, a three day walk. He never quite recovered from the terrifying incident. Padre Schneider cured the physical wounds on his face and chest but emotionally he remained silent and morose.

Before leaving the Indian village, we gave presents for the tribe to Joachim who distributed them to the circle of Indians whilst we looked on. Joachim was extremely careful to give each one an equal share, but his own present, a large bush knife, had been 'forgotten' by Paulo who had deemed it too good and had brought along a very inferior substitute. I saw Joachim's look of disappointment and sent Paulo back immediately to fetch the bush knife, and the chieftain took it with great satisfaction.

Our last night at the mission we dined with the padres in the austere dining-room when there was another visitor, Benedito, who was

Beside Rio Cauaburi

119

bent on introducing cattle and grass to the region.

That evening we prepared for our journey to the Pico. Our rooms were in utter confusion, but we somehow managed to pack in spite of an invasion by the Indians who came to watch us packing and eagerly examined our belongings. Preparations for the journey were only finished by morning.

There was a delay before we got underway, for ten hunters from the tribe had asked to be towed to the mouth of Rio Tucano, a tributary of the Cauaburi, a considerable distance away, and the river leading to the Serra da Neblina. We were desperately short of fuel for the return journey from Serra da Neblina, since so much had been wasted through the malfunctioning of the motor, but we towed them as far as we could and explained the situation to them. They did not complain but pushed off cheerfully in their heavily laden canoe, with five days of hard paddling ahead of them.

At every curve of the river we imagined we had reached the mouth of Rio Tucano. And when we eventually did reach it, after a half day of sailing, we found it completely blocked by fallen trees and branches. It would have been hopeless to try to hack our way through the tangle, for it appeared the barrier continued for some distance. So we disembarked at the old camping site of the 1965 Boundary Commission, where the date of the event was inscribed on a sturdy old tree. Here Murça Pires, the Brazilian botanist, with Bassett Maguire, of New York's Botanical Garden, had made their camp two years before, though the site by this time consisted of a few slightly weathered posts and broken-down palm-roofed huts.

The beauty of this remote forest was awe-inspiring and my excitement overwhelming, to think that at last I had set foot on the cloud-capped Serra at which I had gazed longingly – but always from afar. It was refreshing to bathe in the cool waters of Rio Tucano, and afterwards to retire to my hammock to relax, though it was saturated and my pyjamas wet through, as nothing ever dried.

Early next morning we were up and about, having passed a peaceful night in hammocks hung between the trees, and now eager to start on the climb.

We sent Carlos and Santino in the launch further back down the mouth of Rio Tucano, with orders to sail to navigable waters if the level of the river should fall considerably, and, after carefully concealing the canoe and outboard motor in overhanging bushes of an *igarapé*, we set off, our guides leading the way.

Early in the journey Napoleão shot a large black bird. As soon as we had started the ascent, he explained there would be no more game, news which I heard with concealed relief. So the guides dined on game and the rest of us on our dried packet food.

The ground of the forest was saturated by the incessant rain and the water-filled hollows made climbing difficult, but we walked on through the forests until early afternoon when we prepared to camp for the night. Then a problem arose: we were short of one hammock. Rafael had left his behind, feeling that it was too dirty to bring with him on the journey. He confessed the fact with shame, but Otis drew a nylon hammock from his pack which served its purpose, though somewhat cold and uncomfortable. We were all wet through as the rain had not ceased during the day and continued with renewed force at night. Snug and dry in my tropical hammock, through the dark net windows I could see the rain teeming down in the forest. The Indians, accustomed to these downpours and wet nights, had constructed a shelter for the other hammocks.

On the following day we stopped beside a small stream where the guides, who had by now grasped my objective, collected orchids and bromeliads and even vied with each other as to who could discover the most interesting plants. The rain continued most of the day, but in spite of this the sultry heat was overwhelming, and raindrops mixed with sweat ran down my brow, stinging my eyes.

Clusia aff. *schomburgkiana* and a weathered trunk

Strange spirals of black mud, when trodden on, gave off a sound like the rumble of thunder and I asked Placido what could they be. Beneath these hummocks, he told me, lived *minhocas*, a species of giant earthworm, I imagined. Amongst the hummocks and rotting leaves with which the ground was carpeted I stepped upon the still fragrant though faded flowers of *Clusia grandiflora*.

Rain, and still more rain, and as the light had faded by four o'clock we camped early and cooked our supper and retired for the night. This time, due to the ceaseless rain, my jungle hammock was not so inviting, for it had been hung hurriedly and the water streamed in and I was drenched. Water dripped in my ears and when I turned over to avoid it, water dripped in my face. There was no escape. Paulo shouted above the pelting rain that he was sodden as his plastic cover kept blowing off. When morning came there was no relief, for from wet pyjamas I changed into wet clothes.

Our trek continued. Numerous streams crossed the now almost invisible tracks and we waded through pools of black mud. In spite of these hardships I remained entranced by the beauty of the surrounding forests, their timeless aspect dwarfing all trivial setbacks.

Laughing and joking in their own language, the Indians carried me over the deeper streams which I found difficult to wade across. Later, a steep and slippery ascent proved too much for me. Scrambling up, exhausted and streaming with sweat, my heavy rucksack seemed to be pulling me backwards. Sick and faint I flopped face down in the mud, and I signalled to Rafael, who was coming up the slope behind me, to call Otis or Paulo who both came to my assistance and relieved me of my pack. At this critical moment a venomous ant stung me on wrist and shoulder, an agonising pain! But I was cured of all my ills at the summit of the incline where a glorious array of orchids and bromeliads came into view and amongst them the long sought for *Aechmea fernandae* which I had last found many years ago in Aripuana.

Otis and Paulo, heavily laden with the addition of my rucksack which I was ordered not to carry any more, slipped often on the treacherous ground which was uphill and downhill all the way, the descents almost more difficult than the ascents, but in spite of this they were both well ahead of me.

Suddenly I stood transfixed. At a short distance from the track grew a strange and

Aechmea fernandae

beautiful tree – or was it a tree, or a tremendous mass of lianas? The thick rope–like stems writhed and twisted towards the sky where they were lost in the canopy of the forest. There was not a leaf to be seen on this enigmatic giant.

A tree, or a tremendous mass of lianas?

As I stood wondering and admiring this magnificent arrangement, Rafael, who had been some distance behind me, passed with a strange lingering gaze and I realised with a start that the rest of the group were out of sight and far ahead. Panic seized me as I realised that I was alone on the slopes of Neblina and soon darkness would fall. Following Rafael, well on by now, I hurried on, glancing behind on my way to assure myself that what I had seen was reality and not a waking vision. Eventually I caught up with the others who had already made camp for the night.

The next day, after five days of climbing and torrential rain, with the morning light came bad news. Placido came to tell me that we could not continue on our journey as the track had disappeared due to the ceaseless rains. Early that morning, the guides had gone ahead to discover the state of the path and found it completely obliterated. There was no alternative but to return to the boat – if it was still there. I was bitterly disappointed and could not restrain my tears, but the hope still lingered that should the weather improve we might struggle on.

Painting João's scarlet flowered pitcairnia

The kindly João, seeing my distress disappeared and returned with a scarlet flowered Pitcairnia for me to paint to console me for the disappointment. So in spite of the drizzle I became absorbed in my work until Napoleão ran off with my tube of red paint to which he had taken a fancy, and only returned it unwillingly after my protests. Then the drizzle turned to heavy rain.

All the camping equipment was twice as heavy, being saturated – it was to prove a burden on the miserable return journey. Soon after daybreak, unwillingly, I was on my way down the slopes of Neblina, exhausted and despondent. Added to our disappointment was the doubt as to whether the boat would still be moored at the foot of the mountain, for, in spite of the rain, the level of Rio Cauaburi would be falling rapidly at this time,

Pitcairnia

when *vaziamento* (literally emptying) was well under way. Had Santino and Carlos realised this and, fearing being stranded, sailed back to Maturacá?

Napoleão and Placido went ahead, carrying our food and most of the camping equipment with them, and as the rest of us never caught up with them that day we suffered the pangs of hunger, only finding a little rice and powdered milk in our baggage. However, we gathered unripe papaya at an abandoned Indian village which helped to ease our hunger. There I was able to recline wearily in one of the rough fibre hammocks which had been hanging, maybe for years, in one of the huts. As we walked on we reached another of these sad, abandoned villages. We rested again for a while and Rafael told us, without any sign of emotion on his expressionless face, that most of the tribes from these abandoned villages had died of 'catarrh' (in fact influenza), amongst them his father who lay buried beneath the hut we were in. I was not sorry to leave this place of tragedy, haunted as it was by sad memories of the dead.

Before night fell we were camping at the site of our first night by the soothing waters of Rio Tucano. The men re-roofed the shelters they had built with the huge leaves of ravenella which grew there in abundance. They had just completed this and had succeeded in lighting a fire, when the heavens opened and the torrential rain soon put out the fire. Not discouraged, João and Rafael crept through the teeming rain into the thick forest, returning with an enormous termite nest with which they re-kindled the fire. The nest blazed furiously, giving off heavy, yellow smoke which hung around in the damp air giving off an acrid smell. Shivering and wet we crowded around the fire in the little shelter, having only one hammock between the five of us, for Napoleão and the baggage had still not turned up, though Placido had appeared empty handed on the track earlier in the day.

By the red glow of the blazing flames, Otis was happily taking photos of the lighting effects on the sculptural forms of the Indians. We left early in the morning, greatly relieved that the heavy rain had turned to drizzle.

My plants were becoming an intolerable burden and the ground was slimy under the rotting leaves so that I dragged behind my companions. I was further delayed by plants which I was still collecting. Once I lost the track by following a dried stream-bed which looked for all the world like a path. I was gradually losing grip on the plastic plant bags, and I felt the last of my strength slipping away, when a most welcome sight revived me – Napoleão standing beneath a great tree. 'I was waiting for you Dona Margalete', he said with all his charm, and took my bags of plants, slinging them lightly over his shoulder.

We walked rapidly, I slipping often in my canvas shoes now coated with mud. When we reached the place where we hoped to find Carlos and Santino, what a joy it was to see the launch. On a second look, I noticed with a shock that she appeared abandoned, for all was silent and the shutters were closed. But, on hearing us, the shutters were opened noisily and Carlos and Santino came on deck, relieved and happy to see us. They were eaten up by *pium*, they complained, and had to remain shut in the cabin to escape the plague of these blood-sucking flies – the red variety, they explained, much bigger and more venomous than the small black variety.

Santino had prepared a meal of *paca* and rice which we ate hungrily, even before changing our sodden travel-stained clothes, for it was days since we had enjoyed a substantial meal.

We started off on our return journey after literally extricating ourselves from the Yanomani Indians who had besieged us since early morning with outstretched hands. 'Iba! Iba!' (give me) one of the results of contact with the 'civilizados'. We sailed up Rio Cauaburi passing endless forests, the magnificent peak of Piripira, my plants waving in the breeze. Then brief stops at Maturacá and the friends we had made there. I was sad to leave these beautiful people, dwellers in another world, a world of glorious natures – but for how long?

Galeandra devoniana

Margaret Mee
September 1948

Cochleanthes amazonica
(Rchb. f. & Warsc.)

Margaret Mee
1983

Encyclia randii (Barb. Rodr.)
C. Porto & Brade
Amazonas

1967

RIO MARAUIÁ:
WITH PARROT AND SHEEP

Opposite. *Encyclia randii*

Before we had even reached Uaupés on our way back to Manaus, I was planning another journey. I had already spoken with Paulo who, like me, was keen to sail up Rio Marauiá which rises in the Serra de Imeri and flows into the Alto Rio Negro some twenty kilometres west of Tapurucuará. I had heard so much of the wonders of this remote river from Dr. Froes whom I had met in Belém in 1956. Many years before, this distinguished traveller had flown over the Serra de Imeri and had told me what an interesting place it might prove for natural scientists.

So when we arrived at the Salesian Mission at Tapurucuará, I provisionally arranged for Paulo and myself to go to the mission on Rio Marauiá where a solitary padre, Antonio Goes, lived and about whom legendary stories abounded.

The hospital at the mission in Tapurucuará had not been used since the last epidemic (possibly measles). While arrangements to visit Padre Goes' Mission were being made, Paulo and I were assigned by the Mother Superior to a large, rather dark room with sightless windows in the disused hospital. I chose a bed near to the door from which I hoped to get some light and from which I could see, at the end of a long corridor, the heavy wrought-iron gate giving access to the path to the Indian village. Girls from the mission school brought in my rather untidy baggage.

I had a day working on my plants, collected on my journey to Pico da Neblina. Most of the specimens seem to have survived, but a good rain would be a godsend. Paulo helped me and worked well, whilst Curica, a little parrot I had acquired a few weeks earlier, sat in a tree, observing and enjoying himself immensely. I had opened the door of his cage as soon as we arrived at Tapurucuará for I could not bear to see the fledgling cooped up in a tiny space, and he seemed content to leave it and perch near me as I worked.

But one evening after supper I went into my room and found him hopelessly tied up

Curica, my little parrot

My first thought was for the birds the locals frequently brought from the forests in tiny cages as presents for the sisters

in the fringe of a towel. I hurried the suffering creature to Paulo, who quickly cut the fringe whilst the parrot screamed loudly. When free, he drank water in gasps, then, until it was time for bed, insisted on sleeping under my chin. That night he shared another unpleasant experience with me.

In this region of Alto Rio Negro, vampire bats are as prolific as they were in the days of the mid-19th century traveller Richard Spruce. Spruce wrote in *Notes of a Botanist on the Amazon and Andes* that he was badly bitten one night by these creatures when sleeping, his net having opened slightly. I had noticed the night before that there was a very noisy bat flying around, but did not think anything about it, as my mosquito net was always in use. However, this night I heard the iron gate rattling loudly, and as I knew that there had been a burglary in the mission recently, felt it my duty to investigate. I peered down the corridor but saw nothing untoward. As I returned, the bat flew against my face with an almost caressing movement of its wings, and I rapidly got under my net. I shone my torch around the room, and to my horror, the beam shone on the bat, hanging under the little parrot's cage. Curica, frozen with fear, sat huddled in a corner. I jumped out of bed and the bat flew off as I seized the birdcage and put it under my net. Secure from the vampire, Curica calmed down, though the bat continued to flap around outside the net. Next morning I searched the room and found the lethargic creature hanging under a bed, dripping with the blood of a victim!

That day, the ethnologist Hans Becker arrived at the mission. He had written a book on the Indians of the Rio Negro, and had just travelled up Rio Marauiá with a party of German tourists, so I was eager to meet him. From Dr. Becker I learned that the river is black water, so is relatively free from mosquitoes and *pium*. The group only got as far as the first Indian village at Cachóeira de Irapajé, so did not reach the mission of Padre Antonio Goes, which is at the head of Rio Marauiá.

An interesting Catasetum had flowered and I had just finished painting it on the terrace when Ademar Fontes, owner of a small launch, appeared. Formerly he worked with the Malaria Service and used to spray the *caboclos'* huts with DDT against mosquitoes – hence his nickname Dedé. Happily, he gave up that calling, and was now taking cargo up and down the rivers in his boat, *Santo Alberto*. As he was planning to take provisions up to Padre Goes, I had asked him if there would be room aboard for me and Paulo. Now he had come to say he could take us on our journey. There would not be much space for us he pointed out, as besides himself and a young Indian boy, there would be a sheep and a mule aboard. Fortunately, for us at least, when the time came to sail, the mule, true to character, obstinately refused to get on board, and as soon as we realised the struggle was futile we were ready to leave.

Our first stop was at Dedé's house in the forest, where his wife, a pretty Tucano Indian greeted us, two beautiful children beside her. The house they lived in was constructed in the Indian style, but had a slightly more elaborate interior than I had previously seen. Like the boat the house was spotless. We were treated to a splendid lunch, Curica was given fresh guavas to eat and provided with a more robust cage for the journey, and then we departed.

Our first night was spent in an Indian village At about seven o'clock, when darkness had already fallen, we sailed up a small waterway of Rio Marauiá. On the forested river bank, lights shone intermittently among the leaves, and I imagined that Dr. Becker must have left torches as presents for the Indians. Loud voices rang out across the water, asking in the indigenous language, of which Dedé understood a little, who we were.

'Mea, mea', bleated the sheep

'Mea, mea', mimicked the Indians. 'What is that?'

'It is a sheep', shouted Dedé.

'What sort of person is that?' the Indians asked, laughing

'It is an animal. Come and see her. I am taking her to Padre Goes'.

'Who else is with you?'

'A white woman, Margarete. She wants to stay at your village for the night'.

'Come on then, come now'.

Then several shots echoed through the woods

'What happened?', shouted Dedé

'We have killed an alligator. Come and have a look'.

'No', said Dedé, 'We are cooking supper'.

'Have you got tobacco for us?' cried the Indians.

'No'.

'Let us see the sheep then'.

Two men paddled slowly into view in a dug-out canoe. They were consumed with curiosity and and laughed excitedly at the bleating and sight of the sheep.

They clambered on to the deck to get a better view of the animal lurking in a corner of the dark cabin. They gave their names as Felipe and Domingo, rather than their Indian names, and by the light of the fire I could see I the sculptural form of their faces, high cheek bones and long slanting eyes. Sleek black hair hung to their shoulders. Both had well-shaped, muscular, bronzed bodies. They appeared to be around thirty years of age.

Curica

Dedé's small launch, complete with sheep

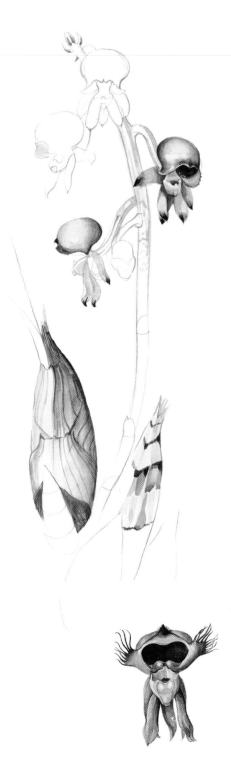

Catasetum discolor

Tall slender poles at the front held the palm leaf roof which sloped steeply

The only concession to the 'civilizados' in their costume were brief shorts. In the tradition of the tribe, ropes of tiny blue and white beads wound around their necks and crossed over their chests and were also worn as armlets stuck with long parrot feathers. Their ears were pierced for parrot feathers, though they were not wearing ear ornaments. I learned later that the German tourists had taken most of them and the Indians were busy making new ones for themselves.

Felipe and Domingo invited us to go with them to their village, so, leaving Dedé and the boy in the launch for the night, Paulo and I left with them in the canoe paddled by Felipe. On dry land, it was a long, dark walk through the woods over rough ground, and I was grateful to Felipe for the help he gave me. When we arrived, we were assigned a place to hang our hammocks in a hut at the far end of the settlement. This consisted of eleven or twelve huts built in a circle around a large, open area. The traditional buildings were very elegant – four tall slender poles at the front held the palm leaf roof which sloped steeply to a Pashiuba palm-covered wall behind, where the hammocks were hung, leaving the structure open on two sides and at the front. As the distance between the front poles and the back wall was quite large, the roof provided sufficient protection against heavy rains and storms. Two more of these shelters were in process of construction. I also saw a few huts which were not traditional and were far inferior in finish and design.

Silence reigned in the forest and the full moon appeared in the unclouded sky, shining between a magnificent group of palm trees. A group of us talked quietly until late, sitting on low, Indian stools in Felipe's hut, while the rest of the tribe were sleeping in their hammocks above the glowing embers of individual fires. The Indians were not, however, very communicative, partly through difficulty with the language, but also, I sensed, because Paulo was asking too many questions and seeming too curious about the village, its customs and religion. Felipe's wife, nursing a baby in her arms nearly as big as herself,

talked more freely with me. She had been to the mission school in Tapurucuará and consequently had a little Portuguese, so was more communicative than the men.

'Who gave you the torches?' I asked.

'Stranger, but they are 'shamin' (no good)'.

'Why?'

'Broken. We did not like him. He treated us badly'.

'Badly? Who? How?'

'Too many photos. Took all feather ornaments'.

Weary with the excitement of the day, I slept soundly, but in the small hours of the morning I was awakened by a man's voice singing loudly. The song seemed to be interspersed with weeping, and wailed on, sometimes sad and complaining, sometimes angry with loud curses when the word *Jurupari* (devil) was distinguishable. Shortly before dawn a soft woman's voice joined in the singing. Then the singers must have fallen asleep, exhausted, for silence reigned again, broken only by the graveyard coughs of many of the tribe. Later, I learned that the singer was a man who had recently lost his wife through measles, of which dread illness there had been an epidemic amongst the tribes in the area. I was told that he had been lamenting his loss in this way every night since her death.

Next morning we set off accompanied by Felipe and Domingo to help us cross the five waterfalls which lay between us and Father Goes, and we certainly needed their help. Below the rapids Rio Marauiá was as smooth as glass. But it changes character at each waterfall, and even with the help of the two Indians it took over an hour to pass the first fall, Bichu Mirim, with much sweating and straining. Bichu Açu was even more of an ordeal, and it took us until lunchtime to pass. At each waterfall we had to disembark and unload the parrot and sheep and the rest of the cargo and then lift the boat over rocks and drag it through the

Below the rapids Rio Marauiá was as smooth as glass

133

Nidularium sp.

raging waters. It was back-breaking work.

Completely exhausted we settled on a big group of stones beside calm waters and cooked our lunch. At each fall, I carried Curica into the forest and there, sitting in a tree, he ate leaves and berries, happy with the long delays and as playful as a kitten in familiar territory. We had moored in a splendid place for plant collecting and there I found *Streptocalyx longifolius, Diacrium bicornatum* and *Aechmea mertensii.*

Their work done and their hunger satisfied, Felipe and Domingo paddled back to their village in the canoe we had towed for them. They had been paid for their valuable help with fishing hooks, nylon line, a small knife each, and plenty of cigarettes, which they did not smoke, but extracted and then chewed the tobacco. The next rapid, Tucum, which the Indians had assured us would not be difficult to navigate, proved quite impassable. After making many desperate attempts to cross, we unloaded the boat and tried once more, but without any success. There was nothing for it but to go back for help. So Dedé, accompanied by the Indian boy, paddled off to get help. They did not return, and as it was growing dark, I began to be afraid that, in their small dug-out canoe, they might have met with disaster in the falls.

Whilst waiting anxiously for their return, I painted *Acacallis cyanea,* seated in the forest. There I also found a beautiful *Heterostemon ellipticus,* which was so fragile that it wilted before my eyes, and a *Pitcairnia uaupensis* in bud.

Eventually Dedé and the boy returned, much to my relief, having been unable to reach the village in time to return before darkness fell, for after dark they would have been hopelessly lost. So in the morning they set off again, and this time returned with Felipe, Domingo and another strong lad. After a terrific struggle, they managed to navigate the boat through the fearsome rapid, but not before Dedé had fallen on the slippery rocks, and was nearly carried into the falls by the strong currents. Whilst the men sweated and struggled, the horseflies took advantage to attack them with their sharp, painful stings.

The water level of the river had fallen considerably since our departure from

We had to lift the boat over rocks and drag it through the raging waters

Tapurucuará, for there had been little rain for some time and none at all for two days, but even so the strength of the falls was considerable.

We did not stop again that day until nearly dusk, when we sighted a solitary hut. It belonged to Feliciano, a rubber collector. The hut was perched high on the river bank, and a long rough hewn ramp, weak and precarious, led to the entrance. It was bounded on one side by an *igarapé*. The room inside the hut was clean and pleasant, so Paulo and I hung our hammocks there, whilst the men lit a fire in the primitive fireplace to cook supper. Peace after a strenuous day.

Round the hut the small plot was being invaded by forest trees and plants and, happily, I found a Solandra bush, its fruit resembling tomatoes. There was also a well-laden lemon tree – lemons had been introduced by the padres in the early days of the colonisation of Brazil. Curica and I ate the tomato-like fruits and lemons ravenously, for there had been a real lack of fruit in our diet in the past weeks. I collected a small *Catasetum* and many other orchids on fallen trees, which had been cut down when this area of the forest had been cleared by Feliciano to build his hut.

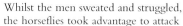

Catasetum purum

We left early next day. The river was falling fast, and would probably give rise to some problems on the return journey from the headwaters of Rio Marauiá. We were hoping to arrive at our destination in the evening, but the journey up Rio Marauiá had been slow, difficult and perilous, and Dedé, experienced pilot though he was, was straining tensely at the wheel, whilst his assistant shone a beam from the powerful torch to light the river banks. As the river narrowed, the rocks became increasingly dangerous. With relief Dedé announced that we must be reaching our destination, as he could hear Indian voices and see the glow of their fires. Indeed, within a few minutes we moored against a steep bank. Hurricane lamps shone down on us and we were welcomed by Padre Antonio Goes, a

Whilst the men sweated and struggled, the horseflies took advantage to attack

Gustavia

tall, heavily-built man with a dark beard, beginning to grey a little. His green eyes twinkled mischievously, and his pleasant smile and manner soon made us feel at home.

'Dedé', he cried, 'You are crazy to navigate the river at night! I never do. At least you have got the sheep, but where is the mule?'

Our explanations made, the Padre invited us to make ourselves at home in his living quarters. This consisted of a large covered area, its roof supported by posts. It was raised well off the ground – essential when the area is flooded – and reached by an open flight of steep wooden steps.

We had a quick meal before we fell thankfully into our hammocks. The night was incredibly peaceful and I slept soundly until dawn. In the morning Padre Antonio, understanding that I would like a little privacy, showed me to a small palm-leave hut, which had the unique luxury of a lock and key. In theory, all possessions there were safe, but the Indians were too quick, and before the rucksacks were stowed, the hut had been invaded. The Indians' curiosity was insatiable and they examined everything with concentrated interest. But at last Paulo succeeded in tactfully leading them away, and I quickly locked the door, eager to change my travel-stained clothes for clean ones. It was a marvellous relief to tear off my sweaty shirt and muddy slacks at last. Standing in the nude, I fished about in my rucksack for clean clothes, when I thought I heard a whispering and tittering. The palm-leaf wall was a-twinkle with eyes! Discovered, the Indians dashed off, laughing..

Only a few of the Indians spoke any Portuguese – usually those who had been in contact with the Salesian Missions. Two Indians who understood a few words of Portuguese led Paulo and me to their village which lay at a little distance from the mission. On the way we passed a small plantation where women were cutting corn cobs. On seeing me, most of them fled or hid behind rocks. But curiosity slowly drew them out of their hiding places.

Catasetum

About seventy adults lived in ten houses in the village, which was very similar in format to those I had visited before, but larger and possibly a little more primitive. The buildings were of the traditional kind but a little larger than others I had seen. I noticed, with regret, the intrusion of utensils and hammocks from the world of the 'civilizados'. They looked quite incongruous among the superior hand-made articles.

I was introduced to two headmen. One, Pedro, took both my hands, holding them for a long time. Then looking intently at my long hair seized it and grasped it firmly announcing 'I am going to cut your hair, Margalete!'

'No, please don't!'

But he insisted, tightening his hold, and looking for someone to bring him a cutting grass or *pirarucu* (large fish) scale to act as scissors. I had visions of returning to São Paulo with a pudding-basin haircut and a large red-stained tonsure, for the women shave the top of their heads and stain them red. I desperately wondered how I could persuade Pedro to desist without giving offence.

'Pedro', I said. 'If you cut my hair, when I return home I will not be allowed into the house'.

Pedro considered long and seriously, looking at me, and then said kindly, but obviously disappointed, 'In that case I will not cut your hair'.

After this incident, we we were led from family to family, some of whom were reclining in their hammocks, many with sick children who were just recovering from measles. The epidemic that had taken its toll in Cachóeira de Irapajé, where we had spent our first night, had swept through this village too. The children especially dragged themselves around, scarcely able to walk, like little wraiths.

The other men of the tribe followed

We exchanged the things that the Indians had asked for, such as mirrors, scissors and beads, for feather ornaments, baskets and arrows. We admired their workmanship, and I felt the exchange was very one sided, and that we got far more than we deserved.

As I walked back to the mission to have coffee with the Padre, a grey drizzle set in. From the river the sound of weeping, wailing and chanting floated up towards us and we hurried out in time to see a number of Indians disembarking and forming a procession which was winding up towards their village. The Padre signalled to me that I should remain silent and keep out of sight, then drew me nearer to the rough palings which formed the limits of his ground. Between the gaps I could see the Indians clearly, but the Padre whispered that I must not be seen or the results could be serious, for this was the funeral procession mourning the death from measles of the wife of the chieftain Praides. The small son of the headman led the way, followed by his father, whose ceremonial paint had been largely washed away by his tears. The other men of the tribe followed in full tribal paint and decorations, the most highly ornamented being the medicine-man, who moved in ritual dance steps beside the leading men. His limbs were painted with black and red dyes in serpentine designs of which two ran from his shoulders over his breast down the the complete length of his body. He wore bunches of parrot feathers in his ears and at the top of his arms fixed to bracelets, which were probably made of monkey skin. The women, who did not form part of the funeral procession (the reason why I was to keep out of sight), carried long baskets so full of plantain fruit that they were bent over horizontally by their weight. Some of them also carried small children. The *xoto*, or basket,

The medicine-man refused to be photographed

Catasetum

A Waika Indian

was carried on the back, resting on the shoulders, and was held by a broad palm fibre strap around the forehead. Earth red in colour, they were closely woven and painted with black dye in the snake-like design used for body painting. The funeral procession wound its way to the village to continue its lamentations with the rest of the tribe.

That evening Padre Antonio told me a little about the region and the Indians inhabiting it. The mission is in the Serra do Chamatá, and its very rich flora at the time of this journey had never been explored by botanists. Connecting channels and rivers link it with Rio Cauaburi, all very difficult to navigate and extremely confusing. The tribe at Cachóeira de Irapajé were the Kemeneté, part of an enormous group of tribes, mostly unknown, who inhabit the mountainous regions from the Orinoco, Serra de Paraima, Territorio do Rio Branco, Serra de Imeri (Pico da Neblina) to Rio Demini. Amongst these tribes are natural blonds. The tribe Paulo and I were staying with were of the Waika, one largely unknown to the outside world. The serra dominating this area is known as Padauari, and is about 2,000 metres high. Here Rio Padauari has its sources. It looked fascinating from afar and I regretted that there would not be time to go there.

We would be returning in two days' time since Padre Antonio was leaving for Tapurucuará, and we had no alternative but to leave with him. This meant I would miss the funeral rites of and feast for the headman's wife, which were to be celebrated at the Feast of Spring, when the dead woman's ashes would be mixed with plantain). The guests and relatives would partake of the mix in the hopes of gaining some of the qualities of the dead. After Padre Antonio explained this tradition to me, it explained the presence of the women walking alongside the funeral procession with baskets of plantain on their backs.

When the Indians received their 'ration' of tobacco, they kept it behind the lower lip, when it was not being chewed, giving them a slightly distorted appearance around the lower jaw. Happily, the majority of these Indians had not taken to the habit of wearing the discarded clothes of 'civilizados' which destroys their dignity and grace. Beautiful feather ornaments decorated their copper-coloured bodies, and the medicine-man always displayed spectacular body-painting of serpentine designs in blue-black and scarlet dyes. But he refused to be photographed, and became very angry when first Paulo and then the Padre asked if he would allow this. I wondered what the objection could be, and the Padre explained the belief that the photograph of an individual took away and imprisoned the soul.

The last three nights of our stay at the headwaters of Rio Marauiá were accompanied by fierce storms, reaching a climax on the last night. I could anticipate each storm by this time, judging by the initial thunder and flashes of lightning streaking through the heavy clouds in the distance. The great hope was that the rain, when at last it arrived, would fill Rio Marauiá for our return journey. Dedé thought that the water level had been rising rapidly, which would certainly make our journey much easier, and the absence of sheep would make it more tranquil. I was by now looking forward to returning to Tapurucuará with Padre Antonio, for I realised he would be an excellent travelling companion. Besides, it would give me another opportunity to collect plants along the wonderful way back

The women carried long baskets full of plantain fruit

We left the mission before 8 am. To save petrol, which was in very short supply, the Padre's aluminum canoe with its 15hp outboard motor, and his large wooden canoe, were both in tow. As I had hoped, the Padre regaled us with his many adventures in the Amazon. He had been lost alone in the jungle for three days; almost drowned in the formidable Cachóeira Manajos, when his motor and canoe were dashed against the rocks; encountered hostility when he first contacted the Indians of Irapirépi who had never before seen a white man. He had an amazing fund of energy and this, combined with powers of endurance, must doubtless have stood him in good stead during the hard days he had passed when he first settled on Rio Marauiá. He spoke the Waika tongue fluently, having lived with these Indians for six years.

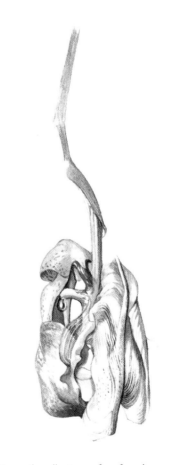

We passed the first two of the five magnificent rapids we had encountered on our way up – the second one so difficult to navigate that it took two hours to pass and the rocks did some damage to the hull of *Santo Alberto*, which had to be repaired. As soon as we had passed the second of these torrents, the Padre left accompanied by three Indians, two of whom we had already met, Felipe and Domingo. Somehow word had got through to them in their village lower down river that the Padre was on his way and looking for guides.

Anticipating another struggle in rough waters at the next rapids, or because of fatigue from passing the previous one, Paulo was in a bad temper. We reached the rapids and were all hanging on desperately to the branches dangling in the water to prevent the boat from being swept over the falls, when, at a crucial moment, I caught sight of a long, pendent inflorescence of somewhat faded, pale pink flowers of a *Coryanthes* orchid. It was within arm's reach of Dedé, whom I begged to get it for me, as it was a great rarity. He tugged at the beautiful plant, then gave a cry as ants swarmed up his arms, stinging ferociously. He flung plant and ants' nest into the river, and plunged his arms in the water. Fearful that the strong currents would carry away my prize, I seized it, still full of ants, and ignoring the bites, put it rapidly into a plastic bag. *Coryanthes albertinae* is often found on the nest of these Aztec ants – possibly a case of symbiosis.

Coryanthes albertinae, often found on ants' nests

Cattleya violacea

Then the struggle to pass the falls started, and Dedé, standing on the slippery rocks, in the midst of whirling currents, slipped and fell, just escaping being carried away by the seething cataract. The freshly repaired part of the hull broke again in the struggle, which caused another delay. But at last we were on our way to Tapurucuará, sailing down Rio Negro, with a marvellous collection of plants from Rio Marauiá, waving in the breeze.

After twenty-four hours' rest and repair, we left Tapurucuará for Manaus at midday and almost immediately encountered a storm. We were six aboard, Dedé, the crew of two (Tonika an Indian, and Ireneu a *caboclo*), Paulo and myself. The wind blew up suddenly and fiercely, and white-capped waves broke against our little boat, so Dedé decided to put into the 'port' of a small group of huts standing on rocks. Rio Negro can be dangerous for small craft in a storm. But though the thunder and lightning passed, the waters remained turbulent, and as the storm threatened to return, we passed the night in this sheltered spot.

Next day Tonika and Ireneu climbed trees to collect for me, as there were a number of orchids flowering in the higher branches. I wished to go further into the forest to search for plants, but just as I was about to disembark, Curica fell into the river. He emerged drenched and terrified and I had not the heart to leave him alone. In rescuing him my watch slipped off my wrist into the water.

Before nightfall we moored beside a group of huts and a house belonging to a Senhor Mercedo, an elderly Portuguese who knew the region well. The Padre had already given me his name as a great orchid collector. We spent the evening in his garden under the cupuaçú trees which were in flower, chatting with his wife and family. It was a hot, sultry night, and the family retired early, leaving Paulo, Dedé and me with Senhor Mercedo. I was fascinated by the things he told me. He had been a participant and witness to all the expeditions to the Pico da Neblina, and had organised the climbers and supplies for most of them. I told him sadly of my attempt to climb the magic mountain, and how I had not even reached the table top at the height of 2,000 metres. He consoled me, saying that from the Brazilian side it was also a tremendously difficult journey; that even the Boundary Commission, set up to define Brazil's frontier with Venezuela, did not succeed in reaching the summit until the third attempt, and that no one had done so at the first attempt. Rondon, a Brazilian (who had set out with two companions who had given up), had made no fewer than four attempts and on the fourth was lost on the slopes for three days – found by 'our' Indian Rafael, who had to carry him most of the way down he was so sick and exhausted.

Next day we continued on our way towards Manaus. An impressive iguana, pale greyish-blue, was basking in the sun on a mass of foliage floating in the flooded forest, but fell with a tremendous splash into the water when we passed him in the canoe.

We spent the night on a wonderfully peaceful beach – in reality the margin of a long, sandy island between two wide reaches of the river. In the swampy stretches grew low bushes, mostly mimosa, and in the deeper swamp, small palms. There I found the petals of *Qualea*, a glorious gentian blue. But I could not find the tree from which they had fallen, for the forest canopy and lianas formed a luxuriant mass of vegetation, every tree and creeper struggling to reach the sun.

While Paulo and Ireneu went fishing I settled down to enjoy the beautiful tranquillity of the place. The fishermen returned with a large ray-fish, with a double sting. They were fortunate not to have trodden on it as it lay concealed in the mud of the river bed. Dedé told me that he has once been stung by this creature, and that, apart from the agony, the wound, like a bad burn, takes a month to form a scar.

I had been attempting to paint the flowers of a magnificent yellow *Apocynaceae*, outside

Opposite. *Clusia grandifolia*

Begonia

the ruins of a rubber gatherer's hut under a great Swartzia tree. But the unwelcome attention of horseflies, small bees and large wasps made it almost impossible, and I packed up having made only a poor beginning.

That night we stopped at about 8 o'clock. It was very dark, and as there were no beaches, we moored in a small channel in a large meadow-like area. The large, waxing moon rose over this peaceful haven, silent but for the frogs' chorus and the sad cries of owls and night birds. There for the first time I heard the most remarkable cry of a night bird, the *saracura*.

A cloudy day dawned, splendid for collecting from the small palms, on which grew a profusion of cattleyas and catasetums, some of the latter in bud, promising male and female flowers.

As night approached, Dedé decided that he would seek a good shelter in view of the threatening storm. It was a wise decision, and we moored in a bay under a group of large trees standing deep in the water. Paulo slept ashore in his jungle hammock, and Dedé and Ireneu spent the night in a little hut nearby. Lying in my hammock in the launch, I wakened to hear wind and rain lashing the boat, and hurriedly got a plastic sheet to stop the rain from driving in. My hammock was already soaked, and I spent the rest of the night rolling from side to side in my hammock as the boat rocked furiously on the choppy waters of Rio Negro.

The following night the storm came earlier. The sky was inky black and a line of storm clouds came rushing towards us while we were still making way. Dedé turned up the motor and we went full steam ahead, searching frantically for shelter. But the wind and rain had caught us. Paulo and I fought the gale, trying to hang a canvas over the entrance to the cabin where the rain was sweeping in. Just as the curtain of rain came rushing up the river, completely obscuring the land, we reached a narrow channel, well protected by the high forest on either bank, and here we moored until the fury of the tempest passed on.

Making colour sketches of a beautiful *Clusia grandifolia* was no easy matter, seated in the boat which was rolling in the swell of the river. It was the first time I had seen this species, coral-coloured inside and white outside, looking like a precious piece of porcelain.

By the dusk of the evening I saw the *Alpha Helix* moored in front of the temporary research station at Carvoeiro, and since it was at anchor this time, decided to pay a call. First we went to the main building, where there was only a young tapir to greet us. In boxes of varying sizes were several species of live snakes, including a big *jibóia* (boa constrictor) curled up in its small prison. The tapir in our wake, we boarded the *Alpha Helix* (the young animal following us in the water, crying to join us in his loneliness), where we were greeted most hospitably. Coffee was served aboard and an invitation to breakfast next morning. To my disappointment, I learned that Dr. Richard Evans Schultes, the botanist, had just left and returned to Harvard.

We continued on our way after breakfast, which was both welcome and delicious. The usual search for shelter began as night drew on. Eventually, the unattractive and obviously abandoned hut of a rubber gatherer came into view, with an entanglement of sticks forming a barricade right down the bank into the water. With some difficulty I climbed up the ramp to inspect the hut, with a view to hanging my hammock there for the night. But the floor boards were dirty and rotting, some had fallen through completely, and the palm leaf roof was crawling with termites. The impression which it created was dreary in the extreme and I decided not to spend the night there!

I started the following day with a fine collection of plants and seeds of the *Bombax munguba,* with its large scarlet pods full of kapok, in which nestled the seeds – very much sought after by parrots. A large bromeliad had attached itself to the launch, but as it was

swarming with ants, I did not bring it aboard.

A large passenger-cargo boat on its way to Manaus stopped by to greet us. Dedé's father worked on it and he generously gave us a bunch of bananas and green coconuts – a great help as we were running short of food by this stage. That morning, I had bought two eggs at a little hut. We were two or three days' sailing from Manaus, and hoped that this new stock of food would last for the rest of the journey.

Bignoniaceae

At noon we were confronted by a terrible storm, with wind so strong that we were unable to move forward and had to ride out the gale, for no shelter was to be found. It was useless to struggle with the tarpaulin, and in any case everything was already drenched, and the wind beat us down whenever we tried. Philosophically we waited for the fury of nature to abate, and then continued on our way. In spite of the still turbulent waters, I collected a beautiful white *Gustavia* with an orange centre. I painted the delicate flowers with great difficulty, as the boat was bouncing and the wind strong.

Our resting place for the oncoming night was the white beach of a steep promontory, where stunted trees grew in the sand. The moon rose with great brilliance, lighting the strange landscape. Cries of night birds broke the stillness, and fishes leapt from the glassy river as they were chased by larger fishes. Dolphins played and sighed. We left this enchanted spot before dawn, as the river was very choppy, and reached an unsavoury little riverside port in Manaus later in the morning. Paulo and I said our goodbyes to Dedé and the two boys, and picking our way over black sludge and offal, our arms laden with luggage and plants, we found our way to a taxi to take us to a hotel.

Pseudobombax sp.

I had some contacts in Manaus who knew of my plant hunting, and one day I was driven to Ponta Negra, a very beautiful part of the Amazon forest. Since my last visit, it was tragic to see how much had been wantonly destroyed and burned. The glorious forest which enchanted the naturalists Darwin, Spruce, Bates, Wallace and hosts of others was now reduced practically to ashes.

A similar situation existed on the Ducke Reserve outside Manaus, named after the famous Brazilian botanist Adolpho Ducke. After two years of being heavily cropped, the soil was finished, leached out, and rivers and channels dried up.

As I flew over the endless jungle of Amazonas on my way home it was announced we would arrive in São Paulo at midnight. I looked at my watch, then realised I had left a world of timelessness behind, for till this minute I had not needed my watch after it fell off and was now lying on the river-bed of Rio Negro at the foot of a purple flowering Vitex tree.

Gustavia pulchra
Amazonas

Margaret Mee

1970

'FORBIDDEN' RIVERS
DEMINI AND ARAÇÁ

It was some two years before I returned to the Amazon. On my return from Rio Marauiá I developed hepatitis for, as I later discovered, there had been an epidemic on the Rio Alto Negro that summer. While recuperating I painted the plants I had found on the journeys to the elusive Pico da Neblina and Rio Marauiá. One of the most interesting was *Coryanthes albertinae*, the orchid I had found growing on an ant's nest. My plants had been sent on after I had left Manaus, and the ants, which seem to accompany this Coryanthes, had died. Since the plant and the ants seem to live in some sort of symbiosis I was worried their death might affect the plant before I had finished painting it. However, I successfully completed the painting, and it was subsequently featured on the front cover of *Orchidaceae Brasilensis* by Guido Pabst.

Many months had passed since my return from the Amazon, and I had been trying to find a sponsor for another expedition, but none was forthcoming. So eager was I to return that I decided to travel under my own steam and, with the help of Guido Pabst and the Brazilian Air Force, at the end of June 1970 I left for Manaus, and Rios Solimões, Demini and Araçá.

The plane bound for Manaus was more luxurious than the other military aircraft I had been in, with individual, upholstered seats instead of the wooden benches to which I was accustomed. Our first stop was Cuiabá, then in Porto Velho, where beautiful forests of palms and hardwood trees grew right up to the runway.

In Manaus my room at the National Institute of Amazon Research (INPA) overlooked the port on one side, where boats were always moving up and down Rio Negro, hooting above the constant sound of motors. In spite of a certain austerity, the room had all essentials, and was well lit for study and painting.

Next day found me wandering in Ponta Negra and Igarapé Leão, where I had hoped to find flowers to paint, but there was little in bloom then and, as the river had flooded the forests for miles around, many plants were under water. My guide showed me an area of *caatinga* (white forest) where two tribes of Indians, now extinct, once dwelt. I picked up fragments of their pottery, beautifully engraved with key patterns, along with coloured Dutch beads, reminders of the Dutch settlers. In this 'cemetery' I felt the spirits of the Indians watching me as I walked sadly across their now desolate territory.

Rio Negro, too, was suffering, for an oil refinery had been built on the banks, and the oil discharge was destroying the vegetation. But the Lake of Januaria was still alive with spectacular birds, and aquatic plants flourished, though the high waters had washed *Victoria regia* (*V. amazonica*) away from the main lake. On a Macrolobium tree I found an *Oncidium ceboletta* – a spray of large yellow flowers. A sloth hung on a dead Embauba tree, looking like a large brown leaf, and on another tree hung a colony of orioles' nests, the black and yellow birds calling noisily.

Next morning, a kind German ecologist took me by car to the Ducke Reserve. When I saw the ghastly 'development' on the way, I became more and more depressed, and on seeing the devastation in the Reserve itself involuntarily burst into tears. I was glad that I would not live to see the final destruction, but sorry that I was not young enough to

Aechmea setigera

Opposite. *Gustavia pulchra*

145

change these things. Before our very eyes, the superb Amazon forests were being laid low and transformed into miserable waste land.

While I was still making plans and enquiries about voyaging up the Rio Demini and Rio Araçá, an opportunity for another trip presented itself. Dr. Heitor Dourado had organised a medical expedition to carry out malaria research along Rio Solimões. Apart from Dr. Dourado and myself, the party consisted of two other doctors and three medical students. The launch we were to travel in was scrupulously neat and clean, and complete with bunk cabins, bathrooms, hospital and dentist's room.

The first night aboard, after a hearty meal, we sat on deck, watching the strange moonlit landscape slipping by – a labyrinth of small islands, and trees of which only the canopies remained above water, because the river was so high. Many of the huts we passed were completely submerged in spite of being built on stilts, as is customary in the region. By the light of the moon and the lantern which swung around, scanning the floating isles of grass and logs, I could see the trees of *Bombax munguba* in flower and fruit, big white blossoms and scarlet seed pods. On many stretches of the river, Embaubas lined the water's edge, hopeful pioneers to protect the forest trees, should they ever return, for massive trunks lay in groups, floating in the river.

We sat talking far into the night, but next morning I was the first to rise, curious to see the passing landscape. Many of the cattle from the narrower strips of pasture flanking the river were on rafts, and a few were grazing on the grasslands between lakes and forest. Chickens, from a hut that was still above the water level, were less fortunate than the ducks, and had sought refuge on the roof or in a canoe. The river was alive with porpoises, and the enormous gourds of calabash trees dangled over the water. It felt good to be alive and back in Amazonas, so we took it in good stead when our pilot made an unfortunate short-cut after passing the town of Manacaparu, sailing up the wrong channel, where the launch became entangled with a large island of floating grass, from which it was difficult to get clear.

At the mouth of the Rio Purus, the Solimões river becomes tremendously wide, and the vegetation flanking it became more varied and spectacular. Leguminous vines covered the trees like massive cloaks hung between the white flowers of the Lecthyds and the golden panicles of the Cassias. Aroids and bromeliads were grouped on the lofty limbs of the Sumaúma. But in the main, the banks had been cleared of the original forest, a feature which became more and more apparent as we sailed past the cultivated margins where only mangoes, cocoa and citrus fruit trees were growing, interspersed with palms. The forests were very dim and distant.

We arrived in the small town of Coarí when a celebration was in progress, and the villagers were strolling around the nearly constructed church of Santa Ana. They were predominantly Indian. Huts nearest the river were still half under water, but not those in the main street. The street was lined with modest wooden huts, through the open doors of which I caught glimpses of hammocks, in many case the only furniture.

Coarí was an unprepossessing place and when the doctors went off to conduct their research I found it frustrating waiting for them for two and a half days. When they returned, it appeared that there had been some misunderstanding, for the medical team thought I had already gone on to the next settlement, Tefé, to collect plants on the way.

We had a new passenger when we started upriver – an old cattle farmer. He had been travelling up and down the Rio Solimões for many years, and knew its every twist and turn. He lamented the fact that recently all the mahogany and other hardwood trees – formerly plentiful in the forests of the Rio Solimões – had gone or were disappearing, leaving only, amongst large trees, Sumaúmas and Couroupitas, whose huge fruit hung down the size of cannon balls. The old man was most preoccupied about the flooding of

Chickens seeking refuge on a roof

Opposite. *Rudolfiella aurantiaca*

Margaret Mee

Rudolfiella aurantiaca Lindl. Hoehne
Rio Negro, Amazonas.
November 1971

the river, which had been much higher than normal, leaving his cattle almost without pastures. He had a keen appreciation of nature, and was genuinely upset by the destruction of the forests, which, he assured me, was becoming worse daily.

Our next stop was Tefé, but before we reached it we passed through a swampy area where we saw a small launch moored, from which three men emerged, obviously hunters, for one carried a gun. Near their boat a beautiful pair of storks were wading, gracefully picking their way through shallow water. As the hunter made to cock his gun, the cattle rancher shouted angrily and I joined in the protest. The birds, alarmed by the noise, slowly spread their great wings and flapped away, whilst the furious hunter struggled with a half-cocked gun.

As we disembarked in Tefé the rancher gave me a genuine Ticuna necklace, and told me that if ever I passed his way again I should go and see his Indian funeral urn which he found in the river bed about two hours' journey above Tefé.

Tefé, originally called Ega, was described by Henry Bates in *The Naturalist on the River Amazon* as being a village surrounded by magnificent forests. Today, the little town is without shade, for the mayor, not liking the great trees shading the village square, had them cut down to their roots, in spite of their antiquity and the shelter which they gave. Any surviving trees had their canopies shorn to look like palm fibre brooms. I left Tefé without regrets and shortly after we moored outside the sleepy, peaceful village of Alvaraes. It seemed to have a preponderance of Indian descendants – perhaps the Mundurucus and the long extinct Passés tribes which extended for 400 miles in this region originally.

In Alvaraes I met an old Dutch padre, Antonio, with a good knowledge of Indian art, who showed me some of the beautiful Indian artefacts in his collection. Thinking I would be interested in meeting compatriots, he introduced me to some Baptist missionaries. Their small house was in terrible disorder, but they kindly served tea, which I was not backward in accepting, and offered to take me in their ramshackle boat to visit the headman of the nearby Indian village.

The Baptists' boat, creaking and belching oily smoke, dropped me in the village where the headman was waiting on the shore, oar in hand, and on either side a son. 'Welcome to our territory', he said with pride and dignity. Later I learned that he had been moved from his land, which was forested and fertile, to this miserable place which was little more than brushwood. Here he had built a hut in the Indian style with bamboo and palm leaves. It was cool and clean inside, though harbouring a tragedy. In a hammock lay his little granddaughter, seven years old, dying as the result of measles. She had a black patch on her forehead, her eyes were dull and lifeless and her tiny face without animation. She could eat nothing now, her sad mother explained, and had not been able to move from her hammock for six weeks. This small family were the only remnants of a once large and independent tribe.

Padre Antonio, true to his word, took me into the forests to collect, accompanied by a number of young boys, to climb the trees if necessary. I was fortunate enough to find *Pitcairnia sprucei,* a beautiful bromeliad, growing on a mossy tree which had fallen across a channel of the river. It was in bud, and I hoped that it would keep fresh and flower in Manaus on my return. The young boys helped me to collect, nimbly climbing trees and swinging on lianas, but collecting came abruptly to an end when a minor accident occurred. We ran into a wasps' nest under the leaves, and one of my helpers was stung on the face and hands. He was in terrible pain and swelling rapidly so we hurried back to the village to get first aid.

My visit to the Baptist missionaries not only resulted in cups of tea and pleasant conversation, but I also gained information which I stored in the back of my head,

Pitcairnia sprucei

Heterostemon ellipticus
Courtesy The Tryon Gallery, London

thinking it might be useful in the future if I ever made a journey to Rio Japurá, a tributary of Rio Solimões. When the flood waters were high, a waterway connection opened up between Rio Japurá and Rio Negro by way of Rio Uneiuxi. The connecting region is known as Primavera, and seemed from all accounts to be completely untouched and uninhabited. I had been told a spectacular tree grew there, its pale violet flowers attached directly to the tree-trunk during October and November. Could this be a Heterostemon, the tree in which the Indian tribe which lived there were said to live?

★★

The journey up Rio Solimões had been brief, for the medical research team had done what they went to do, and since I was travelling on their launch, there was nothing to be done but return with them. Back in Manaus, however, I immediately began to finalise my

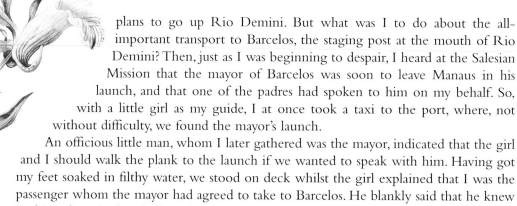

plans to go up Rio Demini. But what was I to do about the all-important transport to Barcelos, the staging post at the mouth of Rio Demini? Then, just as I was beginning to despair, I heard at the Salesian Mission that the mayor of Barcelos was soon to leave Manaus in his launch, and that one of the padres had spoken to him on my behalf. So, with a little girl as my guide, I at once took a taxi to the port, where, not without difficulty, we found the mayor's launch.

An officious little man, whom I later gathered was the mayor, indicated that the girl and I should walk the plank to the launch if we wanted to speak with him. Having got my feet soaked in filthy water, we stood on deck whilst the girl explained that I was the passenger whom the mayor had agreed to take to Barcelos. He blankly said that he knew nothing about it, that the launch was loaded to capacity already, and that he could take no one. He was quite rude, did not shake hands, and would not even suggest another boat. By this time I was near to tears, all chances of that journey having gone.

Galeandra devoniana

I returned, sick at heart, to my room in the National Institute, only to find that it had been turned over to a group of students from California. My disappointment at missing out on transport was compounded by finding myself homeless – until the padres at the mission found me a place in a student hostel run by the Order. It was both clean and comfortable; my room had its own shower, and there was a restaurant downstairs. This cheered me up considerably, and I went for a walk in the grounds where I got into conversation with three charming, chattering monkeys. Things looked even rosier when I heard that there was space for me on a flight to Barcelos – the last time the company was to fly that route.

The morning before I was to leave for Barcelos, I felt my hammock swinging violently; doors banged, windows rattled, and when I got out of my hammock I nearly lost my balance on the rocking floor. It was soon over and a strange calm fell over everything. Then we heard there had been serious earthquakes in Peru, which were reflected as far away as Manaus.

Next day, the plane left early and I was elated to be flying for the first time over the jungles and maze of waters of Rio Negro, landing at Barcelos after only two hours. On the airfield, Sister Elza from the Salesian Mission greeted me warmly and introduced me to the mayor of Barcelos who had come to greet the airplane's crew. We acknowledged each other rather formally.

As soon as I arrived at the Mission, and had put out feelers for transport up the Demini, my first thought was for the birds the locals frequently brought from the forests in tiny cages as presents for the sisters. I started a tour of inspection and found a fledgling *japú* (Orapendula bird) in a sorry state, and a small blue bird with a broken wing. These I fed with grasshoppers and caterpillars collected by small boys, only too eager to help me. But there was a little aquatic bird which ate nothing; we tried to feed her but I despaired of saving her. She ran frantically round the garden, searching for her proper food. However, as a result of my intervention all the parrots were all moved into larger cages.

After the birds, my next thought was to go collecting. Some members of a medical team with the Malaria Service were just leaving in their launch to visit the Paraná de Piloto. We sailed up the river and, after passing a few huts, we entered a narrow channel bordered with Jará palms, a small tree which, during high water, is half or even completely submerged. On their fibrous stems clung *Galeandra devoniana,* an orchid with bell-shaped blooms, purple, brown and creamy-white. Their perfume filled the air. We paddled in the small and very unstable boat over the dark water, between half submerged trees. The silence was eerie. Frequently the trees were so close together that we could not use the paddle at all, but pushed and pulled ourselves through between the tree trunks.

Further afield we encountered a swampy area of a very different character: amongst a

Cattleya violacea

tangle of vegetation, gaunt, dried out trees, some of considerable height, were laden with epiphytes, but some so rotten that it was impossible to climb them. In spite of this I made a fine collection of plants, including Catasetums, Brassavolas and *Cattleya violacea*.

On the return we made a stop at a plantation where the owner harvested *piaçaba*, a palm fibre used for hard brooms, etc. The owner was an eighty-year-old Portuguese named Albino whom I did not see. Instead his son came and talked to me – a middle-aged man with dim eyes, who might have been handsome before heavy drinking had coarsened his skin and features. He wrote poetry, he told me, and by his eagerness to talk, rarely had visitors except from the locality. I felt sorry for this lonely, hopeless man who lived with his elderly father in a house badly in need of repair. But when I told him that I intended to sail up Rio Demini he told me in a dictatorial manner that this was 'forbidden, impossible'. Surprised at his reaction I questioned this, and after a long pause, whilst he obviously sought an excuse, he replied that there were dangerous Indians there. I laughed, telling him that I did not believe him, and that I had met newly contacted tribes and never had any problems.

I left with some misgivings about this rancher, misgivings that were confirmed on my way back to Barcelos, when I learnt that the father, Albino, had a reputation for being a slave-driver and maltreating his workers. All this tied up with what I had already picked up in Manaus, that one could not go up the Rio Demini without the permission of the man who 'owns the river'. More than ever, I was determined to sail up this river and break the absurd embargo! As the crew gained confidence, they told me some more facts about the 'ownership' of Rio Demini and its sister river, Rio Araçá. Up these rivers the Indians worked for Albino, who supplied them with necessities at a cost far above normal. As debt-slaves, they worked for a mere pittance. For these reasons, Albino was unwilling to allow strangers behind the scenes and had already turned would-be visitors away. Apparently he also had the monopoly of all the boats which plied those rivers, as well as of any produce, for which he charged excessive prices.

The black sky threatened a storm, and the Malaria Service launch had covered no distance before the tempest was raging around us. In a few minutes the smooth surface of the river was transformed, and black waves, topped with gleaming white surf, were lashing the boat. The wind swept across the landscape, driving a blinding rain before it. We frantically closed all doors and windows – it was a wonder that our pilot kept his balance in the fury of the storm. Once he was blown from the wheel against the cabin when the launch almost overturned as waves hit her alongside. But he struggled back and headed into the waves.

At this critical moment the rope towing the launch canoe snapped, and as it was cast adrift the Indian boy on the poop was blown into the river. Swimming for the canoe as hard as he could, he got back in, and, paddling into our wake, moored beside us, completely exhausted, just as the launch crashed into the bank. While torrential rain lulled the angry waters into a heavy swell, we waited in the lee of the bank for the storm to pass.

Back at the mission, feeling thoroughly frustrated with waiting for transport to take me to the destination on which I had set my sights – the 'forbidden' Demini and Araçá rivers – I found Sister Elza very excited. While I had been away she had arranged the hoped-for trip for me. The owner of a boat, João Soares, was about to sail to his home on Rio Demini, a journey of about two days. However, without the permission of the agency for Indian affairs, I would not be allowed to go as far as I had planned, nor to the Indian reserve at the headwaters of the Rio Demini. Luckily for me, the agency inspector, Gilberto Pinto, was due to go to the *Posto Indigena*, the local headquarters for Indian affairs, a few days later, more than halfway up the Demini. I could wait for Gilberto in João's house, and then proceed to the *Posto* on the official boat. This was better news than I could have hoped for, and I began to pack my rucksack immediately, then went to the

Vriesea heliconioides

Opposite. *Vriesea heliconioides*

Margaret Mee

Vriesia heliconioides (H.B.K.) Hook. ex Walp.
Amazonas, Rio Demini
January, 1975

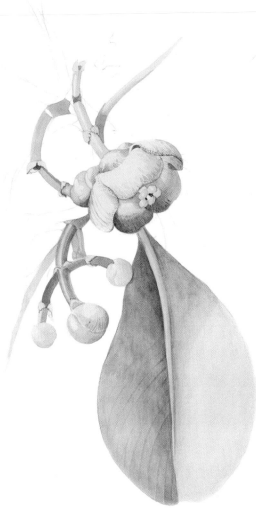

Clusia grandifolia

shore with Sister Elza to meet the owner of the boat in which I was to travel.

It was a small, very primitive palm-thatched craft, with a closed wooden cabin and an inboard motor which gave much trouble on the trip, making explosive noises, stopping frequently and refusing to start until it had been almost completely dismantled. It had obviously been badly neglected for the fumes were suffocating. There were four aboard, besides me, the owner João and three lads who appeared to do little but steer the boat. One of them came aboard completely tipsy, bringing with him a very sick kitten, which once must have been white. Later, the poor thing threw fits. Sorry for the creature, I was at the same time worried that it had rabies. Upriver there would be no possibility of getting serum, so I wore my long collecting gloves and tucked my slacks into my socks, but the kitten climbed on to my luggage and was sick. Its owner said he was taking it as a present to his wife who had just given birth. As he was too drunk to be reasoned with, I did not discuss the matter further with him. I never knew if the kitten had rabies, for it died when we landed.

We only stopped the first night when we met with a boat which, from the depths of my stifling hammock, I could see was enveloped in its own diesel motor fumes. It was obviously in some sort of trouble and needed help, which João kindly gave, and we continued, the other boat in tow, throughout the night. Early in the morning we moored to drop off a passenger from the boat in tow. Then at last, we turned into the mouth of Rio Demini. I saw to my surprise that the water was black, contrary to what I had been told. This was a relief, for insect pests are fewer on black water rivers, which are so coloured by the tannin in them produced by the forest humus.

João's house, at Jalauaca, came into view about five hours after we left the mouth of the Demini. It was completely isolated in the forest, and on the river side lay an extensive area of flooded land. Built in Indian style, the building was large enough to house many families, and probably in the past was part of an Indian village. I was given a large room to myself, partitioned off from the rest of the building by a palm leaf wall, in which a strange assortment of articles was stored – coffee grinders, decorated Indian paddles, feather ornaments, and hosts of other objects. It was very shadowy in my room and I had to paint in the open doorway of the house. But it was a great relief to be left to work undisturbed after the first burst of curiosity had been satisfied.

Dona Claudinha, the mother of the family, worked harder than anyone else. She was a kindly woman, rather heavy, but Indian in appearance. Two of her three sons were away, though their families lived here, including a couple of small boys who were sick with measles. All the family had graveyard coughs except the old people, who had managed to avoid contact with the 'civilizados', from whom these infections come.

During my stay, two boys from the family paddled me in their dug-out canoe into the rain forest beside the house. It was a superb watery place, dark with Jauarí palms, on whose robust trunks are circles of long black thorns, quite a menace to the plant collector. Macrolobiums hung elegantly over the black water, laden with orchids, and from a branch I collected *Catasetum saccatum* in bud, and nearby a charming little red and white clusia. I was busy painting the Catasetum when I heard a motor coming up the river. It was the launch of the *Posto Indigena* from Manaus. I heard it with some relief, for though my stay in Jalauaca had been quite productive for my work, I was eager to go further afield. Besides, food was becoming scarce and I did not like depriving the family of the meagre amount of fish and meal that they were able to procure. Everyone was most hospitable, but it was clear to me that food was not plentiful.

The pilot of the agency launch handed me a letter from Sister Elza. She wrote that Gilberto Pinto had been detained in Manaus, but that I was authorised to proceed to the *Posto Indigena* at Ajuricaba in the launch. (I later heard, with indignation, that a radio

message had been transmitted from Manaus, that I was 'rigorosamente probido' to go to the Indian reserve at the headwaters of Rio Demini, but it had never reached me.) So I bid farewell to the kindly Soares family, thanking them for the hospitality that they had shown me. I left with some regret, though I was very eager to be on my way.

The agency boat was spacious and spotlessly clean, with the added luxury of a lavatory, and plenty of safe storage space for my three baskets of plants Besides the pilot there was a crew of four men, two of them Indians, Xiriana, I believe.

On the first morning, I nearly met with a watery end in the dark waters of Rio Demini. My hammock had been hung to the fore of the portside, and, to keep me sheltered from the cold night wind, the heavy canvas blind had been unfurled. We moved on through the night. I was frozen, and on top of my pyjamas pulled on my peignoir, and wrapped myself in everything available, in an effort to keep out the humid cold. I dozed uneasily until dawn broke, and then, half asleep, tumbled out of my hammock to wash and clean my teeth before the crew were astir. I bent down, over the water – there was no hand-rail – to get water in my tin mug, holding a post with my left hand. But the post was greasy and I lost my grip and overbalanced, falling between the canvas and the hulk, deep down into the black water of the river.

The boat was moving at a good speed, I noticed with despair as I came up in a cloud of dark bubbles, gasping and dragged down by my drenched clothes. I attempted to swim, but failed. So I trod water, screaming my loudest for help. The inboard motor was very noisy, and, fearing that no one would hear my cries over the noise, I pictured myself struggling in the water, hanging on to branches for a week without seeing a single living soul. With intense relief, I saw that one of the Indians had heard my cries. I was nearing my last gasp when I saw the launch coming towards me, one of the men holding out a long pole for me to grasp, so that I should not be sucked under the hulk. I heard a shout that there was a canoe to the right, and I saw an Indian boy paddling frantically to the rescue. My strength had gone when he caught me by the arm and dragged me half into the canoe. Like a log I fell into the bilge, noting the smell of rotten fish, but beyond caring for such trifles.

When the men hauled me into the launch, they were amazed to see that I still grasped my toothbrush and tin mug. The only things that I had lost were my toothpaste, soap and slippers. My mirror remained in my pocket, and in it I saw my ghostly face with water oozing out of my nose, ears and mouth. I felt terribly sick. It must have been an hour that I lay there, then, suddenly, I felt the blood rushing through my body. My colour came back and I started to laugh with relief, and at the absurdity of the episode, realising that they had fished me out of the water still grasping my tin mug and toothbrush. The men came running to me to find out if I had been affected by the incident, and finding me back to normal, joined in the laughter, more with relief than amusement. I became famous for this escape, and for not having been eaten by piranhas, with which, I was assured, the river is infested.

I arrived at Ajuricaba early in the morning. The previous night we moored outside a hut where the crew lingered for a long time, which was just as well, for a terrible storm

Rio Demini is infested with piranhas

Batemannia

broke a little later. It continued throughout the day with rain pouring through the palm thatched roof, though as it was good for the plants I had been collecting I didn't grumble.

On arrival at Ajuricaba, we were greeted by the Indians who had gathered to see us land. At first I thought that they were waving to greet us, but discovered very soon that they were brandishing cloths to keep the *pium* at bay. By this time I was well and truly bitten by this pestiferous insect, and looked as though I had a bad case of measles, except for my face and hands which miraculously escaped. So much for the insect-free black waters of the Demini.

I was introduced to the chief of this tribe of Xiriana Indians, Mattos, a tall dignified man of about forty years, and his pretty little wife who was a Waika. They had a son, Diego, of about ten, who, with his young friend Bernadino, paddled me up the tributaries of Rio Demini to collect in the beautiful flooded forests. There I found an orchid which I think was *Batemannia*. When we returned, I settled down to paint this find.

The first 'room' I had been allocated led off a corridor to which everyone in the large hut had access, and it was impossible to keep the Indians away. They fingered everything and asked for tobacco, clothes, mirrors, etc. At his request, I had handed all my gifts for the Indians to the *Posto Indigena* representative, Paulo, who promised to distribute them. This procedure surprised me, as hitherto, I had always given my gifts to the chief of the tribe, who knew the needs of his people and was scrupulously fair in sharing them equally. Mattos told me of this unusual arrangement and I noticed the offended tone of his voice, and realised that he felt slighted at being subordinate to a young man who was not an Indian, and understood neither their language nor their customs. Unwillingly I handed my fishing line, fishing hooks, etc. to Paulo, promising Mattos that, somehow, I would get a bush knife to him when I got back to Manaus.

At last I was given a hut to myself, one of three huts which had been abandoned by some American missionaries. The baskets for my plants arrived, well ventilated – as I requested when the Indians offered to make them – to let in rain and dew. Once settled, I painted steadily and cared for my collection. I ate my meals with my neighbour Zita, who with her husband was a devout Crente, a small religious sect. The coupled lived in one of the abandoned huts. Mine was just habitable, and, with the luxury of a screen over the window, it was free of *pium*. Of course the dust of years lay on everything, but it seemed fairly wholesome dirt. The river nearby was spanned by a little bridge from which I could bathe, though this was only possible at night, for during the day there were hordes of *pium*. My staple diet was manioc, fish and bananas, and as there was a lemon tree outside my door, I had at least one lemon a day (no sugar), which kept me fit, though very thin. Other than Zita and her husband, my companions were a pair of *graunas*, beautiful birds who watched me curiously and chattered to one another, eyeing me every morning through the little window: They seemed to live in a tree which looked like a guava, but had no fruit at this time.

The flooded jungle, in whose black waters hardwood trees and a sprinkling of Marajá palms grew, was very silent. Small bats, no larger than hawk moths, flitted around when disturbed by the lapping water, but the plentiful birds were shy, hiding in the dark foliage or darting swiftly to cover. When I went collecting there was no sound but the faint splash of our paddles to disturb the tranquillity of this shadowy forest. Here it was marvellous to be free of *pium* and other insect pests, for there were none, apart from ants in every plant and tree.

With Bernadino and a boy named Yon assisting me, I collected some beautiful plants – an *Epidendrum nocturnum* with a large white labello, a deep red *Clusia* and a *Batemannia* with flowers and seed pods together. We would spend whole mornings collecting, when the boys told me in broken Portuguese of the time their families were lost in the *igapó* for three days with nothing to eat, sleeping in the trees at night. 'The young survive without

Epidendrum ibaguense

food, but the old ones die', they said. We paddled into tangles of trees and bushes, and I feared that we, too, might have lost our way, but after struggling through the vegetation, ducking under low branches which barred our way, we saw the light over the *igarapé*.

Two Paqueda Indians had been brought to the Xiriana tribe in Ajuricaba by the agency for Indian affairs, one of whom was very ill. It was said he had been poisoned, but he had recovered the next day. It seems he had been making advances to the wife of one of the Xirianas, and it didn't improve matters that he was from another tribe. I was told that the jealous Xiriana mixed a deadly poison with earth, wrapped the mixture in leaves, and that when the Paqueda trod on this the venom penetrated his skin. That night, as the Paqueda lay dying, Mattos called together his tribe of Xirianas to discover the culprit in order to find out what antidote to use. So the life of the Paqueda was saved.

My neighbour Zita went out for the day, asking me to keep an eye on her house. So I had to get my own meal – packet soup, pumpernickel and lemons. Zita had left me some manioc pancake, but some of the Indians came whilst I was eating, and I had to share what little I had with them. They were all suffering the pangs of hunger. After they had left, a lone

Oncidium ceboletta

Indian appeared, wandering around the huts and trying to get in. He was very strange, and I suspected that he was under the influence of some drug, which also made him aggressive. Very tactfully, I persuaded him to go back to the village with me. Then Zita returned with three Indian women and several small children. They all squatted on the earthen floor of her hut, the women playing with the children and feeding them in turn, whilst the younger infants let forth fountains everywhere. This was treated as a matter of course, and the garment that was used to keep the *pium* at bay was also used to mop the floor. One of the girls was nursing the minute infant of her dead sister and her own child at the same time. I asked about the illness from which her sister had died, and by the symptoms realised that it must have been tuberculosis, and very recently. Complaining that she had not enough milk to feed two, the girl asked Zita's daughter to hold the coughing, wizened infant. Zita refused immediately, obviously aware of this dreaded disease which had already decimated so many Indian tribes.

My journey back to Barcelos had been postponed, and since my food was practically finished and there were only manioc pancakes and a few bananas and lemons to eat, I was quite eager to leave. But there was delay after delay, partly due to Paulo having to make his accounts balance before he got back to head office in Brasilia. Many of the sacks of rice, maize, sugar, etc. intended for the Indians had disappeared *en route* to Ajuricaba, and Paulo had an impossible task, having to juggle with the figures since he refused to try and trace the missing food itself. The Indians will suffer as they were completely dependent on the supplies and all of them were hungry. Eventually Paulo announced that he was ready to leave and we sailed away, more than two days late.

To my distress I left in bad odour with two of the tribe, who came and sat in the boat whilst I was waiting endlessly for Paulo to embark. They looked at me in an aggressive manner, repeating 'Shamin!' (bad), their grievance being that they thought I had brought no gifts for the tribe. As their knowledge of Portuguese was practically nil, I could not make them understand that I had left gifts for Paulo to distribute. Luckily, just as they became quite threatening, and I feared that they would throw me into the river, Mattos appeared and I asked him to explain the situation. It appeared Paulo had not parted with any of my gifts. Very kindly Mattos led the two Indians away, bidding me godspeed. As we sailed off the Indians who had gathered around the boat waved farewell in a friendly manner.

My sombre mood passed as I enjoyed the glories of the river banks, for all the flowers seemed to have opened together. *Gustavia augusta*, white with blossoms, a pink flowered Bignone trailed over bushes into the water, losing its little trumpets in the streams; the yellow panicle of *Oncidium ceboletta* hung below a bromeliad with scarlet bracts, a symphony of colour and form. The crew picked up two turtles at the mouth of Rio Araçá. The poor creatures lay in the boat at my feet, bound and suffering. No respect for St. Francis of Assisi here.

When I arrived in Barcelos at the Salesian Mission, everyone was in a state of great excitement. A woman who had been lost in the jungle was brought to the hospital for treatment and recuperation. She had been wandering in the wrong direction for ten days and nights before she was found by a couple of hunters. I was interested to see someone who had survived such an ordeal. I found her reclining in a hammock before a crowd of curious *caboclos* (mixed Portuguese/Indian blood), being gently questioned by one of the Sisters. The woman's replies were lucid though slow and hesitant. She was little more than skin and bone and looked aged and furrowed, scarcely able to totter along without help when she left her hammock. But in reality, I discovered that she was only thirty-six. Apparently she had been out in the forest collecting wood for her stove. Her dog had accompanied her as usual, but he had disappeared and she didn't know the right path to take to get home. She had a bush knife with her, but found nothing to eat, though on the

Opposite. *Oncidium* sp.

Margaret Mee
July 1985

Oncidium sp.
Amazonas

second day a small turtle crossed her path, but feeling pity for the little creature, she could not bring herself to kill it. Eventually, hungry and completely exhausted, she gave up hope, and lay under a tree, too weak to move, waiting for death. Luckily the hunters arrived in time to save her.

After a few hours of collecting along a wonderful *paraná* one day, I was arranging my plants when a girl from the mission burst into my room to tell me excitedly that my friend Mary, whom I had been expecting, had just arrived on the launch from Manaus. It was marvellous to see her, and to have her sharing my room. Sister Elza took an instant liking to her and soon was arranging a trip for us to Rio Araçá. I heard that Padre Schneider and the anthropologist Dr. Hans Becker were on their way to Barcelos from the headwaters of Rio Araçá, and Mary and I looked forward to asking them about the area.

Dr. Becker and Padre Schneider arrived at the mission accompanied by an assistant, Paisano, whom we hoped would accompany us on our journey, as he knew the region and the people well. He, too, was eager to go with us, we gathered when we conversed with him. He spoke the Indian language of the tribe who formerly inhabited this area. Dr. Becker had published a book on the Suiua and Paqueda tribes, and I imagined that their villages were at the headwaters of the Rio Araçá, the area we were aiming to reach. Apparently, in the face of a good deal of opposition, the agency for Indian affairs was planning to set up a *Posto Indigena* at Cachóeira dos Indios on Rio Araçá. It is said there are only two Indians there, all the others having left and disappeared into the forests. We shall see this for ourselves soon, as we have had an offer from one Alberto, who is leaving in a few days and has agreed to take us in his boat up the river beyond Cachóeira dos Indios, seven hours distant from the spot where he lives.

I was eager to send the plants that I had collected to Rio before embarking on an expedition to Cachóeira, and I hoped that Dr. Becker, who was going to Manaus, would take them that far. But to my dismay, when my boxes of plants were ready, I heard that the passengers had already embarked on the launch for Manaus, and that she was due to sail. As I ran from the mission I was confronted by an inky sky and white topped breakers on the river. The wind heralded a storm, but I hoped that I had time to get to the boat before it broke. The wind reached gale force, a ribbon of lightning struck the ground in front of me, and the tempest raged with such fury that I feared I would be blown into Rio Negro. I ran frantically for the nearest shelter, a little hut on stilts, and climbing up the rickety ladder, banged on the door. A young woman bade me enter. She was tearing down the hammocks and piling them in the centre of the hut, as far from the rain as possible, for it was pouring in on all sides through the gaping walls and rusted metal roof, which flapped disconcertingly as though it would take off at any moment. Her husband stood in one corner hanging on grimly to the shuddering wall. The smell of drains which came from below the hut was indescribable. I stayed there until the storm abated then hurried down to the boat, whose departure had been delayed by the storm. The plank had already been pulled away, but a small boy took my boxes aboard.

Back at the mission turmoil and confusion reigned. A girl had been struck by lightning under a mango tree; the tree had been uprooted, and the girl could not now talk or walk. One of the patients in the hospital had died during the storm, and the mission buildings were flooded.

After purchasing our stores and gifts for the Indians, both approved by Paisano, who was to come with us, we left for Rio Araçá via Rio Demini (the two 'forbidden' rivers). Scarcely had night come when we were overtaken by a terrible tempest on Rio Negro. For greater protection, five launches and two large canoes were lashed together, the smaller canoes in tow, a most unwieldy raft. Mary and I were in one of the launches, swinging in our hammocks, when suddenly a storm wind drove the rain in the openings. We were drenched! The boats were grinding together when the heavy waves and furious wind drove us deep

Aristides with *Anthurium* cf. *sinuatum*

To protect them against the storm, the boats were lashed together making a most unwieldy raft

into the flooded forest. As we crashed around, branches came hurtling through the windows and openings, and the figures in the dim half-light, for all our lamps had been smashed, seemed like ghosts in the forest, as they scurried around, trying to save the boats. Then the crew came dashing in, frantically rescuing the baskets of manioc, worth a month's wages to them, the sole payment for their work collecting *piaçaba*. Meanwhile, Mary and I sat tight in our wet hammocks, the rain lashing us and trickling down our legs until our shoes were full of water. At last, we moved ourselves and our saturated belongings into one of the other launches where we changed into comparatively dry clothes. That night we had a frugal meal of bread and cheese washed down with weak coffee.

A few days later we passed the mouth of Rio Curuduri. There I learned that this river, Rio Demini, Rio Padauari and to a lesser extent, Rio Araçá, are infested with piranhas, the red species being particularly vicious when the waters are low. At the mouth of the next river, Rio Matari, we picked up the wife of one of the crew, Pedro. She was a very primitive woman and brought aboard a huge tin basin, which leaked, full of sour tapir flesh, the smell of which was so repellent, that I had it moved from the prow to the poop, and then, as the fumes were still overpowering, to the canoe in tow. I watched her surreptitiously to see that she did not cover our belongings with grease when she cooked, as she had brought some very dirty saucepans with her. Yet she was a good-hearted person, and later gathered a bouquet of flowers from the forest for me.

Before reaching Sumaúma, we passed through low *caatinga* forest, where plants specific to its light sandy soil grew. When we arrived at the 'port' of the settlement, we found only one hut and not one Sumaúma tree, for they had been cut down many years ago. There the boats with which we had been keeping company moored, whilst we wended our peaceful way up Rio Araçá in Alberto's boat, christened the *Ramshackle,* a perfect description of the skeleton left by the storm.

Gradually the weather turned and we sailed through glorious scenery, the glassy river fringed with graceful Tulia, and dark Buriti and Jará palms on the white sandbanks and beaches. Bacuri trees, covered with pink blossom lined the river banks. This tree bears a small fruit, not unlike the Chinese lychee in flavour. Mary and I bathed in the towed canoe, pouring buckets of water over each other.

As we passed along this most beautiful part of the river, we saw the headquarters of the *piacaba* workers, and a had magnificent view of the Serra da Araçá and the distant Pico Rondon. By midday we were in Monteiro (one hut), where we bathed in the black water, careful not to tread on sting rays which lie in the muddy beds of streams, or even in the

Assai palms on Rio Demini

Clusia

sand. Alberto and Paisano occupied themselves by renewing the roof and walls of the *Ramshackle* with fresh, green palm leaves. Unfortunately, roof-making was no longer the art it had once been, for more often than not plastic and canvas replaced the picturesque *sapé* (thatched) roofs. The two men worked well and rapidly, and transformed the boat.

I wished to explore the forests, and a *piaçaba* collector, Aristides, was persuaded to act as guide. He insisted on taking his rusty old loaded shot gun with him, which he handled so carelessly that I suggested he should lead the way. He became very excited on seeing a great sleeping boa constrictor curled around a Jará palm. His predatory instincts were foiled, as, happily for the snake, a steep bank and deep water lay between him and the serpent. I silently passed by a hummingbird's exquisite nest of moss and roots, with two minute white eggs inside, whilst a *japusinho* screamed a warning nearby. Aristides was no guide, for on the return trek he lost his way. True, the sun was overhead, but he led us round in circles, so that I noticed we were passing the same plants and trees again and again. Eventually Mary and I decided to lead the way, and made straight for the lightest area of the forest, through which the river would be flowing.

Back in Monteiro, we passed a peaceful night in the clean, well-built hut, whilst the others slept under a large thatched shelter At dawn we parted company with the *piaçaba* collectors and crew, with the exception of one, João, for Alberto had wisely decided that he and Paisano would not be able to handle the boat unaided in the rapids ahead. He had to exert all his powers of persuasion, and João unwillingly agreed to stay.

The *Ramshackle* looked very smart in her new attire, but just as we were leaving her rudder fell off. Would she be able to pass the rapids?

We lunched outside an abandoned, derelict hut, collecting hatfuls of limes; the trees had

Tacha

grown from seed brought over centuries ago by Jesuits. After satisfying his hunger, Paisano became eloquent and kept us entertained by his inexhaustible fund of stories. He recounted how he had met Indian tribes for the first time in 1937. There were large tribes in those days in this region, and they lived well from their plantations. He witnessed and even joined in their celebrations and feasts, and observed their customs, describing their tribal dress and ornaments. These stories ran through my mind as I lay in my hammock that night, in a spacious hut with two storeys. The Indian tribes of which Paisano had told us no longer existed, except perhaps for a few wanderers – without village or family, only with memories of the past. The utter cruelty of the situation struck me with force. The night was cold and a brilliant half-moon shone into the river; howler monkeys roared from the forest trees; agoutis, alarmed by a wild cat perhaps, cried out a warning; night birds called plaintively – for centuries these sounds had been part of the lives of those Indians, and now they were no more, though perhaps their spirits lingered still in the shadows of the forests, waiting to return.

We reached Cachóeira dos Indios (or São Francisco de Assisi as it is sometimes called, after the patron saint of the village). It is now a small collection of huts inhabited by Indians of mixed race, though previously it must have been the site of an Indian settlement. Only two of the original Waika tribe remained, the head man Araken, and his wife Joanna. They were about to abandon this ancient home of their ancestors to join their tribe in the middle of the forests, far from the 'civilizados'. No one knew definitely why these Waiká Indians were leaving, though it was assumed that it was because they wished to be independent of the proposed outpost of the agency for Indian affairs.

The patron saint seems to have had little or no influence on the inhabitants we met at Cachóeira dos Indios, for soon after arriving I noticed on the white sand a charming pair of sandpipers, running beside the river, picking up tiny fishes. A miserable fellow killed one of the birds by throwing a stone, and burst into unholy laughter as he saw the little body fall limp and lifeless. He was preparing to kill the bird's mate, when, enraged, I called out loudly to Paisano, asking him as a religious man, in the name of St. Francis, to stop the brute. Did not the villagers treat their patron saint with respect? Paisano reprimanded the man furiously in front of all the families who had come from their huts to see what the commotion was about.

I asked Araken if he would take Mary and me into the forest before he left, and he agreed willingly, and we set off in his dugout canoe. The jungle lay behind a wall of rocks, over which roared the cascading falls. Araken manoeuvered the canoe skilfully into calm waters, and we landed on a rocky shore, part of a great stone which formed the base of

Aristides and some of the piaçaba collectors

Araken and Joanna loaded their canoe

the forest through which he led us. We found ourselves in the loveliest glade, green with ferns and mosses, where little streams trickled through the rock crevices. On a moss-covered branch I found *Clowesia warczewitzii*, an orchid species which had not been seen by botanists for eighty years.

Whilst mist still veiled the river, Araken and Joanna loaded their canoe, in preparation to leave. Two boys were to accompany them on their journey, which would take ten days of constant paddling. Much had been prepared the previous night, and the last thing they had to do before leaving was to catch their dogs. They bade us farewell, insisting that we must return one day and stay with the tribe – if we brought gifts, canvas shoes would be very welcome. Little did they realise the problems to be faced, and the great distances to be covered, if indeed we were ever to visit them in their forest fastnesses.

Joanna looked very regal holding a branch crowned with scarlet parrot feathers, which possibly had a religious or tribal significance. The couple treated their parting with great solemnity, for how many generations of their tribe had looked upon Cachóeira dos Indios as their territory and home? What did the future hold in store for them? Such thoughts probably accounted for the sad preoccupation of these homeless Waika Indians.

There was nothing further to keep us in Cachóeira and the local mixed-race Indians were not very agreeable. But the men wanted to stay and the unceasing rain provided a good excuse for not leaving. But at last a fine day dawned and I insisted on departing by midday. We made a rapid journey to Rialú, where we passed the night. On the way, I was fortunate enough to find the beautiful blue orchid *Acacallis cyanea* in flower. And that night, in the nearby forest, howler monkeys roared in chorus, the most haunting and unforgettable sound of the jungle.

One of the many *igarapés* we passed rises in the Serra de Imajaí and on the curves in the river I caught glimpses of these magnificent mountains. Between the forested slopes shone enormous faces of wet rock, silver in the rays of the sun. It takes two days by canoe up the Igarapé de Imajaí to reach the serra, and one day of strenuous climbing to reach the summit – a wonderful possibility for another journey.

As we progressed downriver we passed the mouth of Rio Jaua which flows through *igapó* as far as the eye can see – the preponderance of Jauarí palms probably gave it its name. Soon after passing this view of the mountains, we nearly met with disaster. The skies darkened early and storm clouds filled the sky. To my disappointment there was no time to collect, as we moved on rapidly towards Sumaúma. The rain was torrential and forced us to take shelter.

Opposite. *Clowesia warczewitzii*

164

Clowesia warczewitzii Ll.L.
Pedraza, Rio alegre, Col.
April, 1974

Then the sun came out and, in the raindrops, hung in a rainbow which dipped down into the river. But as we continued on our way there was no sign of Sumaúma, and darkness obscured the land whilst we were still on the wrong side of Rio Maraí, a river that flows into the Rio Araçá before Sumaúma. Paisano, whose sight was not too good during daylight, and at night was hopeless, ran the boat into a sandbank, from which we managed to extricate her with much difficulty. So Mary and I took over the helm. It was a harrowing journey as the night was black and the sky without stars; the river was wide and shallow with a treacherous sand bed, which in certain areas rose above the river surface. Straining our eyes to penetrate the pitch black, we eventually sighted a glimmer of white coast, where we landed with great relief. It seemed to be a large area of grassland, and we lit a fire and ate supper, Mary and I having decided that it would be an excellent spot to pass the night. The men, however, were not happy with this suggestion, and, in spite of the obvious risks, wished to continue on the way. But we prevailed, insisting on remaining there until daylight.

We did not stop when at midday, Sumaúma came into view. Later, at the mouth of the Rio Curuduri, Paisano became quite excited, knowing that we were near the site of an old Indian cemetery. It was also the site of an ancient Xiriana village. Paisano found two black ceramic jars in the cemetery — how I wished that I knew something of archaeology and the history and origin of those earthenware pots. Once the region must have been the territory of many Indian tribes; now it lies sad and deserted.

As the day wore on we arrived at a small settlement, Nova Esperança, where Paisano, who seemed to have friends all along Rio Araçá, procured shelter for us in a large, open barn. In this outhouse manioc flour was prepared: the roots squeezed to extract the poisonous juice, then the pulp roasted over a stone oven in a huge copper pan, being stirred and turned constantly. The resulting flour formed the staple diet of the riverine dwellers, frequently accompanied by fish or fish soup.

The barn posts provided supports to hang our hammocks, and we were grateful for the shelter of this well-conserved barn, as the night proved wet and windy.

Soon after leaving Nova Esperança, I noticed a large snake swimming across the river. On seeing the launch, it swam towards it, prepared for confrontation. As it came nearer I recognised a *jararacussu* in aggressive mood, but the prow of the boat must have seemed invulnerable and it changed direction, swimming to a white beach, where it slithered across the sand and disappeared in the bushes. The *jararacussu (Lachesis muta)* is usually aggressive, and his great length (up to four and a half metres), combined with a large quantity of deadly venom, makes him a dangerous opponent.

The distant Serra de Demini appeared to the east. Now we began to notice the approach of spring, with trees in flower, the pink and white of Gustavia, the pale purple of *pau rocha* and countless rose-to-white Clusias, the strangler trees.

In Lebom a deserted, derelict hut served as our living quarters. Under the dilapidated thatched roof the ground was full of ant holes, so we hung everything possible on the rough-hewn wood of the walls, including our hammocks, though space was very limited. The night proved hot and peaceful, but at dawn a storm wind brought heavy rain, which poured through the roof and, despite covering our hammocks with plastic sheets, we failed to keep them dry. By morning the river calmed down under grey skies – a sad setting for another Xiriana cemetery. The forests must be stirring with the spirits of these now extinct tribes.

We spent the night at Carapanatuba (place of many mosquitoes). The next day a silent girl took us by canoe into a beautiful, though sterile *igapó*, for the trees had been washed clean by the waters and not one epiphyte was to be seen. In the *igapó* of Carapanatuba, however, densely wooded with enormous trees and Jauarí palms, epiphytes in abundance were clinging to all the branches. To get through this, we had to use our hands more than the paddle, pushing aside branches which trapped the canoe.

Armadillo ('Tatu' in Portuguese)

Whilst we were struggling in this swamped forest, a launch passed by, the first craft that we had seen since Cachóeira dos Indios. But it was not the last, and another launch coasted and moored beside us. Gone was peace and seclusion, for passengers and crew talked long and loudly, and when dawn came they were still talking. So Mary and I had to descend from our hammocks to have a rapid and indifferent wash, in full view of a throng of curious *caboclos*.

When we arrived at Barcelos we were welcomed at the Mission. We also had a good clean up, but could have omitted this had we known our next trip would involve travelling in in a most insalubrious way. Hearing that a boat was leaving for Manaus, and in view of the difficulty in arranging and lack of transport, we decided to seize the opportunity of a reputed twenty-four hour journey. I decided to take my plants with me, as the plane in which I had hoped to send them had left before I was ready. I regretted this decision later, for never were they so badly treated – crushed, covered with petrol and soup. Our sleeping conditions were appalling, hammocks in tiers above beds on the deck. We ate our own food, after seeing meat taken on at one of the ports at which we stopped.

Problems were compounded when the launch developed engine trouble. Everyone had to disembark at the nearby *Posto Indigena* and we were warned that repairs might take time. Talking to an old *caboclo*, I learned that the Waimari and Atroari tribes were imminently about to arrive to fish in the area where we were stranded. They would number about three hundred Indians. A few weeks previously, a group of these Indians had killed ten 'civilizados'. As a result, most of the staff had left the *Posto*, but the *caboclo*, who had been involved with Indians since his boyhood, said he knew how to handle them, and would speak with the chiefs of the tribes in order to avoid any trouble.

Fortunately, the repairs were completed before the Indians arrived, and we embarked again on the overcrowded riverboat, to suffer another night of discomfort. As a storm threatened, we moored in an *igapó* for protection. The tempest came two hours later with such fury that even in our sheltered spot the boat rocked madly, and hammocks swung against each other. The lack of air was suffocating as all the windows had to be closed against the heavy rain. I awoke in the small hours, almost stifled, and managed to open a window with my foot, to let out some of the foul air. It was a great relief to have the fresh air blowing in my face, and to see the sky breaking into a magnificent sunrise. But I was forced to lie in my hammock for another hour as I could not stand below for bodies. Then, at about seven o'clock everyone was madly packing bags, mending clothes and cleaning teeth. We disembarked in the dirtiest 'port' and had to wade through more than a hundred yards of rubbish to reach the nearest road into Manaus.

Installed in a hostel I wasted no time in washing all vestiges of petrol from myself, my plants, hammock and baggage.

Margaret Mee
September, 1975

Clowesia amazonicum Rdr.
Urucará, Amazonas

1971

RIO MAUÉS

GUARANÁ, *PAU ROSA* AND MUTINY

A peaceful mooring on Rio Marau

Fortunately my plants recovered from their dowsing in petrol, and provided me with work for many months. Then, quite unexpectedly, I received a very pleasant surprise. Dr. William Rodrigues, the Senior Botanist at INPA, had recommended me for a Guggenheim fellowship. The project which I submitted was accepted, and the generous provisions of the fellowship gave me the opportunity to make several journeys and visit new parts of Amazonas – I chose Rio Maués on the Lower Amazon, to the east of Manaus.

According to Richard Spruce's mid-19th century *Notes of a Botanist on Amazon and Andes*, Maués was then Aldea dos Mauhés, or Village of the Mauhés Indians, founded by the Portuguese in 1800 with a population of 1,627 of whom 118 were whites. He wrote: 'The progress of Mauhés has been entirely due to this being the great centre of the cultivation of guaraná (*Paulinia cupana*), a stout twiner'. Guaraná is reputed to be a powerful stimulant, and the outstanding Brazilian botanist Adolpho Ducke was supposed to spend his days of research in the Amazon forest sustained during many hours solely on a grated form of the plant.

Maués was also the centre of an oil base for perfume: the trunk, branches, leaves and even roots of the *pau rosa* tree being crushed for this purpose.

In Manaus I was recommended to take as assistant a boy of about nineteen years, Waldemar, and with him and our luggage, which included a small outboard motor I had bought, I boarded a passenger boat heading for the town of Maués.

As the boat chugged along, the commandante, a pleasant man, pointed out the *igarapés, paraná* and settlements as we passed, with information about them all, for he knew the rivers of the Amazon through many years of navigating them.

The boat was overcrowded and overloaded as most passenger boats usually were, and

Opposite. *Mormodes buccinator*

The trunk, branches, leaves and roots of the *pau rosa* tree are crushed to produce an oil base for perfume

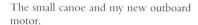

The small canoe and my new outboard motor.

this had led in the past to a number of disasters. Fortunately I had been able to get one of only two cabins on the top deck (the commandante had the other), where I was able to keep my outboard motor in safety, for below deck was a seething mass of humanity with hammocks hung in close tiers over a confusion of baggage.

Soon after supper had been served at a long table on deck, darkness cloaked the landscape, and passing the Paraná da Eva we moved into shallow water where shoals of phosphorescent fishes darted and leapt in the river, caught in the strong light of the ship's lamp.

Well before dawn I awoke to find that we were sailing up the Paraná do Ramos, famed since the days of Richard Spruce for its clouds of mosquitoes. The landscape was typical: emergent Sumaúmas towered above groups of large-leafed Embaubas, Mungubas were hung with large scarlet seed-pods yielding kapok, and the feathery foliage of Macrolobiums drooped low over the margins of the river. Most of the exotic species of trees, avocado, lemons, etc., planted by the riverine people, stood dead and withered for the floods had been exceptionally extensive and the water level was still high for the month of September. A few poorly *Hervea brasilensis* (rubber trees) lined the mud-washed banks, and a handful of bony cattle grazed on the small areas of grass beside huts, or stood lean and drooping on rafts. Many of the huts seemed to have been abandoned. The forests were faint in the distance.

My arrival in Maués was ill timed, for the small town was as overcrowded as the launch, and a room in a hotel was out of the question for the only one in the town, the Victoria Regia, was full, the rooms all taken by supporters following in the wake of a new governor. Loudspeakers were pouring out his speech at top volume to a background of religious music.

However, the Convent of the Sacred Heart had a school attached and, as the pupils were on holiday, I was kindly given hospitality in a classroom. There I was able to hang my hammock and to enjoy a few peaceful nights before the journey up Rio Maués.

Shortly after my arrival I met the *caboclo* 'Jim', who, it had been suggested, would make me an excellent guide. He would be indispensable on such a journey, as he knew everyone and everything along the rivers and tributaries. The wise old padre in from the local mission, however, looked askance when he learned that this man was to accompany me on the voyage, warning me that, following a scandal involving an Indian, the man had been forbidden to enter Indian territory.

Unfortunately, Jim already considered himself engaged for the journey, so I decided to speak with him frankly to discover if there were any problems which could prejudice my work – in which case I would not allow him to sail with me. When I questioned him he protested innocence and persuaded me to accompany him to speak with the local judge

Carará (anhinga or snake bird)

and hear her opinion. Instead I was taken to her landlord, an important functionary in the town, who, of course, spoke in glowing terms of the man. I was still unconvinced, and a little later my doubts were confirmed by an officer of the Government Agency for Indian Affairs. My permit to enter Indian territory presented no problem, but when Jim appeared the officer recognised him immediately, and in no uncertain terms refused him permission whilst Jim listened with a face of thunder.

As I had by this time hired a boat and crew, I could delay my departure no longer. Jim, not to be outdone, appeared on board shortly after we left the town. There was nothing I could do about this, though I worried about possible consequences.

As we sailed up the Rio Maués, the forests which lined the banks gradually became more distant as the river widened to as much as three kilometres or more. In this expanse hundreds of *mergulhas* (large diving birds), were fishing, and as the boat approached they either disappeared completely underwater or, with their heads just above water, watched our course. The leafless trees which stood deep in the river were alive with these fascinating creatures.

I had growing doubts about my so-called assistant Waldemar, for he and Jim had struck up a close friendship. At one point, Waldemar had taken the canoe and outboard motor without my permission and sped round in circles, wasting precious fuel. I shouted in vain but my voice was drowned by the noise of the motor. At last my frantic signals caught his eye and he returned, but not before I had seen him chase and run down a bird with the canoe. My anger blazed as I saw the poor creature hanging limp and dying in his grasp. As Waldemar stepped into the launch I seized the desperate bird whose sharp beak tore my finger. Realising that I could do nothing to save it, I put it on a tree stump in the water, just above the surface, so that it could at least end its life among its natural surroundings. Waldemar shamelessly confessed that he had killed the bird for 'esporte'.

That afternoon we reached the Igarapé do Albino where the men fished and caught a *tucunaré*, far too beautiful to eat; it was a handsome fish with spots of gold and dusky stripes across its black body. Also in the *igarapé* I found a striking species of bromeliad with

A *tucunaré,* far too beautiful to eat

Mormodes buccinator

a long inflorescence of six radiating spikes, already dry with fruit forming, and worth returning for in six months time when the flowers would be in bloom.

Jim's brother had a hut on the banks of this waterway. He was well over forty years with an Indian wife of fifteen. Our visit was brief as it was already getting dark, and we still had to find a place to moor for the night. The men were desperately keen to get flour for they had forgotten to collect our supply in Maués. So before mooring we looked for a hut or encampment where this staple food could be bought, and at the mouth of Rio Urupadi came across a small settlement where we were able to buy some. Amongst the group of *caboclos* there was a very unpleasant man, who lost no time in asking me for sugar and petrol. I gave him a tin of sugar but refused petrol, as I had a minimum supply for the journey. He became quite aggressive and must have followed us as far as the mouth of Rio Cuiuni where we supped on a little beach by the light of a full moon.

As I took my morning dip from the beach, I caught sight of this *caboclo* peering through the bushes, and so gave orders to sail away up Rio Urupadi.

The days passed and I lost count of them, which is not unusual in the wilds where light and darkness are the time keepers. But as the days passed my troubles grew. I was losing time for work, nearly a day lost in giving a tow to a family of *caboclos* – a lift rather than a tow, for, bar the father, the whole family came aboard and sat on deck hungrily eating the only food I had to offer them, dry biscuits. The children were pretty though very pale, in fact the whole family looked sick. At the end of their journey with us, after accepting a few tins of preserves and worm cure, they wearily went their way up a dark forbidding *igarapé*, on the beach of which the crew wanted to pass the night. But I did not like the look of the cramped and sombre place and we retraced our way back to the mouth of the Urupadi. This proved fortunate for me, for day had scarcely dawned when, as I lay in my hammock, I heard the most glorious melody, the song of the *uirupuru*. This relative of the wren is a small bird with darkish plumage. Unfortunately, the

The hired boat and crew

belief that possessing a dead body of the bird brings luck results in many of them being killed and sold in markets. The song continued for several minutes, varied and incredibly beautiful. It is said that creatures of the forests on hearing it listen in rapt silence, then follow the bird far into the jungle.

One of the crew, Bento, had warned me that Waldemar and Jim were up to no good and he offered to stay with me for protection when the other two were nearby, which comforted me considerably, for I had evidence that my initial fears were not imaginary. One day, on returning from collecting by canoe with Bento, as I boarded the boat, a cartridge from my revolver rolled along the deck. Immediately I examined my unlocked suitcase where I found all in confusion – bullets mixed up with my clothes, a shirtsleeve shut in my paintbox. Obviously the two fellows had been intending to steal my revolver. Fortunately I had left it rolled up in my blanket inside a canvas bag and they hadn't come across it during their search. That same night, as I lay sleepless in my hammock, I heard faint scuffling behind me and flashed the powerful beam of my torch in that direction, after which there was dead silence for some moments before I heard someone creeping stealthily away.

After collecting by canoe with Bento

Bento did not escape the notice of the two troublemakers, and constant quarrels ensued until a climax came one lunchtime. Waldemar complained that Bento refused to eat the food he had prepared. I found him in a rage, repeating 'Eu sou Indio! Eu sou Indio!' I managed to calm him and asked what the trouble was but he gave no reply, and I then realised that he suspected that his food had been tampered with. The number of poisonous plants in the Amazon are legion and many of the inhabitants are familiar with them and their effects, and I had heard of many a death through the administration, deliberate and accidental, of these toxic plants. In Igana a widow told me that her husband had died as the result of venomous leaves put inside his shoe. And I remembered that during my voyage up Rio Demini I had heard the story of the Paqueda Indian who just escaped death by poison when the tribal chief obtained a last minute confession from the culprit who named the plant he had used and the antidote was given (see page 157). After this incident the enmity between the Indian and the two *caboclos* intensified.

Bromeliads collected by Jim and Bento

Flooded forest on the Rio Urupadi

These distractions meant I did little work. Since my Guggenheim project had outlined the plans I had to collect and paint living plants indigenous to the region, with particular emphasis on rare and unknown species, I decided that if I were to get any benefit from the journey I would have to ignore the two troublemakers as much as was possible and concentrate only on searching for and collecting plants in plenty. On the banks of Rio Urupadi I found some lovely orchids – *Ionopsis utricularioides* and *Mormodes amazonica* – and, inspired by these finds, decided to investigate other tributaries; one especially, Rio Amoena, seemed promising, for I was told it had a waterfall at its source. Once I had told the crew of this we pressed on with such speed that I wondered if the urgency shown by Jim had any other motive than reaching our destination before nightfall. I soon discovered that he imagined he would find diamonds and gold at the waterfall! I had already noticed that his desire to make money at any cost was intense, and he manifested this aspect of his character later in the day when we moored at a lonely beach where some accultured Indians had landed. After conversing with them, he returned with a roll of skins under his arm which he intended to sell at the earliest opportunity. Knowing they were the skins of forest animals, I refused to have them on the boat, insisting angrily that he leave them in the forest. He was livid.

Whilst this incident was still rankling, we moored at a devastated god-forsaken beach, and the crew, having little or no respect for forest animals, made a rush to find turtles and their eggs, of which, happily there were none. It is no wonder that the unfortunate animal is nearing extinction, for at every little beach where we moored this scramble was repeated.

We sailed on for some distance before I asked Jim to moor the boat as night was approaching fast. He refused, saying that we were less than half an hour's distance from the mouth of Rio Amoena. So on we sailed, twisting and turning through *igapó* and up *igarapé,* until the tunnel of forest through which we were passing became denser and darker and it was impossible to see even with the aid of a torch for which I had no spare batteries, Waldemar having forgotten them in Maués.

We were lost, and had to pass the night in an isolated spot. In the morning, knowing that we only had enough fuel to get back to Maués, I had to make the decision, after

Opposite. *Ionopsis utricularioides*

Ionopsis utricularioides Lindl.
Rio cumina oberim, Pará

Margaret Mee
August, 1984

much arguing with the men, to abandon reaching the *cachóeira* and to return to Maués.

That evening we passed a most beautiful *igapó* at the mouth of Rio Acoará which I saw by the light of a setting sun. Through the years, the waters and winds had shaped the trees in such a way that each one was an exquisite piece of sculpture, and as the wash of the boat reached them it lapped softly around and through them, for many were hollowed out like shells.

We moored that night beside a low *caatinga* forest within sight of a distant hut, and Jim promptly demanded the canoe and motor to get cigarettes from the occupants. In view of our shortage of fuel, I refused, pointing out that we needed every drop for the return journey.

The night was very black, but nevertheless Waldemar and Jim left the launch and made their way on foot through the forest, returning in the small hours of the morning with much noisy shouting. Primed with rum, they did not hesitate to wake me up to tell me about a sick girl who needed a lift to Maués. By all accounts she suffered from epilepsy, and when in a fit four strong men could not hold her down. The two men insisted that we should sail the boat back to the settlement to pick up the girl. When I declined, asking who was to man the boat whilst the crew held the girl to stop her throwing herself in the river, they became insolent and aggressive. Then they insisted we had to take her antibiotics for these cured everything. I replied that I would inform the authorities in Maués that she needed medical attention.

The two men became so abusive and unpleasant that, tired of being harangued, tense with the problems of this journey, I shed a few tears – hidden behind dark glasses. Indeed I longed for the end of the expedition, but as I had not collected enough plants, decided to devote the last few days strictly to collecting. To this end, the next day, with Jim and Bento, I went out in the canoe, but the water was so rough, with waves breaking over the bow, that landing was impossible. The following day, desperate to find more material before leaving the area, I made another attempt in the canoe accompanied by Jim.

It was arranged that Jim and I would go ahead in the canoe and that the launch would proceed slowly in the homeward direction, but without passing the canoe and if possible keeping it in sight. I made this arrangement partly to economise on fuel, partly because I was fearful of being alone with Jim without some sort of back up, and partly because I thought it was safer not to leave Jim and Waldemar together on the boat. After spending some time collecting, the launch was nowhere to be seen. Jim insisted on returning to our last mooring, which was now some way away, but I would not agree, and from then on it became a battle of wills as to which way to proceed. Seeing a white beach across the wide river, I decided to land there and await the launch which must pass. Again Jim disputed. Then I thanked providence for my keen eyesight, for on the shore some distance away I could just discern a craft. Jim swore that I was mistaken and informed me that he had not filled the outboard motor's petrol tank before leaving, and we would not have enough to reach the spot. At this news I became even more uneasy, but hid my fears, and ordered Jim without more argument to make for the shore. Unwillingly and with much grumbling he obeyed. With tremendous relief I landed beside the launch with only half a litre of fuel in the tank. I decided that there would be no more journeys alone with Jim.

The day before we reached Maués I made a last collecting trip with Bento. It was a successful outing, for I found and Bento collected a magnificent bromeliad, *Neoregelia eleutheropetala*, the rosette brilliant scarlet, merging to olive green, with florets ranging from violet to white. Later on I painted it in the deserted schoolroom of the Convent of the Sacred Heart.

As a parting gesture I invited the crew to a farewell dinner at a restaurant in Maués. Only Bento and Waldemar accepted. It was not a success for Waldemar drank far too

Opposite. Neoregelia eleutheropetala

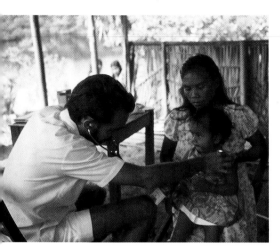

Dr Otto treating villagers

The forest was destroyed for miles around

much and, dinner over, Bento quietly went his way. Waldemar, however, who was meant to be lodging at the mission, decided that he did not want to sleep there and began to shout abusive language in the main street. I was overcome with shame at being seen in his company and told him angrily that he could sleep on a bench in the road for all I cared, and that first thing in the morning I would buy him a ticket to Manaus, as I wished to be rid of him. I did not remind him that he and Jim between them had relieved me of 50 litres of petrol and much of my equipment, but walked away and left him bellowing in the street. In future, I decided, I would pick my own assistant and crew.

After the setbacks of this journey, things cheered up for me when one of the padres at the mission, about to go on a medical expedition to Nazaré, a settlement at the source of Rio Marau, invited me to accompany him. The day before we left I took advantage of an offer to spend a day in the forest with an old ex-hunter, Raimundo.

At the beginning of the day we were caught in a heavy rainstorm from which we sought protection, only to find the only shelter was already occupied by a snake in a large hole. So I ate my picnic lunch of soaking bread and banana feeling icy cold, and suggested returning. It was one of the most disappointing journeys I have made, for the forest was destroyed for miles around – burned giant trees, stripped of vegetation and epiphytes, stood on arid soil, gaunt and white-scarred-black with fire. The only area of green and living forest was being hacked down to make way for a rice plantation.

A little further afield stretched a miserable area of brushwood, once a plantation of the nearly extinct *pau rosa*, though, by a law of 1937, for every *pau rosa* tree cut down another had to be planted. The trees had gone long ago and only maimed stumps remained. This 'cemetery' of these lovely trees had been created by greedy exploiters, who even sent men and women to the headwaters of the rivers to cut saplings when the supply of larger trees had been exhausted.

Towards the end of the day the old man cheered me up a little, relating an experience which had finally turned him against hunting. We had reached a giant tree across our track, where he stopped and told me how he had once encountered a jaguar on that very

Nazaré church of bamboo and palm leaves

tree trunk. He dared not go forward, but feared equally to go back, so stood there frightened and perplexed. Taking courage from the expression of the creature, which was stretched out languidly and looking at him kindly, he spoke to it in a conciliatory tone, promising to do him no harm, but requesting him to let him pass on his homeward way. Obligingly the jaguar rose, slowly stretched and yawned, and walked away quietly into the forest.

It was still dark the following morning when we set sail in the padres' launch, bound for Rio Marau. The sky threatened a storm and as we turned into Rio Urupadi, a white blanket of rain swept towards us, enveloping and obscuring everything.

Eventually we arrived at our goal, the *Posto Indigena*, where some Indians, Dr. Otto, the expedition's doctor, and other personnel from the the Malaria Service launch were waiting for us. We all embarked on the little *Dona Rosa* which was to take us up the narrow Rio Marau to Nazaré.

The *Dona Rosa* was a real chugger, the motor spluttered horribly from time to time, and the rudder failed on various occasions, landing us deep in *igapó* and crashing us against the trees. As we sailed on, the river grew more and more beautiful and we swung around narrow curves brushing against the foliage of the forest trees, then emerging into an *igapó* of tortuous trees, many hollow shells, then a forest fringed with Jará palms where small blue palms covered the water as ferns cover the ground of a *caatinga* forest.

Nazaré

Steep banks of white sand led up to the group of huts which formed the settlement of Nazaré with its modest church of bamboo and palm leaves.

Standing on the shore ready to welcome us were two village chiefs, Paulo and Emilio (the real names of the Indians are not divulged to the 'civilizados'). Paulo was a man of about forty, strong and well built; Emilio was some years his senior, with one eye completely white. I wondered if this was the result of filaria, or 'river blindness', a common disease in the region. Both chiefs were friendly and courteous.

I hung my hammock in the padre's house which was clean and spacious and impregnated with the pleasant scent of dry palm leaves. Whilst Dr. Otto and the personnel of the Malaria Service attended to the villagers, I swam in the black water of the river, rather fearful of the strong currents, and went collecting in a dugout canoe with two young Indian boys, Gilberto and Francisco. With amazing agility Gilberto climbed high into a tree and, from a rotting branch, which I feared would fall with him, threw down a

The water level was still
high for the month of
September

Aechmea polyantha

Opposite. *Aechmea polyantha*

strange bromeliad which I had seen from afar. It was shaped like a Greek amphora, and
from their red bases the leaves turned back sharply, sword-shaped and deeply serrated with
black thorns. The plant was not in flower, but I had no doubt that this was a new species.
It proved to be and was named *Aechmea polyantha*.

Most of the Indians belonged to the Maués tribes and lived at some distance from
Nazaré. There had been little illness amongst them, but the *caboclos,* who arrived from near
and far, were suffering from numerous diseases and as many as three-quarters of them
were quite sick.

The medical team and Malaria Service team had been hard at it, so for relaxation after
the very strenuous work of examining the sick, Dr. Otto suggested a trip in the canoe to
collect plants. A *caboclo* paddled us into a fascinating *igapó* where we passed into deeper
and deeper waters, where the dipping of the paddle seemed not to disturb the birds. There
were highly coloured jacamars, woodcreepers, *picolets* and a large black and white
woodpecker with a large red crest, who, unafraid of the intrusion, continued tapping the
rotting tree.

To my horror, Dr. Otto picked up his gun, cocked it despite my protests and entreaties
and took careful aim at the beautiful bird. In utter desperation I rocked the canoe. Twice
the doctor fired and missed his mark, and the woodpecker, sensing danger, flew off. The
doctor was angrily silent for a long time.

Unfortunately he was a confirmed predator, aided and abetted by the ignorant *caboclo,*
who suddenly became animated, shouting 'monkey!' In fact it was an *irará* climbing
through the trees, with long, silky black fur and tail. Unobserved, in the excitement, I
rocked the canoe again, and the shots all went astray. The men were so agitated that they
had not seen the *irará's* mate approaching through the trees. When she saw what was
happening, she made a detour, carefully concealing herself in the foliage, and with great
relief I saw the pair meet well out of bullet range, and disappear into the forest together.

When I enquired of the doctor why he was so intent on killing the creature, he replied
that he wanted the skin, and was silent when I pointed out that the animal itself had
greater need of it.

Aechmea polyantha Pereira & Reitz
Rio Marau, Maues, Amazonas

Margaret Mee
January, 1975

1972

MAMORI, MAUÉS, TAPURUCUARÁ

IN MY OWN BEAUTIFUL BOAT

I returned from the first of my Guggenheim Fellowship trips, determined that the next one would give me the opportunity to journey to new areas of Amazonia, and that it would run more smoothly. Almost six months later, in mid-March 1972, I left home for the dawn flight to Manaus, from where I intended to journey to the port of Autazes which lies at the conjunction of several interesting rivers. One of my projects in journeying to this region was to investigate and report on infringements of forest laws, hunting, felling of trees and so on, but I was also determined to continue collecting and drawing plants.

Things did not start well. At the airport I was annoyed to learn that, after a great deal of research, time and effort on my part, the airline had no record of my 50 kilos of excess baggage, so I had to abandon the card boxes which I had arranged for the transport of plants. Luckily the outboard motor I had acquired on my previous trip did accompany me. On arrival in Manaus I discovered that there were no rooms available at INPA – and worse, no further talk of the loan of a promised boat.

At first glance the kind offer from a friend leaving Manaus to stay in his empty house in a suburb some way from the centre of town seemed too good to be true. However, after a few days it became clear that I could not possibly stay there if I was to get anything done. There was no phone within reach and the bus journey to town was complicated.

I had arranged to meet Severino who I hoped would act as my pilot on the journey. He had been recommended at the INPA boatyard where I had been investigating the possibility of buying a canoe. Severino was said to be reliable and a good navigator, but I waited for two hours before he appeared – not particularly reliable – and as he was seventy I began to have doubts. In the end his personality won the day and I engaged him for the trip,

Six days after arriving in Manaus I heard there was an INPA apartment available. Splendid news. And more good news – I became the owner of a beautiful boat, 9 metres x 1.50m, in excellent condition. She was spacious, rode the waves with ease and went at a good speed with my 6hp outboard motor. The only problem was the lack of an awning and I hoped to get one made in Autazes.

Four days later, Severino and I set off.

We had sailed about four or five hours from Manaus, when a black sky threatened and Severino decided to take shelter. Fortunately we were not far from a couple of huts, for the storm blew up in about five minutes and a raging gale was tearing at all our possessions in the canoe. We did not even moor the boat but dragged it up on shore with the help of the family from one of the huts, and from their numerous children who ran to and fro rescuing our belongings. We had only just got into the hut when the tempest of tempests broke with incredible fury. It seemed as though the hut, even though it stood on stilts, would be lifted into the swirling black clouds. A sizeable Malaria Service boat was struggling in the raging waters and nearly capsized before reaching shore.

We continued our journey as soon as the storm abated but, as we had left Manaus rather

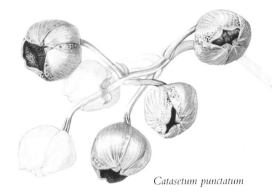

Catasetum punctatum

Opposite. *Catasetum punctatum*

Sunset on Rio Mamori

later than I wanted, the light was beginning to wane and we decided to look for somewhere to pass the night. Two fishermen, eating their evening meal from a big iron pot, advised us to make for the Casa de Zinco, about an hour or so distant. Eventually we saw the house from afar – large and impressive, but impossible to reach. To do so we had to paddle the canoe through flooded grass and then carry our baggage over a long slippery path composed of felled giant trees which must have been there for years.

In this enormous (for that region) and depressing house lived Dona Maria, recently widowed, and her two sons. The interior was prison-like and completely devoid of any sanitary arrangements. But we were made welcome and given a meal of fish soup and fish at a long table, and were offered *macaxhira* to drink, which I refused, since the method of preparing this beverage involves chewing the manioc before it is distilled.

I slept in my hammock on the terrace, deciding that the hacking cough of Dona Maria was probably infectious, and anyway the air on the long terrace was fresh and cool. Hordes of mosquitoes buzzed longingly over my net.

It rained all night and was still raining the next morning, but we managed to get away during a short break in the sky, then had to stop again at a floating mooring as shower after shower blew towards us. When we at last set off again, we made our way through grey weather, expecting to reach Autazes in the afternoon. But there was no hope of this, for we asked three fellows sitting beside the river brewing pots of *macaxhira* how long the journey would take and were told 'three hours'. It was then around 3 o'clock, and the sky still dark and threatening. We had not sailed more than an hour when heavy rain fell, and the bad weather was compounded by the floating isles of grass across the river which slowed us down.

We stopped at a hut to ask, again, 'how long to Autazes?' The owner suggested that we should

stay the night in his house or in the hut of his neighbours, in view of the storm. But I had seen dozens of children looking out of the neighbour's window and decided that the first hut would be more tranquil. I was to regret my choice, for during the night a wretched cat hunted the swarms of tree frogs until dawn, and the cries of the poor, tortured frogs drove me crazy. I threw my shoes at the cat, but in the complete darkness could do nothing about its victims; in the morning I dragged only one away and threw it far into the open towards the river.

The owner of the hut was a Syrian with a finger in half a dozen small pies. He bought a tin of petrol from me, which I was loath to sell, but felt under an obligation in view of his hospitality.

Eventually we arrived at Autazes. Because we had no awning, I had been badly wind- and sunburned, and as the wind continually blew my large straw hat up, exposing the lower part of my face, I looked like a scaly fish.

I had never seen in Amazonas such a well organised port as Autazes, thanks to its mayor, a retired dentist. It included a baggage storage area which was neat and clean, though in spite of appearances, Severino discovered that a number of his tools were stolen. We were given a little shelter to hang our hammocks; treated to lunch, coffee and supper, while I provided a meal for the mosquitoes which were swarming.

A local man undertook to make awnings for the boat which should solve the problem of shelter.

Sr. Luizon, the mayor's brother, told me that the Rio Preto de Igapó Açu – about twenty hours away at the speed of my boat – was very little disturbed, that it was surrounded by many lakes and *igarapés* and would be a good place to look for plants. For epiphytes he advised me to go up Rio Mamori, about half a day's journey. There a wonderful *igapó* was to be found,

My boat and Severino

teeming with ananas and orchids. So I decided to go there as soon as the awnings were ready.

Whilst waiting for them, I met the schoolteacher who introduced me to several people in the village, including the very likeable and interesting French padre. He was young and enthusiastic and we talked together at length. He was trying to cure the Indians of the many illnesses they have contracted, but was meeting problems at every turn. His allowance for medicaments had been cut off so funding had to come from his own pocket – a situation which obviously could not continue indefinitely. In addition to this he had been ostracised by the 'important' people of the town who he felt resented the fact that he was trying to help the Indians and were trying to get rid of him.

The vegetation in and around Autazes was poor, for many areas had been stripped and burned. Indeed, the horrible sounds of a saw-mill, possibly the most treasured possession, reverberated throughout Autazes. I saw few birds apart from some herons, terns and parrots. There were huge areas of swamped land and floating grass, and wherever terra firma could be seen it was inhabited by cattle and people, in that order, for there was no doubt that cattle came before people.

A hospital had been built, but, as the embarrassed mayor explained, the town could not afford a doctor and nurses, so the equipment had to be locked safely away.

The awnings arrived looking large enough to roof a house, and beautifully fresh and green. Severino and the two men fixed them on the canoe where they looked marvellous. We shall leave at daybreak – this will give my burns a chance to heal.

After taking leave of the mayor we left Autazes early one morning sailing up Rio Autuz-Mirim, a dull river with little of interest, and Rio Madeirinha, on our way to Rio

Mamori. We passed Vazea which seemed to consist of small cultivated strips of land and a handful of cattle. Brazil nuts were one of its main products.

It was difficult sometimes to tell if we were on a river or in a lake, so enormous were the stretches of water. Rio Juma flows into a large lake where I longed to stop and collect, but the wind was too strong and drove us into the *igapó*, and Severino was nervous about stopping, not being sure of the way to Rio Mamori. On these extensive lakes there was not a hut to be seen where we could inquire. When we entered Lago Capavari, a huge lake with many outlets, the channel became even more confused because of the islands of floating grass. At last, with great relief, and no doubt having taken a longer way there than we needed to, we entered the Rio Mamori where we were sheltered from the wind.

On the Rio Mamori I passed a disturbed night in Itauba, an isolated spot where I hung my hammock in the open hut of a young *caboclo* who was trying to breed cattle. The smell of cow-dung around the cabin was overwhelming, and I had to tread carefully in the half-light, for we left before dawn broke.

A drizzle started as we moved up the river, and I wrapped myself in my Colombian poncho in an effort to keep warm. But with the day came warmth, and the sight of interesting plants in the trees. On one of the enormous trees I caught a glimpse of what looked like a Stanhopea orchid on the opposite river bank. On drawing near I could distinguish the pendant white flowers against the mass of dark leaves. It seemed far out of reach, until I noticed the natural ladder formed by the roots of a Clusia (Apui), leading up to the huge cluster of plants. But Severino was loath to climb in the rain, muttering something about spiders and snakes, until I threatened to climb the tree myself. Indeed he took so long to select and cut a crook with which to reach specimens, that I had nearly got there myself when he returned from the forest. Seeing me amongst the leafy branches he became alarmed that I should fall and break something and entreated me to come down. He hooked down a plant with flowers and on seeing the magnificent blooms it was difficult to restrain him from bringing down the whole gigantic clump. Thinking of some of the signs of devastation we had seen along the banks, I hoped that those plants continued to thrive for many years, filling the air with fragrant perfume.

Rio Mamori did indeed prove a good river for plant collecting for there I found many orchids, Catasetums and Epidendrums (with fire ants in the roots. How Severino and I suffered!).

Darkness fell early, so when a neat looking hut came within sight I decided to ask shelter for the night. A very pleasant woman, who turned out to be a widow, welcomed us, and took Severino and me to see the room to which we were both assigned. She opened the door of a large, dark room where all the windows were covered, so that it was a while before I was able to distinguish the figure reclining in a hammock in the middle of the room. But when my eyes grew accustomed to the darkness the shock was great, for there lay a man with a cadaverous face, eyes looking from huge dark sockets, and around him an indescribable, sordid confusion. I looked away quickly lest my horrified expression would upset him, and heard a distant voice saying that, of course, we would not mind sharing the room with the invalid. As a hacking cough shook the unfortunate man, I explained that I was accustomed to sleep in the open and would appreciate being allowed to hang my hammock on the balcony. Severino looked embarrassed as he told our hostess that he felt the cold, and if it were not inconvenient to her, would hang his hammock in the kitchen. We left before dawn.

As the sun began to rise I moored my boat to a white-limbed *pau d'arco* (*Tecoma violacea*), covered with purple bell-shaped flowers. I was happily unconscious of having tied up to the bush, within a metre of the venomous *jararacussu*, the most dreaded of all snakes in Amazonas, for it is aggressive and attains a length, when fully grown, of four and a half metres. Stretched along a branch of the bush to which we were tied, its sand-coloured body almost invisible in the dappled light, lay the serpent, watching me with yellow-green eyes, completely motionless. Severino had caught sight of it as he peered into the shadows, and in a panic to leave, started up the motor. Realising that the vibration would upset the reptile and probably pull the bush as well as the serpent aboard, I told him to run the motor very gently. Then, gingerly, I untied the cord of the boat, all the time looking into the snake's eyes with their narrow, vertical pupils. But the beautiful creature did not move, probably fearless in the knowledge of her own power. As we glided away, another *jararacussu* came into view, but lifeless, with a great gash on its four metre long body on which were feasting the most magnificent butterflies.

Perhaps visualising further encounters with snakes, Severino rather unwillingly crossed the river to the bank where I had noticed a group of brilliant yellow flowers. As I neared them my excitement grew for, observing their unusual appearance, I realised that I was seeing this species for the first time. I had seen many vines of the same family, Bignoniaceae, on previous trips, for during June several species had come into flower, mainly pink and purple, and trails of these trumpet-shaped flowers were borne downstream by the currents. But this was different, with its large, impressive yellow blooms. The vine was tangled amongst small trees and the woody stems were difficult to separate from the surrounding vegetation.

The flowers, tantalisingly high, fell in golden showers as I unravelled the tendrils. I painted the plant seated in the boat as we moved upstream, for vine flowers are delicate and ephemeral.

Three weeks after I left São Paulo I could not have imagined myself in such a different situation. Just as Severino and I were crossing the vast lake of Mamori, a fierce storm set in. We looked for a hut in which we could pass the night, but all the shelters and huts were full up for the locals were celebrating the Feast of Judas. At one hut where we asked if we might hang our hammocks, the owner, a middle aged woman, was even quite hostile in her refusal, so we made further inquiries. Some distance away, I was told, lived a young couple who were at home that night.

Memora sp.

It had been difficult enough to moor the boat as waves were beating against the shore and driving us against the maze of enormous tree roots, but it was even more difficult to get clear into the open river. At last Severino managed. A distant light gleamed dimly through the dark haze, and we made our way towards it hopefully.

An *igarapé* on the Rio Mamori

Greatly to my relief when we arrived and landed, a pleasant young man bade us enter and willingly allowed us to hang our hammocks in a large, airy room. There was no furniture and through the open window I had a view of the river and could even discern the dark shape of my boat moored by the bank. I slept fitfully, for my insect bites were torturing me. Suddenly I awoke, a strong storm wind was blowing into my face, and I looked out to check on my boat. To my horror, I saw that it was no longer there. I fell out of my hammock and rushed down to the windswept shore. No, the canoe was no longer there! She must have drifted away in the gale. I returned to the hut and with much effort managed to awaken Severino, who still more asleep than awake, kept repeating dopily 'I've moored it safely'. At last I prevailed on him to go down to the river with me where he regained his wits in the cold air and explained that whilst I was in a deep sleep, he had become fidgety about the boat's safety, and had moved her to a more sheltered mooring. With tremendous relief I saw her there out of danger from the stormy weather.

We left at daybreak and followed a *caboclo* and his large family in his motorboat, a handsome cockerel strutting on the roof and a parrot screaming from a window. As our boats sailed side by side, he told Severino confidentially, interspersed with loud laughter, why the woman who had refused us shelter last night was so hostile. She had heard on her transistor radio, that two thieves were fleeing to the interior from Manaus – a man and a woman. She was convinced that Severino and I fitted the description.

We parted ways at the mouth of the Paraná Mamori, having been shown the direction of Rio Castanha Mirim which we hoped to reach it by daylight. Severino had a relative who lives along the river, in Cotiara, where, presumably, we could pass the night.

Catasetum

Catasetum gnomus (female)

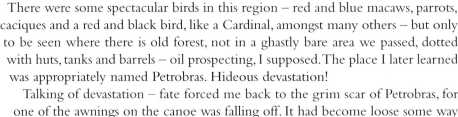

There were some spectacular birds in this region – red and blue macaws, parrots, caciques and a red and black bird, like a Cardinal, amongst many others – but only to be seen where there is old forest, not in a ghastly bare area we passed, dotted with huts, tanks and barrels – oil prospecting, I supposed. The place I later learned was appropriately named Petrobras. Hideous devastation!

Talking of devastation – fate forced me back to the grim scar of Petrobras, for one of the awnings on the canoe was falling off. It had become loose some way back, and I had had to hang on to it with all my weight to stop it from taking off and landing in the waters. Severino, being near his half sister's house, decided that her husband was the man to repair it. Dona Lilli, the half-sister, was one of the nicest people that I have met on the journey, kindly and educated. But we had to spend most of a day near Petrobras while the repair was made, except for a brief and fruitless venture into the *igapó* near the hut where we passed the night. The hut belonged to another of Severino's relatives and, although clean inside, being built on stilts, cattle, pigs and hens had left mountains of manure underneath, and sleeping in that stench with pigs squealing nearby was not easy.

The morning we left his family, Severino seemed to lose his head. First we discovered that he had left the oars behind, then that he had cast off not noticing my only bath towel was drying on the awning. It must have caught in the branches of a tree, and I was furious at its loss. Irreplaceable. But Dona Lilli had given us eggs and tangerines for the journey which made a welcome change to our diet of fish.

Our plan was to take a route through waterways which would take us back to Manaus. Along the way, at a floating mooring, I asked a young boy to take me in his small his canoe so that I could collect in the lovely *igapó* I had spotted. It was a fantastic area, large spreading trees, whose roots started from the trunks about ten metres above water, forming arches and twisting ladders. Clovis, the boy, and I, paddled off in his leaky canoe to collect, leaving Severino to snooze in my canoe. I returned with a good collection, including Brassia, Catasetum and Camaridium.

At Casa Fonseca, which lay across Lake Andiroba, I passed a more or less comfortable night in a spacious, though mucky room, with the luxury of a chair and two mirrors. The large mirrors were not much consolation, though, as I was able to see my insect bites to advantage.

After coffee with one of the widow's sons, we left at 7.15am. Taking Paraná Manicoré into Rio Solimões, we would eventually reach Manaus having made a circular trip. The day was cool and grey, thank heaven, as the plants had suffered in the sun the previous day. As we came out of Paraná Manicoré, there was a good *igapó*, but Severino would not stop, giving as excuse a storm threatened, he would lose his way, had to get home, etc. So we headed for Manaus passing a water slum, where huts cheek by jowl, and pretty miserable ones, crowded on both banks of the river. We reached Manaus in the early afternoon.

An interlude

Once I had got my plants safely installed in the grounds of the INPA building I began to make arrangements to attend the World Orchid Congress in Medellin, Colombia. I heard that Dr. Richard Evans Schultes, the botanist from Harvard University whom I had hoped to meet in Carvoeiro in 1967, was in Manaus and, when I met him he had told me that I really should try to get to Medellin. There were many difficulties to be overcome, including financial, passport and flight problems, but all satisfactorily resolved at the last minute. One excitement was the opportunity which came up to exhibit some of my paintings at the Congress, and Greville arranged to send five which arrived just before I left for Colombia.

Swartzia grandifolia

In Bogota I went through a maze of customs, passport offices, etc, and in traipsing from place to place I managed to lose the precious tube containing the paintings. Only when I sat in the plane for Medellin did I notice it was missing. I panicked, but the crew were marvellous and let me off the plane, together with a young steward to help in the search. Together we tore around the large airport, and after what seemed an age I saw a stewardess waving the tube across the checking-in counter. 'You are an angel', I cried as I grabbed the paintings and ran back to the plane.

In Medellin I spent a marvellously peaceful day in a private house, a lovely place outside the town, full of trees, birds and classical music.

The following day I went to the Botanical Gardens where they were preparing the exhibition of orchids; there was genuine enthusiasm for my paintings which were to be displayed at the entrance.

Scuticaria steelii

Rio Marau

After the excitement of the Congress with its many accompanying social events and the exhibiting of my paintings, I returned to Manaus from where I was to embark on a journey revisiting Maués and its surrounding waterways. But I delayed my departure, partly because I had to wait interminably to obtain permits for Severino, Bento and myself to go into Indian territory when we went up Rio Marau, and then only after pulling strings and mentioning a few names (no mention, of course, that hordes of oil prospectors were working there freely – harmless me, painting plants which are not valued – the world has lost its balance!), and partly because I had an opportunity to go collecting in the nearby *igapó* of Taramãsinho. There I found marvellous plants of *Scuticaria steelii* (which I painted), Epidendrums, Batemannias and Philodendrons, and would have got bromeliads had not the boy (Severino's nephew) helping me been so scared of everything in the forest, and when nipped by an ant nearly fell out of the tree. Nevermore!

Returning from Taramãsinho we went through the market, and there in the crowd a dreadful type grabbed me by the arm, and tried to force me to drink rum from his glass. I turned on him in a fury, much to my own surprise. Severino was useless as a protector, and did not say a word until at a safe distance. 'Was he mad?' he inquired inanely.

I had also to obtain a written permit for collecting from the Director of Rio Jardim Botanico, and this worked wonders wherever I went, especially as I had undertaken to make a report of my journey for the Institute of Brazilian Forestry Development (IBDF). I anticipated difficulties, as I had heard that there are about two hundred men working for the oil company on Rio Marau with a following of fifty prostitutes in their wake, and that Rio Parauari and rivers up to Rio Tapajós were swarming with more prospectors. What a prospect! I remembered only too well my encounters with the prospectors on Rio Curicuriari! I only wished that Severino was more awe inspiring. But for safety's sake I left information of my route, approximate dates of arrivals, etc. with IBDF and INPA, hoping that my fears were exaggerated.

Before I left Manaus, I visited my friend Guido Pabst. I found him kneeling beside a pile of plants, busy pressing them. He was so intent on this work that I stood watching him for some time before he was aware of my presence. We were in the grounds of the new hotel that the company of which Guido was Director was building at Ponta Negra. We sat together chatting over our drinks and Guido told me of the many disturbing things that were happening to our flora and fauna, without any intervention or activity from IBDF, and other related bodies. I left him in despair about our glorious Amazonas.

It was a nightmare of a departure from Manaus. In the first place it was blowing up for a storm, then the promised transport to get me to my canoe on its floating mooring did not arrive. Eventually we reached the canoe – its awnings almost blown off by every gust of wind – and loaded it up, only to find, after setting off, that the spare petrol can had disappeared. So back we went and borrowed a horrid tin one which leaked, a fact we only discovered after we had filled it with petrol. So then we had to make another journey to replace the replacement! By this time I was getting worried that the launch which was to take us and the canoe in tow to Maués might start without us. So we sailed the canoe full tilt to the port and after much questioning found the *Madeiras*, a public passenger launch which was not too inviting, as there were two dirty women aft, cleaning fish whilst spitting noisily. Having stowed our luggage, Severino suddenly said that he had to meet someone, and disappeared. The *Madeiras* was due to leave at midday, and ten minutes before there was still no Severino. I enquired frantically whether the boat would leave on time and was assured that it would. It did and no sign of my pilot as we sailed out of port, I sick with worry about that and the canoe in tow, which was not riding well and looked far from secure. We had been sailing for a good half hour when I felt a sudden sensation

Opposite. *Scuticaria steelii*

Aechmea rodriguesiana

Aechmea meeana

aboard, all the passengers looking at a rapidly approaching speed boat. It coasted beside the *Madeiras* and Severino jumped aboard with a broad smile, bowing like a star actor.

The M*adeiras* was grossly overloaded, as many of these passenger vessels were. The lower deck was a nightmare: people in hammocks hanging cheek by jowl over pools of dirty water, the stench overwhelming..

Fortunately the raging wind abated without tearing off the canoe's awnings, though it made a valiant attempt to do so. A chain was attached to the canoe in addition to the rope, so I felt much easier about it..

Our first stop was to let a number of Crentes disembark. It seemed like in the middle of nowhere – just two huts almost submerged in the river, nothing else. Looking out through the gaps in the hut walls I could just make out a few depressed faces.

On the second day of the journey, my birthday, we arrived in Maués where I was welcomed by the the sisters and padres who invited me to sleep there

Next day we made rapid progress, but only arrived at Piranga at nightfall. The port of Monteiro de Sousa's house, to which we had been directed, was impossible to find in the darkness, so at last we moored at the bottom of dozens of rough steps and hung our hammocks there for the night – that is, Severino and I. Bento slept in the canoe. We left early in the morning, and straight away ran into a maze of *igapó* where I saw many bromeliads but did not dare to stop and collect for fear of missing the outlet into Rio Marau. The *igapó* was tremendous, stretching across the mouth of the river and I decided I would collect there on the return journey as it appeared to be one of the best areas we had seen so far.

The problems I had anticipated and been warned of on this trip were never far away, and I had to keep in the wake of a two-hundred strong gang of oil prospectors and their baggage. Apparently there had been fights and three deaths – two women and one man. The gang seemed to be on another river, nearer to Maués, but no one knew exactly where, so we were constantly alert.

Without help from an Indian in a dugout canoe, we should never have found our way to Rio Marau. The trip had been difficult – Severino grumbling and Bento waving his arms this way and that and directing ineffectually, which did not improve the situation. The Indian lad turned out to be the son of the local headman, Emilio, and led us to his father's hut at the mouth of Rio Marau. There we stopped for a little in his orange grove, where the headman's wife was busy peeling manioc. Opposite was a deserted camp, recently destroyed and burnt by oil speculators with the drilling works still standing, for it was rumoured that they would shortly return.

Emilio told me that a group of soldiers had come to the area to settle the trouble between the local inhabitants and the prospectors. He was annoyed and obviously offended that the officer in charge had not spoken to him about the trouble, but instead had asked the manager of the nearby *Posto Indigena* if he wanted any protective improvements. As a result it seemed the *Posto Indigena* would be rebuilt and a school constructed.

We reached Nazaré at midday, having been directed there by Emilio through a most spectacular *igapó* full of the very bromeliads which I had hoped to collect.

I was interested to learn that this Emilio, an ageing man, tall and thin, with one eye white and blind, had quite a history. As a young man he was living with his grandfather, at the time chieftain of the Maués Indians. The tribe's shaman, an

Aechmea mecana Breva &
Amazonas, Rio Maraú
March 1978

Margaret Mee

Maués Indians at Nazaré

Paulo and Emilio, Rio Marau

evil and ambitious man, persuaded Emilio that his grandfather was the 'mother of influenza', and had to be eliminated. The youth, very unwillingly, yielded to the intrigues of the shaman, and killed the old man. He was arrested, tried in a local court, but was acquitted.

The headman of the Indians in Nazaré, Paulo, and I had a long conversation. He confirmed much of what Emilio had told me, as well as confessing with some shame that he had married a 'civilizada' because she was the owner of a fine launch with a very powerful motor. I met her and realised that this must have been the sole attraction.

Both Paulo and Emilio seemed good men, but saddened and disillusioned by having become shadow chiefs of fast diminishing tribes.

Early the next day I went collecting and filled the boat with bromeliads, species unknown to me, including a magnificent Aechmea in flower. Bento swam to the tree where a huge clump of these plants was growing in a fork branching near to the river surface. He took my powerful collecting knife between his teeth, and when he had climbed nimbly into the tree deftly picked out the big spiders and scorpions with the tip of the knife and started to hack at the roots which were hard and woody. At the first slash, armies of aggressive ants swarmed over him. I shouted to him to stop, knowing how painful these stings were, but he smiled stoically and continued. When he could not stand the pain any longer he jumped into the river to wash off the ants, and then returned to the tree from which he brought me two plants, one in full flower. After we had left, I had a feeling that the Aechmea might be a new species and thought that if so, then I should really have more than two plants. But when we went back, in spite of careful searching, we never found the same spot again, nor any plants of the same species in the neighbourhood.

In another, more open part of the *igapó*, towered a magnificent *ipé rocha*, the canopy a mass of purple blooms. At the top of the white trunk were two massive bromeliads from whose amphora-shaped leaves emerged coral-coloured inflorescences. The plants were far too high for Bento to reach by climbing – there were no branches before the canopy, and not even a nearby liana from which he could swing to the tree. I searched the nearby *igapó* for a plant within reach and found three, without flowers. There were many other plants to collect there, for this *igapó* was one of the least disturbed and most prolific in epiphytes that I have seen. There, Jará palms grow between *pau d'arco* and Cuiras and large hardwood trees. It is also a paradise for humming birds. While we were there an Indian paddled up in his canoe and gave me an interesting orchid with a striped labellum, *Catasetum discolor*.

Opposite. *Catasetum discolor*

We left this marvellous *igapó* and later had to shelter from a fierce storm by taking refuge in a hut occupied by two men. To get to the hut we had encountered several snarling dogs. They were the picture of misery – scabby, ribby and one or two half blind.

Severino and I hung our hammocks in a nearby shelter with a roof showing all the signs of leaking. But it did not rain and was a lovely night with a near-full moon. Owls called from the trees beside me, for the shelter was completely open, and I could hear the distant replies of their mates in the forest.

In the morning I continued to add to my already large collection, finding Catasetums and other orchids, including the lovely *Aganisia cerulea*, with a number of blue flowers.

Eventually the time came when we had to return to Maués. On arrival I found that the mission was full, so planned to stay on the visiting Malaria Service launch. There I lay in my hammock which was hung half in a cabin and half on deck, and all through the night people were coming and going, so I slept only in snatches.

The water in that particular area was filthy – dead rats and other 'things', impossible and inadvisable to analyse, floated past. On a floating mooring a man was waiting to sell a plate of fried fish, whilst a nude baby sprawled in the dirt at his feet, eating biscuits. The heat was terrific and the sun burning hot, and the plants had to be rushed into the shade of the awning after Bento had spent the morning cleaning and arranging them. The heat was so intense it made me feel sleepy, but I decided that the smell from the river would keep me awake.

The next day I stowed all our baggage in and embarked on a passenger boat on the way to Manaus, my own canoe in tow. In an area of swampy meadow we saw some exciting plants growing: red flowers of a Heliconia, a beautiful violet Verbena entwined with the large, white flowers of Munguba. But the forest was spectral only, the giant trees having lain in the water for many years. There is not one large tree to be seen, and all this destruction appeared to have resulted in a few miserable huts, many now abandoned.

I went regularly to look over the stern of the launch to see how the canoe was faring, and on one occasion saw a scene of total disorder. Flowers all over the floor and a tin bucket on top of some plants. I flew into a rage at the thought of losing the entire results of the journey and demanded to get off at the next stop to rearrange things. But when we reached the next 'port' the captain only slowed the boat down, and the passengers scrambled off as best they could while it was still moving. So down I went too, but directly from the *Andrea* to the canoe – how I ever managed it I cannot imagine. I tore off my shoes, stepped over the pigs and hens and muck on deck, and with the help of Severino got into the canoe. The chaos was worse than I had imagined, but between us we did the best we could in the circumstances to adjust things. I prayed that the flowers were not seriously damaged and that petrol had not got into the plants.

I climbed back in the *Andrea* with all my former agility, but feeling myself falling backwards, for there was no firm foothold in the canoe, I flung myself forward against the *Andrea*, and as I did so felt a sharp pain and heard a crack which told me I had broken a rib. But back on board did not mean safety, for the pigs snapped at my bare feet as I climbed over them avoiding their snouts, for they had not eaten for more than two days.

Everything calmed down until Severino noticed that the 'tough' nylon tow rope was fraying and a broken strand was unwinding. So an agile young boy was given a thick cord and put into the canoe to secure it. This type of tow was always a headache, for one had to be on the watch all the time – in addition to paying for the lift.

However, at the end of the journey the captain did agree to drop me off at the INPA floating mooring, thus saving me another headache – getting from the port of Manaus back to INPA.

In Manaus I was faced with many problems. I had no immediate plans for another journey, nowhere to paint or work on my plants, and the usual difficulty finding suitable transport

Igapó forest on the
Rio Marau

once I had decided on my next destination. I seemed to spend hours sitting around while my plants faded, unpainted, waiting to hear about a tow I hoped to have up the Rio Negro.

After a few day staying at INPA, I moved to the Convento do São Geraldo Precessimo Sangue, where I had a lovely little room with a bathroom – tranquil and away from the world, and, most importantly, ideal for painting.

Having arranged for the plants I had collected to be flown to the Botanic Garden in Rio, I spoke to the administrator of the Malaria Service, who told me one of the service's launches was to leave next day for Barcelos. It was arranged that the Malaria Service launch would pick me up at the INPA floating mooring and take me to Barcelos, where they would leave me for ten days while they worked in the area. Then I shall accompany the Malaria Service team to Tapurucuará.

The morning of departure, Severino and I worked on the canoe and its motor, and looked unsuccessfully for the lovely oar – borrowed I suppose. Although we were picked up by the launch as arranged, we did not leave Manaus till nightfall, several hours later than planned, because the Malaria Service was delivering remedies. The horror of the scenes along the banks of some *igarapés* in which we moored to dispense were indescribable – perhaps the darkness added to this impression. One, a slaughterhouse, resembled a scene from Dante's *Inferno* as interpreted in the paintings of William Blake: a primitive, but huge construction consisting of posts supporting a frayed straw-thatched roof, under which dozens of dark men, nude to the waist, were wielding huge pestles in boiling cauldrons, was a veritable witches' sabbath. The stench of blood was nauseating. Piles of bloody meat stood on the ground, while prone, decaying trunks of trees, felled years ago, were black with hordes of vultures awaiting the opportunity to seize fragments of carcass. I had never before seen so many concentrated in one area. But some of the *igarapé* dwellings we visited were not so evil, and even had remnants of lush tropical vegetation and banana palms growing around decaying huts.

My canoe was in tow and, remembering the recent episode when it had been in tow, I was anxious because it kept hitting the side of the launch and I feared the prow would be damaged. So the crew neatly lashed the canoe fore and aft to the launch, and it was transformed into a little river launch, where I could sit alone to write up my diary and even sketch.

The destruction along the banks of the Rio Negro had to be seen to be believed. Small settlements in the midst of large burned out areas produced nothing, or at the most a miserable crop of manioc. Malaria was rife – in places where I was told it had almost been eliminated, it was worse than ever. Wood was being taken out of the forest and *pau rosa* was almost extinct and was only to be found at the river heads where it was too distant to exploit. *Coari-coari,* laurel and *itáuba* were disappearing too. When these and other species are finished, what will happen? What of the future?

An hour or two after passing Rio Cueiras we entered the Paraná de Sumaúma where I saw many interesting orchids and bromeliads in the old trees. Although I had passed it before, it was always worth a visit, but this time it would have to wait for the return journey. It had hardly stopped raining for two days, everything was wet through, and I had to spend time baling out in the canoe.

Chugging up Rio Negro, between strong wind and heavy rain I had a notable encounter with a beautiful toucan, and then, shortly after, with Adolfo Richter, the orchid hunter, sitting in his small grey canoe in a grey hooded raincoat, smoking a pipe and solemnly looking up into the trees with such concentration that he did not hear my calls. He appeared to be in a dream world, enshrouded by the mist which hung over the river.

During the day I noticed that there were few birds to be seen, but as evening drew on I saw flocks of parrots and other birds. As it grew darker, silent nightjars flitted low over the water, fearless of the boat in their hunt for insects.

In Carvoeiro, the river was so wide that it looked like an inland sea, full of little islands.

Erosion of river bank, Rio Negro

Quati (a coati)

The pilot, Nazarene, told me that the Ilha de Anavilhanas is to be avoided as there are many lepers living there. On the left bank we were on the lookout for the mouth of Rio Caurés, for if we passed that in good time we would reach Barcelos by night.

We passed the most extensive *igapó* I have ever seen, stretching away as far as the eye can see. This huge expanse of water was dotted with islets, often a tangled mass of growth centring around a group of strangely contorted trees with trunks covered in white lichen. We threaded our way slowly between them, passing some groups of large, dark trees, but there were few epiphytes to be seen, possibly because the river washed the area so frequently.

As we passed Rio Caurés I saw a mass of *Cattleya violacea*, and I was thinking again how much there would be to collect on the way back.

The pilot forecast that we would reach Barcelos at 9 at night, but as I was sleeping soundly I missed our arrival, and when I awoke found that arrangements had been made for me to stay at the Salesian Mission, where I had a room with bathroom – no running water, of course. The Salesians are charming people, and it is a pleasure to eat and speak with them at mealtimes when they relax for a short time. The sisters told me that my beautiful *japú* died shortly after I left Barcelos [in 1970]. Poor thing, I suppose it was starvation. He was a marvellous bird, intelligent and affectionate.

There was a great deal of malaria in Barcelos and Tapurucuará at the time, and Nazarene, the pilot of the Malaria Service launch, warned me to be very careful, so I decided to take my hammock with its built-in net when I went on collecting journeys from Barcelos, when I hoped to be able sleep in my canoe. Alberto, a kind odd-job man, had undertaken to fix a couple of stanchions in the canoe from which to hang the hammock, and also to make a new awning, for the original one was in a state of decay. These improvements made the canoe really habitable.

Barcelos looked remarkably clean. I met the mayor one day, who must have been responsible for the improvement to the town. On seeing me, he politely turned his back, but later I forced him to be moderately pleasant. Neither of us has forgotten our previous encounters in Manaus and Barcelos.

Nazarene gave me the good news that he had found a good guide for me from Tapurucuará for the trip to Rio Cuiuni which I hoped to make as soon as the awning was ready. I had always longed to collect on this river. The journey will take five to six days and involve a good deal of paddling and movement. But fortunately my broken rib seemed better, and I stopped binding it.

The day and night before departure, it poured with rain, and I feared that this would delay the awning which I was to collect. But Alberto came to the mission to tell me that the canoe would be ready the next day. So I shall leave the day after.

At Sister Anna's suggestion, I agreed to give a talk on conservation. Sister Anna was amazingly well informed and clever. She told me some hair-raising things about Albino, the elderly Portuguese who professed to 'own' Rios Demini and Araçá. I had come across him,

Catasetum

Margaret Mee

Oncidium lanceana Lindl.
Amazonas 1975

and met his son, in 1970 when I was in Barcelos, and had heard of his reputation for ill treating and fleecing the Indians who lived and worked on those rivers. What Sister Anna told me was far worse than I had ever imagined. Apparently soldiers were sent up one of the two rivers when malaria was rife and came away horrified at the conditions of the people working for the rascal. The men were housed in a huge barn with nothing but an open cesspool in the centre around which hung the hammocks of sick people on the point of death. With the exception of the father and a small child, one complete family had died, and the child died on the army boat returning to Manaus, and was buried like a dog on the river bank. The father, too, died later at the Salesian Mission in Barcelos. Apparently Albino was only one of many brutal traders whose only interest was to make money and accumulate wealth.

The keynote of my talk that evening was 'To treat the forests and all that they shelter with respect and with thought for the future'. I was listened to politely, but there was some opposition from the men when the question of hunting for skins and taking wood from the forests was mentioned. But many of the listeners agreed, I think, on the urgent need to protect the flora and fauna of the Amazon.

The following day, Bishop Dom Miguel arrived on the enormous supply barge and launch and this meant I was moved into a smaller room, one I had on my previous visit. But as I was to leave for Rio Cuiuni in the afternoon next day I packed up my things a little earlier than necessary.

My pilot for the Rio Cuiuni trip was Deolindo, and his assistant, Raimundo. There were very few habitations on the river, and as we went along I noticed that the vegetation was very similar until the last two days – when we entered a wonderful *igapó* of great trees, the Boca do Rio Cuiuni por Cima, where I made the best finds of the journey, including *Oncidium lanceanum*. A large frog, two red scorpions and hordes of frantic ants swarmed out of a handsome Billbergia.

Deolindo had climbed up with some difficulty to get the Billbergia. He was very stiff in the joints and getting on for sixty if not more. The older people did not wear well due to lack of good food and bad health. Raimundo, who was young and strong and would have been a more suitable plant collector, was in charge of the canoe's motor, so the climbing and reaching was left to the older man.

There were few birds in the *igapó*, which I thought had been burned until I realised that the enormous expanse of strange vegetation was due to what was known as the great *Quaimada*. In 1925 the heat was so intense that spontaneous combustion started forest fires in the area and many parts were burned out; only forest bordering rivers escaped. Presumably, man did his best to continue the destruction of nature.

I returned from Rio Cuiuni earlier than I intended, mainly because the *Cattleya violacea* which I found – a beautiful specimen with four perfect flowers – seemed to be the last one in flower, for I found no more, and this made me think it might not survive in its perfect state long enough for me to paint. In any case, I was running short of macaroni, the staple diet, and this presented a problem with two hungry men to feed. On my return journey, the boat was filled with baskets of cut plants. Curious hummingbirds came hovering over the flowers. Flights of macaw flew overhead, and there were many *curicas* and parrots – one unusual parrot with bright yellow body and dark green wings; *japims* and *japú* had hung their long woven nests on the taller trees, and occasionally I saw toucans and black ducks. A male howler monkey was swimming across the river and nearing the shore after crossing the wide expanse, making for a Jará palm on the margin of the water. Deolindo leaned out of the boat, his arms outstretched to catch the poor creature, whose expression was of fear and despair. I sternly ordered him to leave the animal alone, and told Raimundo to start the motor but to run slowly and was rewarded to see the animal, limp with exhaustion, clutch the trunk of the palm and slowly, with tired limbs, climb up and make his way to

Opposite. *Oncidium lanceanum*

safety through the trees of the *igapó*. His fur was a magnificent shade of chestnut.

Curious to know why Deolindo wanted the monkey, I asked him what he intended to do with it had he caught it. To my horror he replied that he would have killed it and sold it for meat in Barcelos.

Back at the mission, Sister Anna told me that malaria was rife and spreading and that many cases had come to Barcelos by canoe from the various rivers. She said things would probably not get better until the weather was cooler and that the services dealing with the disease were quite inadequate. I kept taking my malaria pills and hoping for the best.

After I returned to Barcelos I painted solidly, bar preparing for my next journey – to Tapurucuará on the Malaria Service launch, with my canoe in tow. Unfortunately Nazarene had terrible influenza, and as the voyage took two days, and I seemed often to be in his company, I just hoped that I wouldn't catch it.

At one stopping place a family came aboard – mother, father and two of the sickest looking children I had ever seen or hoped to see. They were both puffed up and yellow, almost like transparent balloons, even their eyes swollen. It must have been a combination of malaria and hepatitis and heaven knows what! Poor little creatures! And the mother looked little better. Nazarene was taking them and their canoe, which he stored with their chattels on the foredeck, to the Santa Casa of Tapurucuará.

All day we passed through the most wonderful forests, starting at São Tomé and extending for about forty kilometres. The long island, which forms the *paraná*, opposite this beautiful coast, is lovely too – Jauarí palms mixed with hardwood trees. The mainland seemed to have a preponderance of what they called *macucuzinho* – Erisma. The trees were veritable giants, standing high in the deep waters. It was such a magnificent area that I decided to visit IBDF on my return to Manaus to ask them to consider making it a forest reserve. Nearer to Tapurucuará most of the big trees had been stolen. We could see the gaps and confusion where smaller trees had collapsed when they lost the support of the mature trees.

Quite suddenly the launch's motor broke down – almost seized up judging by the fumes which poured out. Fortunately two of the men on board were good mechanics and managed to get the motor running smoothly again. Though not for long, for it broke down again almost immediately, and this time it seemed impossible to repair. So Nazarene put my canoe and outboard motor in front to tow the launch. We wondered if the canoe's motor would be strong enough to tow the heavy launch, but though our speed was much reduced, we managed to reach Tapurucuará safely.

The rooms at the Salesian Mission were all taken and I was directed to the Santa Casa where the unfriendly sister in charge of the hospital directed me to the infirmary full of sick people and, when I refused this, to the girls' dormitory in the main building. Again I politely refused. Eventually, hearing that I would have to look for lodgings outside the mission, the charming Sister Superior kindly vacated a classroom for me. I had met her previously in Içana and I was so happy to see her again. Another pleasant encounter was with the distinguished Padre José Schneider who had been so hospitable in Maturacá on our journey Pico da Neblina in 1967.

My time in Tapurucuará seemed to be one of renewing old friendships and remembering earlier journeys. For two days after I arrived I heard that the amazing Padre Antonio Goes who had been so helpful and informative when I visited him on Rio Marauiá was also expected on his way to Manaus. He arrived, looking much thinner with a beard which was nearly white, but after the years he still retained his old vivacity. All this time he had been in the one-man mission in the Serra do Chamatá with the Waika Indians. I was told that another padre went up there to take his place, but the Indians sent him packing and insisted that they would only have Padre Antonio. Then, as I was still remembering old times, a familiar voice called my name. It was Dedé who took me up to the headwaters of Rio Marauiá in 1967. His lovely

Opposite. *Billbergia decora*

Margaret Mee
July 1978

Billbergia decora Poepp. & Endl.
Archipelago das Anavilhanas

Opposite. *Selenicereus wittii*

Tucano Indian wife had died in childbirth, and he had married again, but he still lived with his wife and daughter in the same little house, now also a grocery shop. He had looked out for me in Manaus last June, having heard that I was there. He is someone I shall never forget.

My motor and canoe were being looked after by a Señor Aljimiro, who I was informed was extremely reliable. I felt somewhat embarrassed for I mistook his wife for his mother, but did not say so, of course. I was not sure whether he noticed my mistake or not, but was too polite to say anything.

The guide whom Nazarene found for me was named Leonardo, a Tariana Indian, the brother of Carlos who was my guide on Rio Cauaburi in 1967. Leonardo (not his real name) was busy working on the boat which he said would take a day or two. About forty years old, he spoke and wrote fluent Portuguese. He was stocky in build, similar to the Tucanos, with high cheekbones and the long slightly sloping eyes common to Indians. He was proud of being an Indian and had nothing to do with FUNAI. I suspected that he had been a village chieftain originally. His wife had been badly disfigured by burns and, as I did not see her, I supposed that she kept herself hidden away in their hut on Alto Rio Negro. Altogether, Leonardo seemed another reliable man, independent and resourceful, and had taken on a young Indian, João, to assist him on the river journeys I had planned.

As soon as the boat, Leonardo and I were ready to leave for Rio Daráa, we came across another problem – we could not find a dugout canoe to take in tow. It seemed that, as so many of these dugouts were working boats, we were going to have difficulty in buying. Furthermore, time was not on our side, for Leonardo was keen to leave immediately because of favourable weather prospects. In the end we decided to leave and try to buy a dugout on the way.

Rio Daráa was good for collecting, the main prize being the water cactus, *Strophocactus (Selenicereus) wittii* (now called *Selenicereus wittii*), which I had first found near Tapurucuará, when the boy who was helping me collect had left it behind because of the thorns. From across the river I saw the gleaming scarlet leaves catching the late rays of the sun. I had borrowed a dugout from a forest dweller, so was able to go right into the *igapó* where it was growing flat against the trunk of a large tree. The large variable leaves looked almost like transfers, for the roots grow from the veins on the underside of the leaf. There I also found *Aganisia cyanea* flowering profusely and a pale almost white Scuticaria.

At night I slept in my canoe, the hammock strung between two posts and my mosquito net over me, while Leonardo and João found a deserted hut at the top of a steep bank. It was marvellously peaceful but for the splashing and sighing of dolphins who were in playful mood at night.

As we progressed upriver, I went collecting in the *igarapé* and coasting along the banks of the river. But we did not get far on on Rio Daráa. Even before we reached it, Leonardo had expressed doubts about passing through the *cachóeira*. As soon as we came to it we realised the impossibility of passing this tremendous foaming cataract, which hurled itself against the great stones in a raging torrent, and with a very narrow channel through which to pass. To get to the higher reaches of the river, boats had to be dragged for a considerable distance over the ground, which had been worn smooth, and at least six men would be needed to pull my little canoe far enough to reach calmer waters.

While we decided what to do we walked through the forest behind the deserted hut of the keeper of the rapids. But there was little interest for me there, as the old trees had gone, leaving a rather poor secondary growth.

It was pleasant to be with Leonardo, who told me with pride that he had been born in the forest and mentioned with some scorn that the *caboclos* were afraid to walk through them, having been born and bred in towns, by which he meant settlements of huts.

The prow of my boat was filled with plants by this time, which made moving around difficult, even more so because I had a painfully swollen hand, resulting from a *tocandira* sting

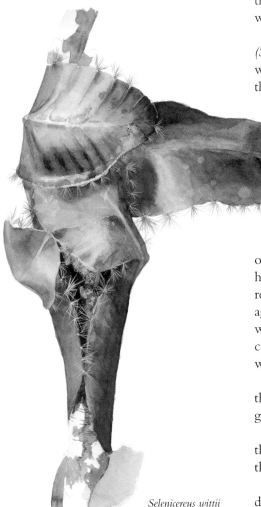

Selenicereus wittii

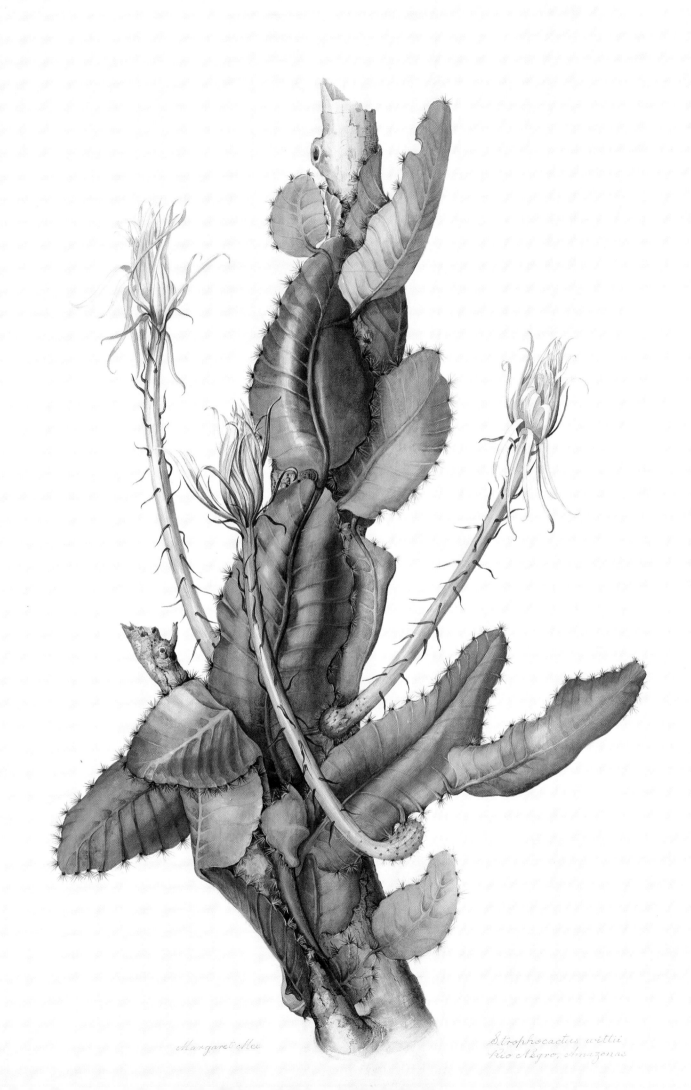

Margaret Mee

*Strophocactus wittii
Rio Negro, Amazonas*

João and Leonardo with my boat on the Rio Daraá

João and my boat, Rio Daraá

between thumb and finger. It was quite agonising, but my own fault as I got it through not using my gloves when I was collecting. The hot sun of earlier in the day had disappeared and a cool wind was blowing a heavy rain across the river. It would be cold in my hammock that night! An hour ago I was buying fish from a *caboclo* who came alongside in his dugout.

Next day we turned back and headed for Rio Jurubaxi, but when we came within sight of the mouth of the river it was almost obscured by *chuva branca* – a sheet of rain!

Shortly after we reached Rio Jurubaxi I had the good fortune to meet a man willing to sell me a little dugout canoe for collecting in the *igapó*. It was strong, well made, amazingly cheap – compared with prices I had seen in Barcelos, and was worth its weight in gold. All my plants were transferred to it making way for the petrol I had bought on Rio Daraá, which I was hoping would last until we got back to Tapurucuará. I was only allowed one tin, so with that and a little in the tank, we meandered with the strong current, trying to eke out the petrol.

Collecting on Rio Jurubaxi was fantastic and resulted in some magnificent finds – amongst them the orchid *Gongora quinquenervis*, growing on a deserted ant's nest. Strange how, coasting along, I stopped and entered the forest at the very spot where it was growing. *Aganisia cyanea* (the blue orchid) and a pale form of Scuticaria were quite common; and bromeliads were legion – many Aechmeas, Neoregelias, Guzmanias, Aerococcus and Billbergias.

Sheltered by the dark Buriti palms in which the river banks abounded formerly, there stood a small tree, deep in the water, full of cerise coloured fruit. From the brilliant pink bracts black and green berries hung, reminiscent of spindleberry. I made a rapid painting of this in the boat and then sketched a very lovely red Clusia which I had found in flower nearby.

The destruction of the magnificent Buriti palms along this river, was unbelievable. Instead of climbing up the tree and cutting the bunches of fruit, the whole Buriti was chopped down, with the result that the species was dying out. Compounding this, the massive trunks floating just below the water's surface endangered the river craft. In the *igapó* the destruction had created a confused tangle of vegetation, and on the banks erosion. Not only was this most spectacular of all palms being destroyed, but many hardwood trees had also been stolen, and a desolate waste of blackened stumps and burned vegetation left behind. This damage was extensive all along the river, but still the *caboclos* talk of *muito fatura* (great turnover) in the *Tapuacuzza* of Rio Jurubaxi and other neighbouring rivers. Nothing was cultivated, all was extracted. There was scarcely anything to buy, only lemons and occasionally fish. The *caboclos* went up river for a few days, slept at night in the leaf-thatched shelters, which Leonardo and João used frequently when uninhabited, collected the natural products – rubber, Buriti fruit, Brazil nuts and palm fibre, and went back again to Tapurucuará having taken all and left nothing. And this was what they meant by *muito fatura*.

One night we moored the canoe well out into the river, protected by a group of trees.

Opposite: *Ouratea discophora*

Margaret Mee

Ochna
Amazonas, Rio Curicuriari, June, 1972

The men found a small shelter – four posts and a palm leaf roof – out of sight, as it was far up the river bank. Opposite lay a beautiful stretch of sheltered *igapó*. We were far from any habitation and the silence was almost eerie.

In the morning I thought that the men looked a trifle jaded and pale, and asked them if they had slept well. They had scarcely closed their eyes, it appeared, for all night long they had been hearing a jaguar roaming in the forest bordering the rainforest. I laughingly reproached them for not warning me of the danger, to which they replied in all seriousness that they could not divine whether the beast would come to them or go to me.

Soon after this I was to pass an unsettled night, for we landed at a settlement where a festival was going on. At first Leonardo and João were eager to mix with the *caboclos*, having scarcely met a soul for days. But the loud and horrible music, the bonfire belching clouds of smoke and the violent quarrels amongst the men soon wearied them. At 6am the radio was still screaming and I was crazy with an aching head through lack of sleep and Leonardo's eyes were bloodshot.

My canoe and dugout by now looked like the hanging gardens of Babylon, for I had so many plants that they could not accommodate them all. The thorny water cactus hung under the 'eaves' of my canoe along with a Neoregelia which looked like a candelabra. Leonardo was most inventive and of his own initiative made a rack for the plants in the canoe. I mentioned that the roots of the orchids were getting saturated, and shortly afterwards saw him deftly constructing the rack which perfectly follows the contour of the canoe. He also made roll-up curtains from my large plastic sheet, to protect me from rain and mosquitoes..

On the return journey to Tapurucuará we landed at a hut where on the journey upriver we had been able to buy fish, in the hope of buying more. We were fortunate, as the man had been fishing in the morning. He also told us, with much excitement, that one known as Alberto Doido (crazy) had shot fourteen wild boar at the Boca de Jurubaxi, just as they were crossing the river, and had made a fortune selling the meat in Tapurucuará. Alberto Doido was a well-to-do man, it appeared.

A few days later, with Leonardo and João, I set off from Tapurucuará bound for Manaus. We had not been sailing for an hour before we ran into a storm – a real tempest. We had just returned from collecting in the canoe when I noticed that the sky was inky black, so we hastily returned to the motor just as a terrific wind driving the blinding rain before it, swept across the forests and rivers. Fortunately we were coasting near an *igarapé* and were able to take shelter there, but after a bit there was not enough shelter from the fierce wind in the *igarapé* and Leonardo made for the *igapó* in haste, driving right into its heart. The last heavy shower opened the sky to a glorious sunset, as we reached a fisherman's hut to buy fish for the journey. By the quantity it seemed that we would be eating it until we reached Barcelos – but it kept the men happy. With the fish and the oranges, lemons, onions and green bananas which Sister Claudia had given us, and the two dozen eggs I bought from her (there seemed to be a few extra), we shall not go hungry on this long trip.

One morning we left our mooring early in time to see a magnificent red dawn, and almost immediately ran into a *banzeiro* which only abated because we took shelter in a *paraná*. But in spite of a good deal of rough water on our journey to Manaus, I was able to collect and draw a splendid specimen of Gustavia – pure white with an enormous flower. The large tree had fallen into the river and the flowers were on branches at shoulder height. Leonardo, with careful manoeuvering in the choppy waves and avoiding getting entangled in the tree's canopy, triumphantly handed me some perfect blooms. My plants were beginning to look a trifle sad, but I did not think that I would lose any completely, though they still had a long journey ahead. Nevertheless, just in case they wilted, I managed to complete sketches of all of them, though the constant wind and rain made drawing difficult.

For three days after we left Tapurucuará we journeyed until 10 o'clock at night and later

Acacallis cyanea

We did not get far on Rio Daraá

still, finding it better sailing then as the waters were calm and mirror-surfaced.

We had a long wait one morning when it was quite impossible to sail as waves were breaking over the prow, so Leonardo took a well-earned rest, whilst João and I took the dugout into the *igapó*. Almost directly we were under the dark and shadowy trees there was a tremendous crash, and I thought Leonardo must be banging on the side of the canoe to attract attention for us to return. But João laughed heartily at this idea, saying simply '*guaribas*'. Then, just above our heads the howler monkeys set up a deafening roar. The troop was so close I could distinguish the leader's husky voice. João looked at me inquiringly, to know if I was alarmed, and asked if I wished to abandon collecting. If the monkeys objected to our presence there, he told me, they might throw branches at us, or relieve themselves on us. But we continued to collect and no harm came of our decision to stay. In fact, I found a new species of bromeliad with a delicate, candelabra formation, whose small individual cups had tiny florets as transparent as blue crystal.

It must have been 9pm one night when we found a shelter for the men to pass the night. The deserted hut, long abandoned, lay far from the port, a fallen tree, where the canoe was moored. It was very silent among the tall trees standing in the river. But I slept soundly until nearly five o'clock when the rain came teeming down. This delayed our start, and as soon as we set off we ran into a stiff *banzeiro*.

On the fourth day of the journey I became concerned about the petrol. We had the greatest difficulty in getting four tins and one 'empty' – this with an additional half tin over from Rio Jurubaxi was all we had to last us until Manaus. In Barcelos, I was told that the mayor had

Clusia

211

petrol to sell. So whilst Leonardo carried out some running repairs on the boat, I waited to buy some petrol. After waiting for forty-five minutes, the mayor sent a message to say that he had no petrol to sell. This confirmed my dislike of the arrogant man, whom I had met twice before. The first time his behaviour to me in Manaus in 1970 had been as offhand as this time, though this time he knew who I was, so was able to disappoint me without coming face to face with m. In the end I bought some fuel from one Francisco and paid him with borrowed money, since I had spent all I had, not expecting to need any more money on the trip.

Then we were speeding along, the surf flying. The weather had been bad on this journey, one *banzeiro* after another, yet in spite of this Leonardo managed to sail most of the time. One night, when we were enveloped in a *chuva branca* followed by a curtain of mist over river and forest, Leonardo sent João to the prow to watch for obstacles, and stood with his chin above the awning and drove and steered the motor with one foot. It was a spectacular performance but with one moment of peril, when a completely unlighted boat met us head-on. Leonardo saw the dark shape when nearly upon us, and with amazing rapidity changed course, saving us from what might have been disaster.

The long fine leaves of *Streptocalyx longifolius* dangled from a large tree standing deep in the river. Through them I could see the pale pink flower which in this species lies almost hidden in the cup of leaves. João climbed to the fork of the tree and prised out the plant and threw it down into the boat. With a shock I saw black scorpions emerge from the plant, a huge one with his tail upturned, about six writhing centipedes of a type reputed to be poisonous, at least a dozen black cockroaches, also venomous, for I remember being bitten by one in Curicuriari, and thousands of frantic ants. It took time to wash this menagerie into the river, and I hoped that the plants were uninhabited after this, for they were soon after sent to Rio's Botanical Gardens.

The men sheltered in a two-storey house on the last night – an unusual building for these parts. In looking curiously through the straw side of my canoe to see who could own such a luxurious house, I stuck a small bamboo into my eye. And what a night it was! Even though we were moored in the shelter of a small bay, blustering wind pushed the prow of the dugout against the canoe's motor, and I had to get out of my shelter in the canoe to secure it. Wet through, I was attacked by hordes of mosquitoes which followed me in, after which I had no rest. I lay there, itching with their bites and wondering if the rope by which the canoe was moored to a tree would snap, and the canoe with me in it would be blown along the choppy waters of the river, for outside the shelter of the bay I could hear the storm was still raging.

During daylight, Rio Negro is turbulent as one approaches Manaus, and only after passing the mouth of Rio Tupi do the cross-currents die away. As we sailed past the Arquipélago das Anavilhanas down the vast expanse, the waves tossed my little boat about like a cork in the water.

I was sad at the thought of leaving my beloved Rio Negro and the forests of the Amazon, but I was also rather weary and battered after more than three months of journeying through the wilds. The canoe looked like a floating forest – plants hanging around the 'eaves', baskets bursting with leaves and flowers, many of which had opened during the voyage. The hummingbirds which had come to take nectar from them were left far behind, and instead vultures wheeled above and quarrelled over scraps of refuse. We were approaching the noise and pollution of a city. Small craft dotted the water and sea-going ships were sailing into and out of Manaus. We passed familiar landmarks, the big closed market and the floating moorings bobbing up and down on the agitated waters.

As we entered the harbour, a sickle-shaped speed-boat shot by, turned, and almost upset my canoe as the owner shouted loudly, 'Got any jaguar skins?' Leonardo answered angrily in ringing tones, 'Get away, smuggler!'

The Tariana Indian was defending his territory in the camp of his adversary.

Opposite. *Sobralia margaritae*

Margaret Mee

Catasetum fimbriatum
Morren Lindl.

1974

JOURNEY TO RIO ANDIRÁ
SHIPWRECKED IN THE BAY OF SAPUCAIA

The diminutive Hotel Paris is tucked away in Avenida Joaquim Nabuco, Manaus, cheek by jowl with FUNAI headquarters, where I had called after my wanderings through the town.

I had been arranging the loan of a dugout canoe, for the beautiful one I bought two years earlier on Rio Jurubaxi (after much searching) had either been lost or stolen from INPA's floating mooring. I ended up with a much inferior one, and then turned my mind to arranging a crew to accompany me on my proposed journey up Rio Andirá, which I had briefly seen in 1971 when I was in Nazaré, and felt would be an excellent area for plant collecting. After much waiting to interview three possible pilots, two arrived, one after the other. They were both completely unsuitable, but the third, Carlos Tadeu, who had been recommended, did not arrive, so I sent a taxi or he would never have come, and in the end I chose him, though he did not want to go further than Barreirinha where he had relatives.

Weary, I was looking for a place to rest, so called in to have a chat with Capixaba, the owner of the Hotel Paris, who greeted me in his usual friendly manner. As I sat drinking a small black coffee, a British airline bag swung by. I did not see the tall owner, but inquired of Capixaba whether he had an English guest staying in his hotel. Yes, he would fetch him. His name was 'Cristovão'. I looked in the visitors' book, and saw to my astonishment, the signature of a friend from Gloucestershire.

Young Christopher was drooping a little, disappointed at not getting a permit to journey to Alto Rio Negro and Rio Uaupés. Why the refusal, he could not understand. He wished to meet the Indians on those rivers, and to see something of the glorious Amazon. Some British journalists had recently been to that region and had incurred disapproval through their articles and photographs, I explained. Hence the refusal, perhaps.

So here was a heaven-sent opportunity not only for me, but also for Christopher who enthusiastically accepted an invitation to journey with me. He would have to rough it, I added, remembering the rather luxurious and highly civilised surroundings in which I had met him in Gloucestershire.

Before we left, we had to transport all the stores and belongings to the floating mooring, and make an awning. Christopher managed to fix this – in mid-blue plastic (not *too* revolting – and disguised it well with palm leaves (a Manaus Port Authority regulation stipulated that only canvas, plastic or wood should be used for awnings, but no straw, the usual material).

One afternoon a few days later we were sailing along the Amazon river, on our way to Rio Andirá. The water was calm and a fine evening promised. We had arranged to meet an uncle of Carlos soon after we left Manaus. He had a 50 hp motor on his canoe and towed us to the mouth of Rio Madeira – a great help. I was glad when we left the urban landscape behind and got into the wilds, for there had been a good deal of destruction along the banks of the great river, though the change was not so great as I had imagined.

The promised evening and night were wonderful – a star-filled sky, glassy water and a waxing moon. But we ran into a *banzeiro* later and were drenched, mainly because Carlos

Opposite. *Catasetum fimbriatum*

215

would not slow down. Large boats were passing all night long as we slept, I in my boat and the others in a floating mooring. The next day, having said goodbye to Carlos' uncle, we sailed up Paraná da Eva, a very narrow channel and highly populated.

That day the motor on our dugout gave trouble, stopping dead three times, but after the spark plugs had been changed, it ran well.

Next, when we were preparing our evening meal, to my dismay I discovered that the stove I had been lent to substitute my 'lost' one was worthless – no, worse, a liability, for it caught fire when we lit it, and but for prompt action the boat might have caught fire too. We would have to starve until we could buy one in Itacoatiara.

When we reached Itacoatiara next day, I searched in vain for a little gas-stove, and eventually came away with a wretched alcohol burner and two bottles of spirit. The cost was pure blackmail! But needs must. I bought it from a very grasping woman, at a small cottage outside the town. When we were cooking on the river bank bordering a cocoa plantation the wash of large boats almost dragged the stove away.

We spent the night in the Paraná do Ramos. It was agonising! More mosquitoes than I ever remembered. As we stopped only at 10 o'clock all the huts and shelters were shuttered and dark. So our three hammocks had to go up on the new frame which had been fitted to the canoe. Fortunately it stood the test. But we did not. The mosquitoes bit me through the thick cotton hammock and a cat got in and clawed Christopher's net. We thankfully left this unhappy situation at dawn, and continued along the tremendously long Paraná do Ramos. Magnificent birds appeared, much to Christopher's delight - macaws, parrots, *mergulhas*, herons and an aquatic bird which I had seen pictured in Zimmerman's book of birds – there was a large flock of them with young and they set up a-screaming at us as the boat passed by. There were hundreds of dolphins popping up from time to time.

In Barreirinha a small Catholic mission and school stood beside the river port, and it was there that I asked for hospitality for one night. I also asked if they knew a pilot whom they could recommend to take us up Rio Andirá. Manoel, a small but sturdy man of Indian descent, was chosen, and I agreed thoroughly with the choice. So after a peaceful night, supper and breakfast in the mission we set sail at 11.30 a.m. The sisters and a crowd of onlookers were there to see us off, but the motor failed before we were even out of the port.

The gasoline, we decided, was at fault, so we changed it and got along splendidly until we stopped to collect Catasetums in muddy water fields along the river edges, and had difficulty starting it again. Then a storm blew up with such heavy rain, and we took shelter in the *igapó*.

More trouble. The motor refused to start, so Manoel paddled away in the canoe to fetch help, and just as night was falling, came back with a lad, the 'mechanic', who had not a clue as to what was wrong with the motor. So Manoel and the lad paddled us to the nearby village, no great distance, and we moored for the night in a small inlet where the men were able to sleep in the cabin of a launch. In the morning the lad returned and fiddled about with the motor, but to no avail. In the end we were taken in tow to Parintins, where I hoped to find a mechanic from the Malaria Service to help. Eventually we landed, but I still had to walk for half an hour in the burning sun, no trees – as usual, and not a vestige of shade. But eventually the Malaria Service mechanic came to our aid and solved the motor problem.

While I collected various Catasetums in the *igapó* I was stung by a wasp but without any reaction. I wondered if I was immune after so many stings? Crossing the great Lake of Andirá we ran into a *banzeiro,* much to the alarm of Manoel. Thus I missed some good collecting, but I decided to return if possible. In the *igapó* beyond Tucumanduba, to my joy I found *Catasetum macrocarpum* male form and female form. It was sheer magic there,

Opposite. *Catasetum macrocarpum (male)*

Margaret Mee
August, 1981

Catasetum macrocarpum L. C. Rich.
Amazonas

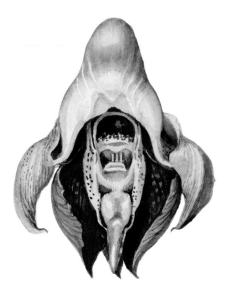

Catasetum macrocarpum var.

with the water so still that I could not distinguish the image from reality.

We stopped at a deserted hut in an ideal situation where we slept. The men were up at dawn fishing and returned with three piranhas – one less than we supped on the night before.

Another night the men found a beautiful abandoned hut in which to sleep. I was just dozing off after having rehung my hammock which had slipped down in the small hours, when I heard a loud thud, followed by a commotion – flashing torches and much laughter. Christopher had fallen from his hammock too.

We wended our way through the waterways of this part of Amazonas, heading for Ponta Alegre, where I hoped to pass the *Posto Indigena* without difficulty, as we did not have the necessary documentation. In the end we spent a night there, after handing over cameras, revolver, etc. on the insistence of Daniello, the youth in charge. He was Amazonense, so had better relations with the tribe than other officials I have met. But the old Indian headman, França, lived there, and it seemed he had a good deal of authority. I had a somewhat heated argument with Daniello about relinquishing my camera and getting his consent to proceed to Molongotuba and Simão, two very interesting Indian villages of the Maués or Sateré tribes. In the end I mentioned that the IBDF in Manaus was aware that I intended to collect on the river as far as Simão. At this Daniello's manner changed, for he had been an employee of Forest Defense and knew of the IBDF's work. But he was adamant about leaving our cameras, although I pointed out that photos of Indians who looked healthy and happy could do no harm to FUNAI or the *Posto Indigena*.

We had Guilherme as guide to Molongotuba and Simão. The houses we passed were made of *babaçu* palms and were very well ventilated and spotlessly clean. From Molongotuba, we took the village headman and his two nieces for an outing to Simão, and the headman in return sold us some oranges from his orange grove. One of the nieces seemed to have river blindness, as one eye was an opaque white; otherwise they were sturdy and nice looking.

Simão was some distance beyond Molongotuba, at the headwaters of a sinuous river which flows through the plains. It was under the domain of the headman Manoel, who spoke Portuguese, unlike most of the tribe.. He took us into the spacious *maloca*, where Christopher and I sat on either side of him, whilst half the village assembled and sat in a

Opposite. *Catasetum macrocarpum (female)*

Margaret Mee
July, 1981

Catasetum macrocarpum
L.C. Rich. (fem. form)
Amazonas

semicircle along the wall facing us. We conversed with these delightful people, the headman Manoel translating for the tribe. The Indians appeared to be very independent of the outside world, and their quiet courtesy was most refreshing.

On our return, darkness descended about two hours before reaching Ponta Alegre. It was a difficult journey, but luckily there was a large moon to help us.

On our return Christopher and Manoel were invited by França to hang their hammocks in the village *maloca*, and I slept in my boat. Early in the mornings the kindly Guilherme brought me plants to add to my collection, including a bromeliad, *Neoregelia leviana,* a very beautiful specimen with five plants forming a candelabra.

Money seemed to be a rarity, and I needed change to pay Daniello for Guilherme's services. On the outskirts of the village there was a small shop belonging to a trader, a most unpleasant man, who almost refused to change my money, perhaps because he saw my expression as I looked askance and disapprovingly at the beautiful spotted skin of an ocelot which he was displaying on the wall alongside other skins of forest animals.

The *igapó* of which I had great hopes yielded nothing but one Catasetum and a few Streptocalyx. But collecting was not the main thing on my mind following the ordeal we went through after returning from Simão. We were literally shipwrecked, and the boat went down in the bay of Sapucaia. Now we are heading for Freguesia over the choppy waters of a large lake. We should pass in an hour or so and then reach calm waters.

The evening before the disaster had been calm followed by a beautiful starlit night. But the following day had been squally from the start and we decided earlier than usual to look for a place to camp for the night. We found an ideal hut – abandoned. It was scarcely a hut, for all the walls were missing, though the roof was fairly waterproof. We moored the boat on the sandy beach, and then Christopher and I paddled into the nearby *igapó* which was silent and lonely. I kept a watch for the *hoatzin*, a bird I had seen earlier that day, when he had followed the canoe with curiosity. He is known as *ticuán*, an onomatopoeic name given him by the Indians. Fearing that we should get lost when we reached a very complicated area of *igapó*, I suggested that we should return. On nearing our shelter, we heard Manoel calling frantically to hurry, as a tempest was threatening. We had scarcely disembarked before the fierce storm wind started blowing. The canoe was moored both fore and aft and we were stowing possessions when the waves, whipped by a gale-wind into a turbulent fury, broke over the stern and the canoe began to fill with water. We frantically began throwing things on to the beach, rushing our possessions into shelter just before the planking floor in the canoe began to float away. The rain was teeming down but we persevered, drenched to the skin, till everything was saved. I looked at Christopher whose hair hung streaming over his face and burst into laughter, as he did when he looked at me – a couple of drowned rats! Manoel seemed puzzled by our strange outburst and odd sense of humour.

Gradually the boat went completely under water. We were literally shipwrecked. But Manoel's knowledge of the river and living in the wild proved a godsend, for he knew how to refloat the canoe. He cut a strong fork from a tree and, with Christopher's help, forced it under the prow, standing neck deep in the river. So, together, they raised the boat and being a lightweight I went aboard and baled out, whilst the waves were still breaking over the prow. Eventually we beat the waves and emptied the boat completely just as the light faded.

Christopher and I spent the night under the shelter of the frail roof as I gave up my berth in the boat to Manoel who had no hammock, his being drenched. I slept scarcely a wink, not because of the sounds of the forest, but because I shivered without a blanket having lent it to Christopher who had lent his to Manoel, and Christopher had a terrible cold. We left after a hurried breakfast, sailing over the choppy waters of a large lake before reaching calmer waters.

A few hours to go before reaching Barreirinha, we met a strong wind which drove

Opposite. *Neoregelia leviana*

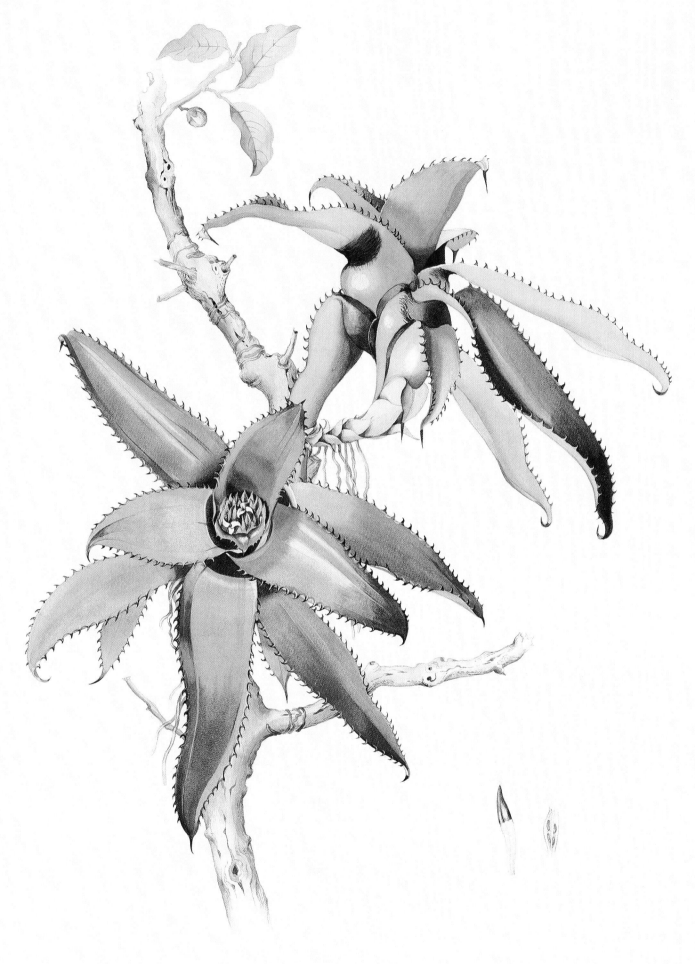

Margaret Mee

Neoregelia (unclassified)
Proc. Amazonas, Rio
Uaupés   Dec. 1964
Neoregelia leviana L. B. Smith (1965)

Catasetum macrocarpum

against us and we dipped and tossed across the vast waterway. Now we were on our way to Barreirinha, Manoel was like a horse returning home, and could not be restrained from galloping on at top speed, though on the journey his pace has been slow.

I have picked up my pen again after a terrible storm. We came through the Boca de Andirá into foul weather. A dreadful wind was blowing, but we went with it until the sky became too threatening and there were peals of thunder, so, fearing to repeat the ordeal of another shipwreck, we moored to a fallen tree in the port of a tiny hut, hoping to sit the storm out, until the owner came in his boat. So we had to leave, only to meet another tempest with heavy rain. Just at the peak of the storm, I caught sight of a magnificent Catasetum in flower high on the trunk of a large tree. Before it lay a great barrier of floating grass. Heroically, Christopher volunteered to get it, and, trying to avoid the impenetrable grass, sank waist deep into the black mud of the river bed, whilst mosquitoes and ants tortured him. He returned, crestfallen. So Manoel, who was familiar with these grass islands, took the canoe and with the paddle fought his way through until he reached the tree, and was just able to reach the orchid, detaching it with the oar blade. It was a beautiful *Catasetum macrocarpum* and I could not wait to paint it.

When we arrived in Barreirinha we moored, as before, in the little port beside the mission, where another drama took place. Christopher had been harangued by a drunk, a great burly *caboclo*, who insisted on explaining that all food, when eaten, passed through the heart. Christopher had scarcely time to warn me about this type before he strode over to me in a most aggressive manner, demanding the orchid which Manoel was holding to be photographed. I explained kindly, that this was not possible, whereupon he offered bananas in exchange. Using all the tact I could muster, I turned down the offer firmly. He flew into a rage and, brandishing his large bush knife, advanced, shouting that I must move my boat, that I was a smuggler, and so on. As he advanced, knife raised on high, Manoel, who scarcely reached to his waist, ran at him heroically and pushed him in the stomach, shouting to him to clear off. A small crowd had gathered by this time, and I grabbed an Indian girl standing by, telling her to run quickly to fetch the Italian padre, a large and vigorous man. He came at the double, took hold of the drunkard by the shoulders, leading him off to the local councillor. The councillor himself appeared very soon after, with a troubled expression on his kindly face, and apologised for the incident. I assured him that I realised every village had one black sheep.

We waited in Barreirinha looking for a tow to Itacoatiara or Manaus. I was running short of money and desperately needed a new pump for the motor.

The water in our mooring in Barreirinha was filthy and I could not wash anything – clothes, equipment or the boat. I tried to settle down to some drawing, but dozens of *caboclos* gathered round to watch and it was impossible to concentrate. And as soon as I stopped drawing the *caboclos* drifted away. So all I could do was to sit in the port, waiting …waiting…and no news of anything going to Manaus. It was a really depressing time, for we had been moored in the dirty little port for too long and it looked as though we should be there for all eternity, unless I made some move. None of the pilots who worked for the Malaria Service had any suggestions, but suggested that Inspector Monteiro might be able to help, and that they would ask him to call on me. But he never came, and by the end of that day I had lost hope. It looked as though I would have to go under my own steam, but first I had to find someone to cash a cheque so I could buy a pump, petrol and pay a pilot – if it was possible to find one.

During the night, whilst I slept on the canoe, and Christopher slept fitfully (to judge by his constant coughing) in the nearby Malaria Service launch, someone came aboard and stole the paddle, leaving behind a large, jagged stick – perhaps as a weapon if necessary? Presumably Christopher's coughing had disturbed the thief. I felt that we were terribly vulnerable in the little port, and the characters whom I had observed during the too long days were, on the whole, not very friendly. So I took the decision to search out Inspector Monteiro myself.

In the morning Christopher paddled me across the river to a broken down wooden construction where I landed with some difficulty. This strange jetty was a maze of planks leading to slum dwellings, with filthy waters flowing sluggishly below. My chief preoccupation: would I ever find my way back? I felt as though I was making this journey in a nightmare, wondering what I would encounter at the end. Once on terra firma I found my way to the main street and to the headquarters of the Malaria Service. Closed. After much enquiring and searching I found 'the house of Monteiro', but not the Monteiro I was seeking. I took a taxi through the village until I came to the house of Inspector Monteiro, and explained the situation to him – no money, faulty pump, no guide, and no sign of transport to Manaus. He was most sympathetic and took me on the pillion of his motorcycle to Inspector Benedito's house, travelling through the puddles and pools of one of the roughest of roads I had ever seen in any Amazon village. Then, together the two men went off, leaving me in Benedito's house. Eventually Benedito returned with the welcome news that a passenger launch heading for Manaus had moored at the main port. Paulo, Benedito's son, would guide us to the launch once I had returned to the other side of the river.

My relief was overwhelming and even the terrifying return to my boat could not damp my spirits, though I crossed the river in the most perilous manner seated in a rudderless boat, paddled by two small boys who both pulled in the opposite direction. I visualised myself falling into the highly polluted water and swimming to my canoe across the filthy water.

Safely back, Christopher and I met Paulo with much rejoicing and followed him to the *General Osorio* where all was arranged and stowed most efficiently – even the plants, which were in the hold, while the canoe was in tow.

Back on the great Amazon, we passed Urucará, São Sebastião, and the mouth of Rio Uatumã which flows into Rio Jatapu – a very interesting and uninhabited region. The captain told me that tragically many of the Indians who lived there had died, and remnants of the tribes have abandoned the area for Ponta Alegre.

At São Sebastião, a *caboclo* had come aboard, and our conversation turned to manatee and turtles. Manatees, or sea cows, existed, he told me, in *paranás*, but were becoming scarce. It is a large and defenceless mammal which has young only every two years, and then only one at a time. Because a young calf relies entirely on its mother's milk, if she is caught, the calf perishes. The cries of these animals were pitiful to hear, the *caboclo* said. This had given rise to the legend that the manatee was a woman in disguise, which for a long time protected them from hunters. Now, my informant went on, they were hunted to near extinction, and their meat bought in the open markets. Hunting, with harpoon and knives, was carried out with incredible cruelty. The *caboclo* pointed out a man seated in a boat by the river bank, who hunted manatees and turtles, the latter with hooks on a line. Apparently his main hunting ground was about an hour beyond the mouth of the Rio Urubu, a charming little bay with a thick growth of Aninga. I pointed out that it was illegal to hunt or catch these creatures, but was told that inspectors never appear and nobody cares. Along the coast off São Sebastião, he said, the fishermen brought in catches of around two hundred turtles, although on his beach he did not allow line fishing for these creatures.

We passed many beautiful river mouths, all of them giving tempting glimpses of possible collecting areas. But before that we had to return to Manaus and sort out the plants and equipment before thinking of the future. After the adventures and disasters of the last two weeks, the journey back was smooth and the waters remarkably calm.

Margaret Mee
July 1977

Aechmea rodriguesiana
Rio Marau, amazonas

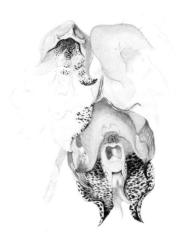

1975

RIO UNINI, RIO NEGRO
LUXURY BY MY MODEST STANDARDS

Catasetum macrocarpum

Less than six months later I was back in Manaus preparing to show parts of the Amazon to some English friends: Sally, Duchess of Westminster, and her companions, Michael Szell an outstanding designer and decorator, and David Vickery a distinguished architect. They had come to Brazil to experience a journey through the Amazon, and Michael to seek inspiration from the tropical flora and to find orchids for his collection.

But the spectacular start to this trip had taken place on dry land. The night before we left we had, in the cold light of day, been in the realms of fantasy for we had attended the reinauguration of Teatro Amazonas by the President of Brazil.

The famous theatre, built during the rubber boom of the 19th century, had remained unchanged for many years, and was somewhat neglected. The lovely wrought-iron banisters had lost their glow, the original cane chairs in the auditorium were dusty, and the back-stage was badly in need of ventilation. A complete overhaul was needed and now it had all happened. The exterior had been beautifully repainted in white and grey, the interior redecorated throughout, the paintings and chandeliers cleaned and repaired, and in the auditorium red plush seats replaced the humble cane chairs – whose disappearance I regretted along with the wrought-iron banisters. Behind the scenes everything had been brought up to date.

Following the inaugural celebration and programme we were introduced to the President, and then attended a reception at which there was a beautifully prepared buffet and plenty of champagne.

But at dawn next day I was in the port of Manaus to take over the splendid launch *Jaragua* which had been loaned to our party by the Ministry of Agriculture. The launch was spacious and even luxurious by my modest standards – for I always travelled 'rough' – and had been thoughtfully equipped with everything for our comfort and convenience, even to four hammocks hanging temptingly on deck. Bunks had also been provided, though when on the Amazon I always preferred to sleep in a hammock on deck breathing the perfume of the jungle and pure air of the river and listening to the plaintive notes of night birds and sounds of the forests which became more mysterious during the hours of darkness.

The *Jaragua*'s crew had been taken on by the Ministry; it would be a pleasant change for me to have a cook to prepare meals, and be free of the problems of purchasing fuel and constant baling out. I had employed a guide myself, Paulo, who, in spite of his name, was an Indian both in appearance and character. He had the reputation of being an excellent man in the forest, and this he proved to be, for no tree seemed too difficult nor too high for him to scale, armed with my heavy bush knife.

In the afternoon, leaving the noisy port of Manaus behind we sailed up the broad Rio Negro on our way to Rio Unini, a tributary of the great Rio Negro. About three hours' sailing brought us to the mouth of Rio Tarumã, one of the beauty spots of the last century, when Richard Spruce journeyed through the Amazon. In *Notes of a Botanist on the Amazon*, 1882, he wrote a scenic description of the magnificent towering trees and the

Paulo, an excellent man in the forest, for no tree seemed too difficult nor too high for him to scale, armed with my heavy bush knife

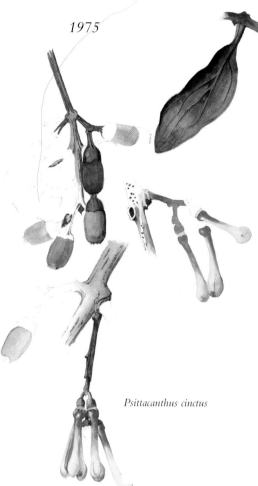

Psittacanthus cinctus

rocks over which the clear waters of the river cascaded. But what we saw was that much of the surrounding woodland had been senselessly destroyed, and the giant trees of which Spruce wrote, which could have lived for centuries, had disappeared giving the scene little more than a mundane aspect. It was a sad sight for my companions new to the Amazon to be introduced to its delights by this sad scene.

However, we all rose early next day, eager to reach Rio Unini, and as soon as the sun had lifted the mists from the river were sailing upstream again. The air was fresh and cool, ideal for paddling up inlets and streams to look for the wonders we expected to see, and we were not disappointed, for in a patch of sunlight perched a large toucan with red and black plumage and ivory neck and bill. Alarmed, he called his mate, and together they sat protesting at the unwelcome creatures intruding on their territory.

Next afternoon we reached the mouth of Rio Unini, half an hour after passing Old Airão, once a settlement, on the south bank of Rio Negro, the only remnants of the abandoned town being three 18th century buildings, now in ruins. As we passed one of the crew told me that in November, when the waters were low, the manatees bred in the shallows and were hunted. The ruthless hunters butchered adults and calves indiscriminately in spite of the female manatee only bearing young once in two years and then only one calf, as well as being a protected species nearing extinction. The loss of this mammal in the Amazon would have serious repercussions, living as it does on aquatic vegetation and thus keeping rivers clean and clear. Happily a number of these creatures were being studied at INPA with a view to preserving the species.

Edge of *igapó* forest on the Rio Unini

The launch *Jaragua,* spacious and even luxurious

The conversation about manatees had been so disturbing that we passed the mouth of Rio Unini and were heading for Barcelos (four days away) before getting back on course. Next day we confronted the rapids of Rio Unini.

It was early morning when we called on Raimundo, known as Keeper of the Rapids, to pilot us past this great underwater rock which extends for some kilometres. It took us an hour and a half to pass this impressive series of waterfalls, and even with our experienced pilot the *Jaragua* struck rock, fortunately without damage to the hull. The water level was unusually high for January, which made it easier to pass the falls, but the channel was most devious and the river had to be crossed more than once. Old and wizened though he was, Raimundo navigated with ease, admitting however, that his sight was beginning to fail him. On the return journey his grandson, also an Indian, was our skilful pilot.

We landed in a very dark forest where many of the towering trees were as artfully ribbed as Gothic columns. From the branches of one hung coils of heavy rope-like lianas, and in the midst of them a snake of about two metres, dangling from the canopy, silver-green in colour and almost invisible against the background of sinuous vines. Above the serpent circled two parrots uttering angry outraged cries, obviously defending their young against the marauder. Ignoring the drama being enacted beside him, a woodpecker tapped loudly on dead wood, searching for insects. Our stay was cut short as angry wasps emerged from a fallen tree where we were detaching an orchid.

On the sixth day of our journey we were still on Rio Unini, passing our days pleasantly in the forests and in the warm waters of the river. We had passed the mouth of Rio Anamari, so knew that we were nearing the small Rio Papagaio, and after inquiring of

Aechmea sp.

some peasants in a canoe, eventually reached this stream's narrow inlet. The *igarapé* merged into an extensive lake and there was scarcely any firm ground on which to stand to collect, though there were areas of swamp which we managed to wade through. As we struggled through this marshy scrubland we were rewarded by seeing, even stroking, a sloth who was hugging the base of a small tree, sound asleep. Paulo, trying to be helpful, removed the struggling animal so that he could be photographed at closer quarters, and the poor creature fell into the water. Lifting him out of the mud, Paulo then tried to put him up a tree, but the dazed sloth sat with his bottom in the stream, clinging to a branch, his little head drooping and a sad smile on his face. I stroked his shaggy grey coat, full of fungus and insect life, and left him to his dreams.

Before dark the crew moored the *Jaragua* in a creek, having decided that it would be impossible to navigate further up the *igarapé*, as our boat was too large. So Paulo paddled us in the canoe to an area where we found small orchids and enormous clumps of bromeliads, mainly *Aechmea setigera* and *Aechmea tocantina*, both species armed with terrible thorns and impossible to collect. Plants were not as prolific on Rio Papagaio as we had been led to believe, though parrots of all kinds were, and in the dawn chorus toucans, *japims* and hosts of birds added their cries to those of the parrot family. Nights were no more silent than the days, for frogs provided orchestral music through the dark hours.

Rose-pink dolphins were playing in the broad expanse of Rio Unini as we sailed through the mouth of Rio Papagaio. Full of *joie de vivre*, they were leaping and diving, the large males shooting sparkling fountains of water into the air.

Sally and Michael, full of enthusiasm at the sight, dived into the river, whilst I hesitated, having recent memories of having been chased by a pink dolphin into an *igapó* in a small canoe, paddled by a boy who told me in alarmed tones, that a dolphin will overturn a canoe in playful mood or anger if one had trespassed in his territorial waters.

From this sunlit area we glided in the canoe into a strange, dead world where the forests were disintegrating. The surviving trees stood stark and dried out, some black where fire had charred their limbs, others spindly, white and rotten. Many orchids still clung to the crumbling branches, Catasetums and Galeandras in flower, but it was hazardous to try to reach the higher ones, so Paulo took his long crook and prodded the dead wood to loosen the roots. More than once, not only the plant but also the bough full of sawdust came crashing down narrowly missing us and the canoe.

According to the local people this forest had been water-logged for two years instead of the usual six months in each year, and as a result they could no longer keep cattle, having nowhere to graze them. The trees of the *várzea*, having adapted to a pattern over

Aechmea tocantina

Opposite. *Aechmea tillandsioides*

Margaret Mee
1976

Aechmea tillandsioides (Mart ex Schult)
Amazonas, Rio Negro

Galeandra dives

Aechmea tocantina

countless years, were rotting as a result of the changed conditions. People blamed a *fura da terra* (hole in the earth), for the catastrophe, which we understood to be earthworks for a dam. I had seen a great deal of this rotting forest on this journey and concluded that it was not only burning which was wreaking widespread destruction, but also interference with the river system.

On our homeward journey we spent time sheltering from the frequent rainstorms, stopping to scan the forest for plants or to swim in the black waters, often in company with large grey piranhas. Thus the days passed pleasantly until we reached Manaus with its noise, bustle and pollution.

It was sad to part company with my travelling companions. Alone again with my work, I soon felt I should take advantage of being in Amazonas, and planned a visit to Urucará where I had friends with whom I had been invited to stay. I had passed Urucará on other trips to the Lower Amazon, but never collected in the region. It would be a two-day

voyage down the Amazon and the Paraná da Silva.

Reinaldo, a mutual friend, had also been invited, so together we went down to the port, weaving our way through the milling crowds, to book a passage on the *Cidade do Parintins*, a launch which sailed two or three times a week. She was due to set sail in the late afternoon, but we hung our hammocks immediately, an hour in advance, for the launch was filling rapidly with passengers and cargo. Most of the passengers were country folk returning to their riverside huts, laden with baskets of *pirarucu*, fruit, clucking, fluttering hens and white cotton bags containing other possessions. There were a few prosperous looking farmers and less prosperous small traders and a sprinkling of students on holiday. Unfortunately a group of unruly youths embarked who gambled throughout the night playing radio transistors at top volume, vying with the noisy boat's radio which provided permanent background music.

During the night a storm blew up and the launch pitched and tossed so violently that my hammock and I nearly hit the ceiling, and on the rebound collided roughly with Reinaldo in his hammock. Waves splashed over the upper deck creating panic, but the river calmed down later on, when I could have slept had not the brilliant, swinging ship's lamp and the interminable radio prevented me.

At last morning came with the usual flurry of passengers cleaning teeth, snatching a miserable wash, drinking coffee from thermos flasks and packing up scattered baggage ready for landing. It was already midday when we arrived in Urucará in the pouring rain which completely obscured the village from view. But our hosts awaited us with a supply of umbrellas.

During the days that followed the weather improved and trips in the aluminium canoe driven by an outboard motor, took us into fascinating areas. Landing on a sandy beach, we followed a hunter's track through the forest, past an impressive group of scarlet-hearted bromeliads (pineapple family) which seemed to be the stronghold of large black scorpions.

On the beach the heat was intense, but escape was always nearby in the cool shade of the *igapó*, where our host manouevred the canoe through the winding tree-tangled

The port of Manaus, with its noise, bustle and pollution

Aechmea cf. *tillandsioides*

Maxillaria multiflora

Mormodes buccinator

channels. Hummingbirds hovered over nectar-laden Norantea, a parasitic bush like European mistletoe, but with more colourful flowers, which are orange and yellow, contrasting strangely with the blue and cerise fruits.

As I wandered along the sandy shore of the *igapó* I saw an electric eel in the shallows between the tree roots, almost indistinguishable from the brown river bed. The small, keen eyes observed me and the creature remained quite still except for the slight twitching of his tail fins. This harmless looking eel can give an electric shock of 600 volts, which in the water could prove fatal.

Before leaving Manaus the previous year I had arranged to have my canoe painted, the roof re-covered and various other repairs carried out. I left it with some doubt at the back of my mind, which on my return proved justified, for I never saw the little boat again. Its loss was a tremendous blow both for me and for my work, for transport was always the main problem on these river journeys. A canoe of my own meant freedom of movement and added tranquillity in which to collect and draw.

I made enquiries of everyone I thought might be able to tell me about the boat and gleaned that it went down in a storm. It was seen again in port at close quarters a month

Ananas bracteatus

later when the viewer identified it by the holes drilled in the wood to hold the supports for my hammock, for I was accustomed always to sleep aboard. Later, it was seen again, sailing on the Rio Negro. In spite of all this information I was unable to trace it, yet still had hopes of discovering its whereabouts or even seeing it on one of the rivers.

I had been unlucky with my boats, to which I became attached, having braved many difficulties with them as well as having enjoyed the freedom which they gave me. The beautiful little canoe which I had purchased on the distant Rio Jurubaxi was the first to go, having disappeared from the jetty in the same mysterious manner as this latest loss. I had used it in tow to carry petrol tins, too bulky with the rest of the cargo, and as the tins were emptied, plants took their place on the rack which Leonardo the Tariana Indian pilot had made for them.

The third boat, bought in Maués, I had sold, much under priced, when I was unwell at the end of a journey and without the fare to get home. The purchaser, aware of my plight, beat the price down to rock bottom

So the loss of my fourth boat was a disaster, and with it went all my travelling equipment and, at the time, any hopes for future journeys.

Psittacanthus sp.

Margaret Mee   Philodendron arcuatum Krause ex descr.
                                              Near Manaus, Am. Oct. 1977

1977

RIOS JUFARI, JAÚ AND NHAMUNDÁ

SUCCESSFUL COLLECTING BUT NO 'BLUE QUALEA'

A bitterly cold wind had been sweeping across the unprotected plains when I left the airport in Brasilia, so that it was quite a shock to step out of the plane in Manaus into a temperature of 42°C.

The headquarters of INPA were shaded by remnants of forest, for the building lay some distance from the town of Manaus in a relatively peaceful area. Here the kindly Director provided me with an apartment where I was able in peace and quiet to plan my next journey to the waterways of the great Amazon. My object this time was to travel to Rio Jufari, whose mouth I had sailed past several times and always been tempted to explore. There were problems over my equipment, partly because of the loss of my little boat and its contents, and partly because INPA denied that I had stored anything with them in the past, so I was busy arranging transport and getting together the belongings I would need.

My planning was constantly interrupted by the busy and varied animal life in and around the INPA site. One day a band of squirrel monkeys invaded the trees near my apartment and I fed them them with bananas, with the result that they reappeared regularly. They were black around the eyes, with a black smudge over the nose and yellow gold limbs. They were playful, fascinating little creatures. The Director of INPA introduced me to his tame parrot who was persecuted by an opossum, and pointed out the nesting places of owls and toucans in the lofty old trees, sole survivors of the former great forest.

Phragnipedium vittatum

Other birds and animals I saw during my stay at the Institute included *pacas*, lizards, scarlet ibex, curassows, and a tiny anteater which was being raised by one of the staff. One night I fed two large spectacled owls with raw meat. They landed on my shoulders and arms, which was rather painful as they have powerful claws. But they were magnificent birds.

A few days later, at 5.30 in the morning, and not too hot as there had been rain in the night, Reinaldo, a friend from INPA, drove the 130 kilometres on the Manaus-Porto Velho road to Igarapé das Lajés where INPA was concerned about damage to an area rich in vegetation. The new road was a disaster – at least the 130 kilometres we travelled – both for destruction of the forests and consequent erosion. Many stretches were flanked on either side by sheer precipices of eroding ground. Rio Preto must have been a lovely waterway, but mounds of excavated earth had been deposited in and beside it and, like most of the *igarapés*, it was choked by the road cutting across its course. Instead of the land being drained as nature intended, great pools of stagnant water had collected in which trees had rotted and fallen. Thousands of trees must have perished in this way, to which the tragic appearance of the scenery bore witness.

But, in spite of this, there were still areas of beautiful forest, and where it had been ruthlessly destroyed, pioneer Embaubas were valiantly trying to protect new growth.

At last we reached Igarapé das Lajés, and here further destruction awaited us. Apparently a few months before the unique rock formation had been adorned with quite spectacular plants: a white flowered Sobralia, Catasetums, Gesneriads and a rare Philodendron, but in

A tiny anteater was being raised by one of the Institute staff

the course of the road building the area had been set on fire and much of the adjacent forest sprayed with defoliant. At one point the net result of this destruction was one Mamao tree, a few pineapples, and goats which were helping to wreck any remaining forest which was being hacked away when we arrived.

INPA was endeavouring to get the area protected as a forest reserve, but Reinaldo and I thought it was doubtful if there would be anything left worth saving if the devastation was allowed to continue on the scale we witnessed.

Wandering among the rocks, away from the destruction, I came across a grotto of amazing design. Within it were beautiful caves which seemed to be used by hunters as night shelters, for fires had blackened the cave walls which doubtless were once covered with mosses and ferns.

Outside, light filtered between the leafy canopies of the trees in untouched forest, falling on swamp plants around a small lake, whilst a short distance away a black river flowed through a *caatinga* forest teeming with plants, many in flower – *Acacallis cyanea* – the blue orchid, *Scuticaria steelii,* delicately perfumed, and the lovely climber *Philodendron arcuatum* (= *P. brevispathum),* with white, pink spotted spathes and stems covered with what looked like the russet fur of a forest animal.

I walked until I was exhausted, wading through streams and then, with soaking canvas shoes, ploughed through black, swampy ground. But I was delighted with the results of my journey, for I had material for many paintings.

The trek over, I sank down in the comfort of the little car, noticing strange black clouds which seemed to dangle from the sky like streamers. When they reached the ground a violent storm broke and torrents of rain fell, making driving difficult on the slippery mud road. Then Reinaldo saw through the rear view mirror a bus bearing down on us, the driver obviously blinded by the sheets of rain. To escape being hit, Reinaldo deliberately skidded into a deep ditch which had been transformed into a raging river. Eventually, with the help of a young soldier who had observed our plight from a passing lorry, and passengers from a bus which the fellow commandeered, the car was lifted on to the road and we arrived at INPA well after dark

To everyone's sorrow the tiny anteater had died while we were away, and one of the spectacled owls was ill, but when I gave it water it drank avidly and seemed to recover.

At last I was able to finalise arrangements for my journey to Rio Jufari. INPA lent me their smallest launch, the *Pium,* and with a crew of three – Adalto the pilot, Paulo the cook and Pedro my collector – I left early one morning for the port of Manaus where we spent a tedious time arranging and stowing supplies and getting the boat's gearbox repaired. Everything seemed to be delayed or difficult to organise. Just as we were ready to leave, the crew asked me to buy bullets for them, but I told them that I had my own defence and that their guns and ammunition were their responsibility. The launch is fine, full of life-belts!

On the way to Rio Jufari I hoped to be able to collect in the Arquipélago das Anavilhanas, a collection of isles which are waterlogged for many months when the rivers rise. I also intended to hire a dugout canoe at the mouth of Rio Cueiras, opposite the Archipelago.

As we continued up my beloved Rio Negro, the banks were almost unrecognisable – fire after fire on the horizon. Only two years had passed since I came this way, and this time not a big tree to be seen on the banks. No birds. The remnants of the forests thin and poor. The rapidity of the destruction was appalling.

We moored at the mouth of Rio Cuieras beside a little hut where half a dozen Indian children were playing, and asked for their father. He was out, but I waited in the shade for nearly four hours and when he returned I managed to hire a canoe from him at a most

Trunk of *Philodendron solimoesense* on which various orchids were growing in the *igapó,* also lichens

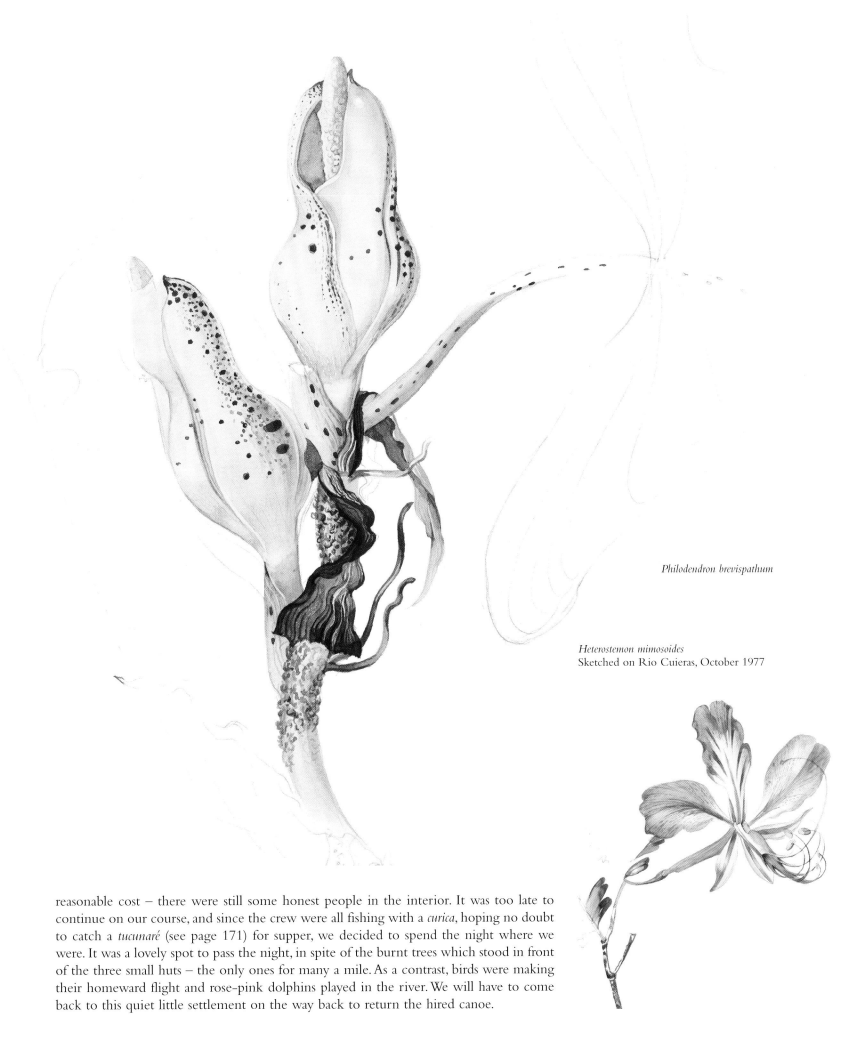

Philodendron brevispathum

Heterostemon mimosoides
Sketched on Rio Cuieras, October 1977

reasonable cost – there were still some honest people in the interior. It was too late to continue on our course, and since the crew were all fishing with a *curica*, hoping no doubt to catch a *tucunaré* (see page 171) for supper, we decided to spend the night where we were. It was a lovely spot to pass the night, in spite of the burnt trees which stood in front of the three small huts – the only ones for many a mile. As a contrast, birds were making their homeward flight and rose-pink dolphins played in the river. We will have to come back to this quiet little settlement on the way back to return the hired canoe.

Selenicereus wittii

Next day, in the Anavilhanas, Pedro climbed a rotting tree to get *Strophocactus wittii* but without flowers. In spite of a long and unsuccessful search for a late bloom, for the flowering season would have passed some months previously, I did find a few fruit with the leaves. I had found *Strophocactus wittii* (now called *Selenicereus wittii*) in 1967 and 1972, both times higher upriver. It is a remarkable cactus which is immersed in water for months of the year without the leaves under water rotting.

We sailed on towards Rio Jufari. Wildlife was becoming more plentiful and interesting – flights of parrots, large black ducks, solitary kingfishers with vivid plumage skimmed the water, hunting fishes; toucans flew from the trees as we passed, unmistakable in flight because of their large beaks, and at dusk myriads of nightjars darted low over the river, dark and silent.

One evening we moored in a *paraná* earlier than usual due to some problem with the fuel. I passed a wonderfully peaceful night there, only awaking briefly to hear a nocturnal bird, the Great Pootoo, calling its beautiful and melancholy cry. There were no Howler Monkeys here, though further downriver on previous nights we had heard plenty of them howling away.

When we sailed past the mouth of Rio Jauaperi, and an hour later Paraná de Cuperi, I saw that the exposed and drying root structures of giant trees were ready to fall into the water when the banks were further eroded. A happier sight was a flock of *anú* flying low and weaving in and out of the vegetation, their indigo plumage glancing in the sun. The beautiful *Bombax munguba* (Kapok) was in fruit, great scarlet pods hanging from the boughs.

Paraná de Floresta was followed by Paraná de Gavião, where a pair of storks with enormous wing spans rose from the river and flew into the luxuriant forest which seemed to be primary.

We sailed through steaming water after a storm, crossing a wide expanse of river beyond Moura, a small town, and reached the first rocks on the journey, a group of great rounded stones known as the Pé de Gavião. After passing this landmark more appeared in the river.

At about 5p.m. we sailed up the Jufari, after much searching. The mouth of Rio Jufari seemed to be one tremendous lake merging into Rio Negro, and very wide at that point, without apparent boundaries. As a result we spent a great deal of time looking for Rio Jufari, not realising till late in the afternoon that we had already passed it.

As we sailed up I was breathless – the scene was primeval, not a habitation, nothing but enormous volumes of water and a distant complex of *igapó*. Herons and toucans perched in the stunted trees and four black ducks on the river seemed scarcely aware of us before they flew low into the *igapó* where all was gold and green in the evening sun. Groups of small delicate palms stood along beaches of white sand. It was a dream world and I felt that I must be the first stranger to have entered it. The crew, however, did not share my enthusiasm for this glorious place, but, shuddering slightly, proclaimed it 'Muito deserto' (a lot of desert).

Exploring up Rio Jufari, we reached a small settlement and a little church where a festival seemed to be in progress with the old mayor from a nearby village, Carvoeiro, presiding, a strange old man whom I remembered having met in 1967 when *en route* for Pico da Neblina. He was unfriendly and unhelpful, and the *caboclos* took their cue from him and, with hostile looks, refused to sell me baskets for my plants.

But plantwise the river proved disappointing. The forest was walled by *molongo* and a low, sterile *igapó*, and was quite impossible to penetrate without cutting a path which would take hours. So, after spending one night there, surrounded by storms, battered by waves and strong winds, we decided to head back for Rio Jaú, a river which had shown great promise when we passed it earlier.

Strophocactus
wittii
Seavelinhas, Amazonas

Margaret Mee
February, 1978

Maguarf (Maguari heron)

There had been much deliberation and discussion about this change of plan. Rio Jaú was on our route back and to get there meant crossing Rio Negro where it was not too wide. The crew's opposition to this was based on their claim never to have journeyed on the south bank of the river and visualising problems if we did so. In the end we decided to cross Rio Negro at a point where there were no isles and where the south bank could be clearly seen, aiming to arrive not far from Old Airão.

When we left Rio Jufari and came into Rio Negro I did some collecting, or, at least, Pedro did, climbing trees which seemed impossibly high to get me epiphytes. I was also able to draw a tree with fan-like adventitious roots which indicated the tremendous annual rise in the water level. I found *Oncidium ceboletta* growing on a tree which had been ripped out of the forest and was floating in the river; although the plant was completely saturated, it was still managing to flower. After the exertion I drank copious draughts of tea, my one extravagance in the wilds.

Then there was a problem with a chain on the motor which broke for the third time, and we had not been under way for long, when we stopped again, this time to buy *pirarucu* at the hut of a trader who kept a small bar a little to the west of the mouth of Rio Branco. As I sat drawing my newly found Oncidium, *pium* attacked me – there seemed to be hordes of them in that area. It was a disturbing thought that a *pium* transmits the disease of Leichmannosis and it appeared that the owner of the bar had been infected, as he had a large red sore on his leg. The disease was prevalent in areas where trees had been felled, as the insect normally lives in the canopies, coming down to suck the blood of small animals. In the absence of this source of blood, humans are a substitute and easily encountered

Since my last journey to this area destruction had been widespread, and the capuchin monkey which I saw in the forests then, have doubtless left the region or died out. The only plant which I wished to collect, an interesting Aroid, was the home of wasps and in my attempt to get it wasps poured out of the nest and we fled.

As we passed the mouth of Rio Branco a storm was brewing. Not what I wanted in view of the crew's anxiety about crossing to the south bank. Brilliant white clouds half masked by black ones piled up, and suddenly a storm without wind broke over the glassy river. Then as suddenly as it broke on us the storm went on its way.

Evening added mystery to the forests; flights of macaws, parrots in pairs, crossed the water on their way to roost, and a white heron skimmed the river to do some late fishing before the sun sank. The red moon rose behind an arabesque of trees, more like a setting sun than a pale, cold planet. Towards dawn another tempest swept over with a terrific wind and torrential rain, and though the crew rushed to pull down the storm blinds I was drenched in my hammock.

A group of three old houses marked Old Airão, colonial buildings, long since abandoned. A line of washing showed that one of the houses was in use again (as a meteorological station, it seemed). One of the crew, mistrusting my directions, landed to make enquiries as to our whereabouts, and was told that we were one kilometre from the mouth of Rio Jaú.

We moored the *Pium* outside the first habitation on the Rio Jaú, as the owner was a relative of Pedro. In the morning I had breakfast with the owner's wife, Dona Francisca Vianna, who was angry because a safari from São Paulo had recently been up Rio Jaú hunting birds and animals of the forest. Some of the *caboclos* had collaborated with the hunters, catching birds in nets (especially the friendly *socco*), and releasing them for the visitors to shoot. Often, she said, they caught animals and birds in cages, taking them back to sell in Rio or São Paulo. These safaris were a menace to the riverine dwellers, who depended on controlled fishing and hunting for their food, which consequently was becoming scarce. The river dwellers, especially those living beside the rapids, were happy to act as voluntary forest guards, and willingly took on the task.

I decided to explore the surrounding forest and sailed as far as the rapids which could only be navigated in a canoe. Beyond the rocks the journey was unrewarding and depressing. I went into the forest beyond a façade of live trees and was appalled at what I saw – an area of death. There was not a spot of green to be seen. The trees which were not already leeched out and crumbling looked sick, the bark peeling and rolling off the trunks. A strange chemical smell hung in the air. I waded through piles of dead leaves up to my knees and felt contaminated by them, though I avoided touching anything with my hands. The forest which we had passed in the days before were full of new shoots and fresh green leaves, but here there was not a sign of regeneration. I felt certain that some diabolical defoliant had been sprayed over the area.

To counteract this experience I found an area of 'normal' forest where I stood admiring a beautiful tree with a fluted trunk of enormous size and breathing the scented air. Rude voices broke my reverie: 'Clear off! You are trespassing on our land!' The voice came from a large boat moored across the river. A group of toughs were cutting down trees behind the shelter of their boat. My pilot revved up the *Pium*'s motor and Pedro and I embarked, sailing towards the clandestine craft. The thieves left in great haste, hiding

Oncidium

Catasetum gnomus

themselves from view. 'That gave them a shock,' laughed the men, 'They thought we were inspectors of IBDF'!

Our next stop was in the Paraná de Camanaú, at the mouth of the river where the Indian tribes of Waimari and Atroari fish during some months of the year when the level of the waters falls and fish are plentiful. They travel from Rio Alalaú which connects with Rio Camanaú. I was told that there are many Indians in the *maloca* of Alalaú, and that they are hostile, for in the past they had been attacked by the plantation owners who had killed many of them. In the forests bordering the Rio Camanaú I heard the dreaded wail of the mechanical saw, and heard a giant tree crashing down. The beautiful *paraná* is being devastated by charcoal burners.

As we wanted to be near enough to Manaus to arrive at 8 the following morning, the last evening of our trip Adalto moored in a *molongo* about three hours sailing from Manaus. Not far off, but well out of sight of our mooring, was a floating bar, which we had passed on our way, and I had noticed that it was rowdy and unpleasant. The mosquitoes, usually minimal on black water rivers, proved exceptionally vicious and attacked in force at dusk. They were so aggressive that I could not eat supper, but rapidly swallowed some soup then dived into my hammock beneath my mosquito net. Adalto and Pedro left in the canoe to buy *guaraná* at the bar. When they returned, late, they decided they would like to do some fishing from the canoe, whilst Paulo was to stay on board and take charge of the *Pium,* to which I agreed. The generator was roaring and I lay dozing in my hammock. Suddenly I had a strange feeling of being alone in the launch. Braving the hordes of hungry mosquitoes, I slipped out of my hammock and called Paulo. There was no reply. I looked everywhere for him – he was nowhere to be found. I was alone and became alarmed. Anything could happen here. The generator stopped roaring and I was in complete darkness. Over the river it was pitch black. I blew my shrill police whistle until the pith ball flew out. Then I fired a shot from my 32-calibre revolver, but to no effect. I waited some time and fired again. Still no answer. I was alone in the silence and darkness. A good four hours later, I heard the distant popping of my outboard motor. It drew nearer, then shut off. I heard low voices and the dipping of a paddle. The men disembarked from the canoe, silent as mice. Standing by my hammock, revolver in hand I challenged them to say who they were and threatened to fire if they did not comply. It was the crew – all three of them. They answered quickly, and their equilibrium was somewhat upset when I reminded them that deserting the boat could mean instant dismissal.

To Rio Cauhy and the Qualea

On arrival in Manaus I immediately started to arrange the trip Rita, companion of my first journey in 1959, and I had planned to make. This was to Rio Cauhy, in the Lower Amazon, where I intended to search for a tree which I hoped would be in flower then, *Qualea ingens (Erisma calcaratum)*. In the Mato Grosso in 1962 I had seen the forest canopies brilliant with gentian-blue flowers which I was unable to collect because the truck, in which I had managed to get a lift, had faulty batteries and the driver dared not stop. I was desperately eager to paint the flower, and was inspired by a report of the great Brazilian botanist, Adolfo Ducke, that he had first found this beautiful tree with its gentian-blue flowers on the verges of Rio Cauhy in 1955. I hoped that as November was the flowering season there I might at last find it myself.

Rita and I embarked in the port of Manaus on the *Colonel Sergio,* one of the Barcos da Linha, sailing between Manaus and Urucará. We had chosen the *Colonel Sergio* principally because it did not have a noisy radio as the other boats had, was clean and above all had a pleasant *commandante*. Our plan was to visit friends in the little town of Urucará, and later to sail to Parintins and then up Rio Cauhy.

The exquisite sun bittern

In Urucará the guest room was separate from the house and was reached by a flight of wooden steps and thus was ideal for my work. It stood amongst dark, old mango trees, which were in fruit and attracted hundreds of noisy parrots. At night the garden was perfumed by the star-like flowers of a cactus, as big as a small tree. When morning came the flowers closed, never to open again, having been pollinated during the night by bats or night moths.

One night there was a terrific storm, but I slept deeply, recovering from the effects of a prophylactic against malaria, and so heard nothing of it, but the next morning, as we sailed up Rio Taracuá, all was fresh and green after the rain. As we glided silently up the little river the most wonderful birds appeared – *japim, japo, socco,* egrets and the exquisite sun bittern. An electric eel watched us with curiosity from a hollow between tree roots in the river bed. We were told that they have a unique way of killing cattle which stray into the river, by coiling around one of the animal's legs and biting the other, giving a shock which can reach five hundred volts, so that the beast falls into the river and is drowned.

In the *igapós*, where Cuia de Macaco (Monkey Cup), and a true parasite of the Lorantaceae family were blooming, hummingbirds were numerous; amongst them I saw one, metallic blue from beak to tail. I was also pursued by wasps when I landed, but fortunately had my head veil with me and thus escaped their stings.

The trees on the banks of Rio Taboari were laden with orchids, including a brilliant yellow Mormodes and *Catasetum gnomus*. From there we encountered a road being made to connect Castanhal, a tiny settlement, to Marajá, an even smaller settlement. The road

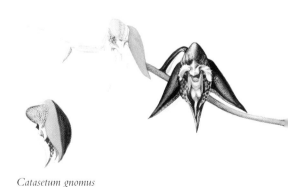

Catasetum gnomus

had been cut through the most spectacular forest that I have ever seen – enormous trees, many of which must have existed when intrepid scientists, among them Martius, Spruce and Bates, were exploring the Amazon jungle. Apparently the road was being built by the settlement's mayor, for he had property in Marajá, and it was rumoured that it would facilitate the lumbering of seven of the giant Red Cedar trees, of which there had been nine, each worth a fortune as the species is nearing extinction in Amazonas.

Nearer to Urucará there was a small lake on the edge of luxuriant forest, too near to devastation to be safe from axe and fire. It was teeming with life, and on the Buriti palms which stood deep in water grew vines and epiphytes. *Nymphea rudgeana* opened its white flowers to the sun, and myriads of dragonflies skimmed the surface of the lake.

From Urucará Rita and I embarked on a crowded passenger launch bound for Parintins. An official at IBDF had advised this, and that at Parintins we should hire a small boat for the journey to Rio Cauhy. After studying the map, the most direct way to Rio Cauhy appeared to be from Parintins across Lago de Faro, from which there was access to the mouth of the river.

Aboard the crowded boat there was scarcely a space left to hang our hammocks, and even when they were hung, a passenger arranged her own, cheek by jowl, so that we found it impossible to get to them, and I had to ask the captain to intervene. Sleep was impossible, and the toilet door was barricaded by a group of men gambling with cards. Below Rita's hammock an old countrywoman was enveloped in a cloud of smoke proceeding from a 'cigarro da palha', literally a straw cigarette! Suddenly I awakened from a doze to see flames rising towards Rita, as the old woman lighted up again with wrapping paper. I roused Rita and shouted to the smoker to put out the flames, which she did, only to repeat the performance throughout the night, keeping us in a continual state of panic.

It was four o'clock in the morning when we disembarked in Parintins, exhausted and bewildered, but amazed to see one or two taxis. We bundled into one and asked the driver to take us to the nearest hotel, which he was at pains to assure us was the only one in the town. It was an appalling place and we were shown to a miserable room and, enquiring about a bathroom, were told that the kitchen sink could be used for washing and that there were two showers just round the corner, which turned out to be cupboards, black with lack of light and dirt in which hordes of cockroaches were scurrying. We decided not to wash that night. Tomorrow we would scour the town for another hotel. So we hung our hammocks on the hooks provided, and endeavoured to sleep until dawn.

Some short distance out of the town we found the pleasant little Hotel Joia where we breakfasted and then purchased supplies for the journey to Rio Cauhy. We called at the town hall where we met the agreeable mayor who kindly sent a colleague to accompany us to help in hiring a good boat for the journey.

We sailed at 9.30 the next morning, in the *Izabel Maria,* a small cabin-boat owned and crewed by brothers, João and José, who were pleasant and good-hearted, though rather stubborn at times. It was difficult to persuade them to put the canoe in tow, though when I insisted, explaining it was essential for plant collecting, they saw reason, and the dugout rode the wave behind the boat for the whole journey. The cabin was spacious enough to hang our hammocks; José hung his beside the motor, ready for any eventuality. The boat was spotlessly clean and newly painted.

At first we sailed on the Amazon towards Lago de Faro. The night before we reached Rio Cauhy had been very disturbed, with boats coming and going to the town of Nhamundá at the mouth of the lake. Even so, the forests were not far distant, for we heard the howler monkeys roaring from the treetops.

The landscape we passed through was wonderful – sandy beaches on the margins of the river, and beyond, forested plateaux and wooded plains. Habitation had disappeared, and

Nymphaea caerulea

Galeandra devoniana

Aechmea huebneri

the country seemed unpopulated. Once we were on the great lake, Lago de Faro, at one of the white beaches we made our first stop to collect from twisted, contorted trees which the winds had bent into strange forms. The sweet-scented *Galeandra devoniana* clung to the fibrous trunks of Jará palms, and *Aechmea tocantina,* armed with formidable thorns, clustered on the hardwood trees. As we passed alongside the forest, every few kilometres we saw large Ipé trees full of yellow blossoms, and in one spot the towering trees of *Symphonia globulifera,* a Guttiferae with red flowers covering the spreading canopies. The birds were numerous and varied.

The lake system was extremely complex and vast here. Behind the gleaming beaches lay wide gullies, tree-filled and dark. These depressions would become small lakes when the waters rose. Beyond them were lakes and *paranás,* the land behind rising to high, forested hills. There was little destruction on this most beautiful river, though unhappily some signs of it were beginning to appear. But as we sailed along it gradually became evident that prospectors were at work in the area with their usual lack of respect for nature, eroding river banks through the felling of trees and the consequent silting up of the river bed. João and José told us that a great number of labourers had come to work in mineral companies who have works along the rivers, and that in many places devastation had followed in their wake.

Moving slowly up the river we searched in vain for the mouth of Rio Cauhy, inquiring of one or two solitary fishermen who could give no information as to its whereabouts. The narrow mouth of Rio Nhamundá, bordered by an attractive *igapé* appeared, a complex mass of islands where the stunted trees were almost obscured by masses of epiphytes in their branches. Red was the dominant colour, bromeliads with scarlet leaves and inflorescences (*Aechmea huebneri*) grew together with black-green clusters of orchids (Schomburgkia) and large leafed Anthuriums. As Rio Cauhy was proving so elusive, we decided to explore this promising and fascinating river, and on the return to search again for Rio Cauhy.

The forest landscape gradually became darker, with many Jauari palms and trees whose ribbed trunks towered like Gothic columns; below them the fern-like leaves of spreading Macrolobium dipped over the river.

When spume started to appear on the water we knew that we were nearing rapids, so we sailed cautiously as the river was particularly shallow at this point. Luckily, we were able to follow in the wake of a boat, the *Fernando,* probably heading for a mineral company's camp, which we were told was situated just before the rapids – so they had some uses!

When we reached the beginning of the falls of Rio Nhamundá we could go no further. As it was we struck rock, fortunately without any damage to the *Izabel Maria.* Perhaps it was just as well that we were forced to return, for on our way back we saw some of the mining company's encampments. The men there seemed pretty villainous types, so when José suggested that we should stop at an attractive beach for the night, about fifteen minutes away from the last camp, I firmly vetoed the suggestion.

At one camp we noticed at least ten men squatting under a blue plastic tent, half hidden by the trees. They glowered at us in a very hostile manner. Long white tubes connected to a pump in the river disappeared into the undergrowth of the forest. On a platform constructed on the bank sat an Indian lad, the same one I had noticed on our way up river, obviously a watchman on the look-out. So we moored far from the gang and slept soundly, though, taking no chances, I had my gun ready in my hammock.

The silence of night was only broken by nocturnal birds, owls and *pootoo,* and a chorus of frogs singing from deepest bass to highest treble. At about 2 a.m. the howler monkeys set up a deafening roar on the other side of the river – one of the most thrilling sounds to be heard in the forests of the Amazon. Ju-tapu! cried a bird in harsh tones and the toucans, *curicas* and parrots joined in the dawn chorus.

We moored by a sandy promontory and as soon as I landed I nearly stepped upon a

Erisma calcaratum, Barcelos, the 'Blue Qualea'

small nightjar sitting on the sand among a few dry leaves. She was hardly visible against this background, her mottled feathers and beak whiskers in perfect harmony with her surroundings. I called to Rita to come and look at her and, startled, the bird flew up, uncovering two mottled eggs the same colour as her feathers. She sat on a branch a few metres distant from us, but soon overcame her fear and returned to her nest. After seeing this lovely creature it was a shock when we discovered that this beach was a veritable cemetery of wildlife; alligator skulls, turtle shells, bones of capybara and other large animals, black wings of *jacu*, curassows and other galliformes. All around there were hunting look-outs, rough constructions of branches about six feet from the ground and others built in the low canopies of the trees.

As we sailed down the river after a night of heavy rain, having slept in wet hammocks, and now wearing saturated clothes, we were hailed from the bank by a gang of men armed with rifles. When they insisted on us crossing the river we became very wary. Employed by the mineral company, they were going upriver to look for unauthorised workmen. Had we seen any? Rather maliciously we replied that we had seen some much

Aechmea polyantha (fruit)

further back in a broken down launch being paddled by two men. On hearing this the men demanded that we should pick them up and take them back to the camp by the rapids. Instead, we left hastily lest they should take the law into their own hands.

Hunters had occupied the beach where we had hoped to bathe and dry our clothes and hammocks; and other sandy spots which we considered suitable proved to be covered with bones of hunted animals. At last we found a wonderful grassland plain where four rough hewn crosses stood in the sand. There were no bones nor wings there, so perhaps the hunters had some respect for the dead, or maybe feared that spirits still lingered there.

We moored beside the trunk of a fallen tree on which orchids were growing, including a Catasetum, the first that I had seen in this area. Under the arch formed by the tree trunk, standing in the canoe, I tried to detach the plant with my bush knife which disturbed wasps in a nest nearby. I felt a piercing pain in the cheek, elbow and behind and, stunned, fell into the canoe moaning 'Caba!'. The sting was agonising, and from then on I understood why the *caboclos* are so terrified by *cabas* (wasps). But not so João and José, for when my pain had subsided slightly and I was getting ready to collect the Catasetum they intervened, got into the canoe despite my protests and, approaching close to the angry creatures, very carefully and cautiously detached the orchid without getting one sting.

Not all collecting was so hazardous and one day in particular proved excellent, for early in the morning I collected a wonderful bromeliad which I had seen from afar on the way up the river, a crown of coral plumes on a palm tree *(Aechmea huebneri)*. The climax came, however, when another bromeliad, *Aechmea polyantha,* appeared in the fork of a large tree. In 1971 I had found it on Rio Urupadi when it was described as a new species. It had not been found since. In my enthusiasm I drew until the light faded, when we made for a promontory of a remote white beach to pass the night. It was not remote enough, however, to escape hunters who had left a dead alligator on the sand, which had been slashed in half, probably too young and too small for profit. In that region the riverine dwellers seemed to assist clandestine gangs of hunters, for outside more than one hut alligator skins were hanging to dry in the sun, and on the ground beneath a bloody mess of flesh and entrails, which I was told would be used as bait to attract the big cats. Earlier in the day we had heard that we had been mistaken for IBDF inspectors, and that as a result a crowd of these hunters had thrown illicit skins into the forest in fear of being caught red-handed. From the slaughter of forest animals to the murder of mankind is not a long step, when João and José told us a grim story concerning the death. of their father, late owner of the *Izabel Maria.* They recounted with emotion how the old man had been carrying valuable cargo up Rio Jatapu, a tributary of the Amazon to the west of Rio Nhamundá, and had moored there for the night. Five bandits invaded the boat, killed the father and his cook with hatchets, leaving their bodies in the river, and made off with the spoils. They eventually moored the *Izabel Maria* in a deserted *igarapé* a short distance from Belém and repainted her. By coincidence a friend of the dead man happened to pass the boat and noticed the name *Izabel Maria* appearing through the thin paint. The police were informed, and four of the bandits were caught, spent a short time in jail and were released.

Perhaps as a result of this horrible story I passed a rather uneasy night, awakening from fitful sleep to hear a shot ringing through the forest at no great distance and, on looking out from the depths of my hammock, saw a fire burning on the shore. Hunters of course!

The last few days of this journey were spent in quest of the blue Qualea. After many inquiries about the location of Rio Cauhy, as a forlorn last hope I asked the owner of the only shop in Nhamundá where I had bought additional stores. The proprietor, a former mayor of the town, introduced us to a friend, Pedro, who offered to accompany us to the headwaters of Rio Cauhy, while at the same time asserting that no river of that name existed any longer. We arranged to meet him and he eventually appeared after we had

Opposite. *Aechmea huebneri*

at the Selby Gardens
Sarasota, Rio Hammock   December 1977

waited more than two hours for him. We sailed to Faro, where Pedro led us into 'Big Bar' and introduced us to a wide selection of Faro society. There we met an elderly man who, it turned out, had met Adolfo Ducke, without having any idea who the great man was. He described the botanist as exceptionally tall, about two metres, with his wife who reached little above her husband's waist. When he learned of Ducke's fame, our new friend was most upset that people had not treated him with more deference. The botanist had lived in the neighbourhood for a year or so, going into the forests for days on end – a very kind and modest man, we were told.

Cattleya violacea

I treated everyone in 'Big Bar' to beer, then hired a car to take us on the next stage of our mysterious journey in search of the blue Qualea (*Erisma calcarata*). Rita, myself, João and José, Pedro and the driver, squeezed into the car and we set off. The car broke down frequently but eventually landed us at an abandoned airstrip. From there we proceeded on foot along a rough track leading to a devastated area, once the course of Rio Cauhy. Adolfo Ducke would have been turning in his grave! Except for a sprinkling of Bacaba palms, everything growing had been destroyed. Burning was still going on at the site of this now extinct river. A small swamp marked its former bed – little wonder that no one remembered its existence. And, of course, no Qualea tree.

Pedro, who had had too many beers at the 'Big Bar', was hopelessly drunk, and laughed so much when he learned that I was looking for a particular tree that he fell into a helpless heap. As neither João and José would help him up, I had to whilst he burbled that trees meant nothing to him, he could well do without them.

We drove back to the 'Big Bar', where I told my sad story and the conclusion of our search. Our elderly friend's eyes filled with tears when I told him that Adolfo Ducke's discovery had been ruthlessly destroyed. 'Que vergonha pare nos!' (shame on us) he kept repeating.

I was told that a part of the river still existed which could only be reached by boat and foot. So the next day we took our boat and, having found the mooring, walked through swampy forest, feet black with mud, without seeing any sign of *Qualea ingens*, and not a trickle of the now extinct Rio Cauhy.

The next day we left, heading for Parintins and thence Manaus. The great Amazon was flowing swiftly. It was a grey day and few river craft had come into view since we set sail from Nhamundá that morning. Every so often a handful of huts appeared poised on the very edge of the river bank, steep and sheer at this point. They seemed so frail that a strong wind would blow them all into the choppy waters. Then suddenly, as if from nowhere, a shabby launch, larger than the *Izabel Maria*, appeared in our wake. Clearly its crew – of five – were trying to catch up with us, reaching within a couple of metres of our stern in a deliberate and vicious effort to ram us. We could see their sinister expressions so close were they.

João and José, doubtless remembering the fate of their father on the *Izabel Maria*, revved up the motor to top speed and shot ahead, as luckily our boat was lighter than that of our pursuers. If they had not done so, we would have stood little chance if the five characters had been able to board our small boat. Fate was on our side, however, for the pursuing boat seemed suddenly to develop a list so bad that it limped slowly towards the shore. As it faltered in our wake, Rita and I waved exultantly, laughing aloud at what might have been a narrow escape.

After this we passed an Amazon river slum, depressing in the extreme, both landscape and population. The banks of the river, once rich with the enormous trees of an exuberant tropical forest, were now so eroded that they showed the white clay base, nude of soil.

Here and there were remnants of forest – though only trees which yielded fruit for the inhabitants, and even these seemed to be dying – Castanhas do Pará and *sapucaia*. Many of the huts were abandoned, and the people who still lived there made a bare subsistence and looked worn and unkempt.

When we sailed away from this sad scene, we passed through the Furos, where pairs of yellow and orange canaries were nesting in holes in the river banks. The most magnificent hawks sat proud and motionless on the bare branches of dead trees and did not stir when our noisy boat passed by.

But the small of burning wood polluted the wonderful clean air of the Amazon, for the *caboclos* had taken to destroying the river margins, which, of course, aggravated erosion and destroyed the soil, in which, presumably, jute is to be grown.

We arrived in Parintins at night and moored in a secluded port. José went home but João stayed on board, and the night passed peacefully. At Parintins we said farewell to the brothers who had looked after us so well, and embarked on the passenger launch to Urucará, where we were met by our friends who made us tea and where we enjoyed our first hot baths since we had left them six weeks earlier.

I had thought there was a law that forbade the cutting of trees within 100 metres of the river banks. If so, and if it had been observed, how much of the Amazon forest would be spared! And how much erosion of the river banks prevented!

But no. As we left Urucará and headed for Itacoatiara, devastation continued uninterrupted. What *is* to be done? The banks fell away as we looked at them, the only growth on them grass and occasionally miserable beans. The grass, growing in unstable clods of earth, eventually fall into the river, float away and form grassy islands, which become a menace to navigation. Melons had been planted along some of the banks but had done nothing to secure them. But, in spite of all this, mimosa was striving to survive. With pale purple flowers and dark leaves it was growing happily beneath the water's surface and creeping up over the banks. Perhaps one of the ways to reclaim the banks?

We arrived in Manaus at dawn. Rita, my wonderful companion on this journey, left for the airport, while I returned to the IBDF offices to give an account of my journey, one that had had its successes from a collecting point of view, but had been dispiriting in not finding the Qualea, and especially so in encountering so much devastation.

Teju açu, a large lizard

Margaret Mee

Loranthaceae
Rio Negro, Amazonas
May. 1982

1982

RIO NEGRO
GILBERTO'S HOUSE AND THE
ARQUIPÉLAGO DAS ANAVILHANAS

Four and a half years after my search for the blue Qualea I was in a Brazilian airforce plane, leaving behind the spectacular mountains and seascape of Rio de Janeiro *en route* for Manaus. After a brief stop in Brasilia, we landed at the unsophisticated airport of Carolína, when the passengers made a concerted rush for the little bar. Undisturbed, I was able to observe my surroundings. A number of Indians, mainly children, were trying to sell small artefacts to the tourists. One small girl had the traditional blue circles of the Caraja tribe on her pale cheeks and she and the other children were all beautiful, though thin and undernourished. Small boys were playing with a tame parrot and inviting visitors to hold him – laughing slyly when the bird nipped the proffered fingers.

Carolína was left behind and a swamp landscape lay beneath us, a dream world of sombre olive green, sparsely dotted with trees in some areas, in others dense copses, all surrounded by water and marshland. Storm clouds, which had been hanging above threateningly, dispersed leaving white domes of iridescent radiance.

For five ecstatic hours I looked down on dense forests which clothed this part of Pará. Here and there a shadowy line traced the course of a hidden river, where doubtless the enormous silver ribbon of water flowed through a mysterious tunnel of overhanging greenery.

I was so elated to realise that so much forest still existed untouched, that even the dreary sight of factories belching smog on the outskirts of Manaus could not completely quell my spirits. A later journey – and the sight of miles of decimated forest and man-made desert – would disenchant me.

A friend, Gilberto, had lent me a small house on the banks of the lovely Rio Negro, opposite the newly proclaimed Biological Reserve of Anavilhanas. His boat and boatman, Paulo, were also at my disposal. In Manaus, Paulo met me and my travelling companion, Sue Loram who worked for INPA.

Paulo seemed rather a surly fellow, so without more ado we made our way to the market to buy provisions for the journey. It was pouring with rain and we splashed through muddy pools in which the port abounded. We had planned to leave Manaus in the cool of the early morning, but eventually left under the burning noontide sun. When we finally set off up river, we found Paulo had brought along his wife Maria and grandchild, as well as another family with three children so, with Sue and me in addition, the little boat, the *Secorro,* was crowded. Unfortunately there was a dearth of shade aboard and the first comers had claimed it, until they moved to the bows eventually to cook their meal. But the damage was done and I was burned to a frazzle, face and feet, and how I suffered for my large straw hat was of no avail against the tropical sun and reflection from the river.

My suffering was not only physical, for the first few hours sailing on Rio Negro were more than painful to one who had known and loved this river and its glorious forests for many years. The transformation was a visual shock, for all the trees of any size had disappeared, sacrificed by the neighbouring plantation owners to that ghoulish *Jurupari*

Opposite. *Psittacanthus cinctus*

Psittacanthus sp.

Macrolobium

Riverside palms

(devil), the charcoal burning factory, which turns the glories of the Amazon forests into fuel. But those who had destroyed the native woodlands were discovering that problems grew as fast as the poisonous weeds which thrive on the devastated soil and kill the cattle.

Five hours brought us to the outskirts of the Arquipélago das Anavilhanas, a maze of forested islands, harbouring magnificent trees and plants. Massive Philodendrons crowned the ancient trees, their air roots forming curtains; arabesques of bromeliads hung against the sky on branches beside the scarlet foliage of Phyllocacti.

As daylight began to fade, bands of parrots crossed the skies to their roosting places in the lofty trees and *secorro* skimmed silently over the water's surface, taking toll of myriads of insects. We lounged on the roof of the boat; watching the sun sink behind the forests, gilding the complete horizon. Long after it disappeared from view, glowing embers hung in the night clouds. Sunsets over Rio Negro surpass all others for beauty.

When we arrived at our destination, it was completely dark, and we landed barefoot, stumbling up a grassy slope which led to the house, whilst Paulo unlocked the cottage door. Then he left us and went his way, having kindly offered to stay with us as a guard that night, under the impression that we were doubtless nervous foreign tourists.

Exhausted by the day's happenings, we sank wearily into our hammocks, and I, despite my painful sunburn, slept soundly.

At break of day, with a light mist hanging over the river, masking the forests of Anavilhanas, we hurried out to explore the surroundings of the cottage. The garden was an orchard of Assai and Buriti palms, cashew and cupuaçú trees. An *igarapé* bounded the land upstream; on its banks, supported by sapopama roots, spread a lofty tree, the remote upper branches hung with a colony of *japús'* nests. Here the birds had built their purse-shaped nests – in this case below a large white wasps' nest – and at least eight of them swung in the breeze.

I soon discovered that the Buriti palms sheltered hordes of parrots who roosted in them at dusk, descending on the palms with deafening cries which reached a crescendo as they shuffled for the best places, after which silence reigned. At dawn they would leave again, flying in groups across the river to the Archipelago. Perhaps the most beautiful of all the birds was the exquisite sun bittern which fished on the river banks at dawn and dusk, and was only equalled in charm by the hummingbirds, regular visitors to the native flowers.

The next day we waited eagerly for Paulo who was to take us to the Biological Reserve of Anavilhanas. As we approached it we saw three white buildings on rafts which marked the entrance. When we landed, guards questioned us, and only when they were satisfied that Sue worked for INPA, and that I was a botanical artist, were we allowed in and were even invited to stay for a few days.

Paulo and his wife Maria left for Novo Airão, a comparatively new village, where they could buy fuel for the *Secorro*. It was some hours distant but they planned to return that night.

Sue and I took a canoe and paddled into the swamp forests up overshadowed waterways in a silent world, and there I found endless subjects for my sketchbook. As I worked rapidly the sky darkened and ominous rumblings of thunder could be heard as a storm approached. We left this enchanted area as quickly as we could, Sue paddling her hardest, for we knew that the little canoe could never survive a tropical storm and had visions of being swamped whilst struggling to take shelter in the *igapó*. Fortunately Raimundo, one of the reserve guards, had thought of our possible predicament and at the first signs of the

Buriti palm

Rio Negro with *Philodendron solimoesense*

Psittacanthus cinctus

storm took to his canoe and came speeding towards us, and we landed on the floating rafts just as the first enormous drops of rain fell and a tremendous *banzeiro* developed.

Needless to say Paulo and his wife did not reappear that night to take us back. When they returned in the morning they related with gusto, how, in the dark hours, the boat had become entangled in a tremendous grass island at the height of the storm, and how with great difficulty they had eventually managed to get free.

While we waited for them, Raimundo took Sue and me by canoe to explore the Archipelago, and I was able to do some hurried sketches. An area on the outskirts of the reserve was 'owned' by a *caboclo* living in a small hut bordering the stream. He gave me permission to collect there and offered to guide the canoe through the tangled trees of the Furo de Castanha, a complex canal dividing into many channels.

From a hole in one of the trunks in a group of old trees, many hollow and riddled with termites, emerged the head of a toucan, curious to see who was invading its territory. Not liking the appearance of the crowd it flew away rapidly, displaying its brilliant plumage. Raimundo was convinced that the toucan had a nest in the hollow tree which the *caboclos* would return to raid, and later sell the young birds. Unhappily he could do nothing to prevent this, he said, as the Furo was outside the limits of the reserve.

These remarks led to a gruesome story about a hunter of turtles, who lived beside the *igarapé*, and carried on his clandestine trapping on a commercial scale. The man's first son was born deformed, and now at three years old the child's feet were crossed in the way that those of a captured turtle were tied, whilst his hands hung down like a turtle's flippers. Perhaps this unfortunate infant's fate has saved some of the persecuted reptiles from hunters, for the hunter's superstitious neighbours believed that the father had been punished for his cruelty by the birth of a deformed child.

There were, however, other ways in which turtles were being destroyed, along with fishes and countless aquatic species. For every day but one whilst in the cottage on Rio Negro, I heard dynamite explosions nearby. After the blast there was dead silence – not a bird's note, but just an awed hush as though nature's heart had stopped beating. Then later a lifeless young alligator might float past on its back in the still water of the *igapó*, just one of the explosion's victims.

One day I rose early, awakened by the cries of parrots and toucans. I painted all morning – a superb Norantea, one of the true parasitic plants which flourish on the bushes and trees of the *igapó*. The flowers, which are brilliant yellow and orange, attract hosts of hummingbirds, and are still in bloom when their blue and cerise fruit is ripening. After a piranha lunch (Paulo had caught them that morning), Sue and I paddled into the *igapó* beside Gilberto's house, where I attempted to collect a bromeliad, *Streptocalyx longifolius*, but at the lightest touch of my collecting knife, hordes of furious ants swarmed out. As the flower was very fresh I decided to wait until the next day. While I was thus deliberating I was being observed from the tree above by a handsome black and white striped woodpecker with a large red crest and a pair of completely black toucans.

I neglected writing my diary as every night I collapsed into my hammock, completely exhausted by an appalling cough allergy.

In spite of my cough, we went out for a day in the *Secorro* with Paulo – and wife and grandchild – to Lago Surubim. This lake proved to be all that Paulo had claimed, and I was to realise that his enthusiasm was due to it being well stocked with fish, especially a fish for which the lake is named. For one and a half hours we sailed without passing a single habitation – just forest and *igapó* until we reached the lovely lake. It was isolated from the river by barriers of grass, which formed little islands, the hunting grounds of wild ducks, and before we landed long black necks reared from the green, and a flight of huge black ducks took to their wings.

Opposite. *Streptocalyx longifolius*

Opposite. *Clusia* sp.

Paulo moored the *Secorro* and released the two canoes which had been in tow. He got into one of the canoes with Sue and me, but quickly abandoned it when the water came over the top. So Sue and I paddled off on our own and Paulo and family went off together to do some fishing in the other canoe. Dipping along beside the shore and up shady waterways I was able to observe the magnificent plants by which the lake was surrounded, and to see some of the spectacular birds – golden woodpeckers creeping up the trees, black ducks flying in formation, toucans and parrots. But the thunder had been muttering as we arrived at the lake, and the rain which had masked the distant forests approached rapidly, driven by a wind that raised waves on the wide surface of the shallow lake. Just as Sue and I clambered into the boat escaping a heavy downpour Maria arrived, paddling calmly – drenched but unconcerned – with Paulo and the child, the latter completely nude and enjoying the heavy rain.

In 1977 I had found *Strophocactus wittii* in the Archipelago before it had been proclaimed a Biological Reserve. I had made a painting of the plant with fruit and was determined that on a future journey to find the flowers which had eluded me. I was convinced the logical place to find the Strophocactus would be in the *igapós* bordering the reserve. As I sat painting recently collected plants, Sue, who had been paddling the canoe in the nearby *igarapé*, came in greatly excited having found leaves of this very plant. I abandoned my work at once and together we paddled to the spot where the Strophocactus was growing. Not only was a long strand of scarlet leaves growing flat against the tree trunk, but two large flower buds were just within reach. The stalk of the flower was very long, about twelve inches, the sepals reddish-green, the petals white, not red as I had been led to believe. Above the plant in the fork of the tree grew a large, red-veined Philodendron, a very distinctive landmark.

Every day after this discovery we visited the *igarapé*, watching the Strophocactus flowers and waiting for them to open.

On the outer fringe of nearby forest there was a strange area where dried out shells of trees, riddled with ants and weathered by the beating winds and rains, mingled with young trees bearing luxuriant foliage, many in flower. Epiphytes clustered in their branches – Philodendrons with large dark leaves, spiny bromeliads – *Aechmea setigera* and the very aggressive *Aechmea tocantina*, armed with black thorns and giant clumps of *Schomburgkia*

A well-camouflaged lizard

Margaret Mee
November 1984

Clusia sp.
Alto Rio Negro, Am.

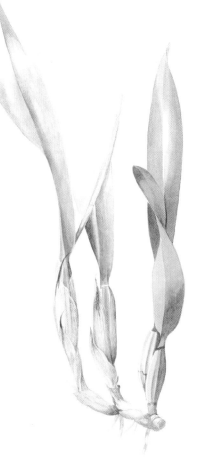

Schomburgkia crispa

The sky blackened with an approaching storm

orchids with long spikes of flowers. As so often when I found a good collecting area, the sky blackened with an approaching storm; the tranquil scene took on a dramatic aspect, and we paddled hurriedly for shelter.

Later, when the weather had cleared, and hopeful that the heavy rain had encouraged the Strophocactus flowers to open, we again made for the *igarapé*, but they were unchanged. As we were leaving, two dark shapes loomed in the densest part of the *igarapé* – monkeys with thick, bushy tails and dark brown fur, but on sensing intruders they left their feast of beans they had been collecting and disappeared rapidly into the depths of the forest.

On our return to the house, we found a miserable dog in the garden, just skin and bone and so weak she was scarcely able to walk, poor creature. She was munching the green fruits which had fallen from the palm trees, so hungry was she. We gave her what little food we had over which she devoured ravenously. She smelt appalling and heaven knows what parasites she had! She refused to leave us.

The next morning we made an early start in the canoe, paddling straight for the tree on which the cactus grew. The flower was opening. With much hesitation and in fear and trembling I decided to take it lest it should never open more, or close during the heat of the day, for being a white flower I imagined that it would be pollinated at night by moths or bats.

In spite of Sue's intense care the flower fell into the canoe and was slightly damaged, for it was no easy task for her to detach it from the tree with my bush knife while she balanced on the prow of the canoe while I secured the boat by hanging on to a bush in the water.

Holding the precious bloom in my hand I examined it carefully. The twelve-inch stem was very robust and fleshy and the white silken petals of the large flower seem to have a hidden light in the centre giving it a yellow glow. The arrangement of the stamens was intricate.

That evening, as I watched a glorious sunset, the sun bittern came fishing, uttering soft, plaintive cries and snapping up tiddlers at a great speed. She was the daintiest and most delicate of creatures. As the light faded the parrots came home to roost in the Buriti palms beside the house with their usual noisy flurry, bickering and arguing until darkness silenced them. It was a perfect end to a successful day.

During the days which followed the heat was intense and for respite we sought the cool shade of the *igarapé* where the cactus grew, and from there moved on to the lake. We were not alone in seeking the shade of the great trees which bordered the water, for as soon as we arrived a band of about fifty monkeys were leaping from tree to tree, a line of sturdy chestnut-coloured animals with long prehensile tails. As they sped by they uttered shrill whistles.

Whilst observing the monkeys antics we were being watched closely by a nun bird, magnificent with her orange beak and dark green plumes flecked with white. Another onlooker, a large grey hawk tucked into the cranny of an enormous tree, stared unblinkingly at the strange intruders disturbing the tranquillity of the lake with the splashing of paddles and foreign voices. Tree creepers flitted silently from tree to tree, their tails spread against the branches in their search for insects. Myriads of tiny bats emerged from tree roots and disappeared as suddenly as they came.

Later, when the weather had cleared…

The iguana climbed with
incredible agility

Recovering from the torrid heat of the morning and trip up the river to the *igapó*, I was relaxing in my hammock under the pleasant shade of the trees writing my diary, when the clanging of a bell disturbed the peace and a vendor in a well-stocked boat, accompanied by Paulo, pulled to shore. Sue and I hurried joyfully down to the cheerful looking *caboclo* to buy such luxuries as bread, onions, and tinned butter, for our supplies had been down to rock bottom for some days.

In the evening the weather broke when a *chuva branca* (white curtain of rain) came sweeping across the river cloaking the landscape with a fine mist. During the night I thought that the roof would cave in with the weight of the torrent and raging wind. The bathroom and terrace were flooded, and the next day everything in the house was saturated.

Paulo did not appear after he came with the merry trader, and we decided that the two of them had probably gone on a spree up Rio Jauaperi, which was the trader's next destination.

Following the torrential rain, Rio Negro rose at an alarming rate. The situation was compounded by the melting snows coming down from the Andes into the Amazon basin. The river crept up the banks so quickly that many of the bushes and small trees were under water. We had to move the canoe from its mooring or one morning we would have found it out of reach in the middle of the river. It was impossible to go collecting, but there was plenty of sketching and painting to get on with, and much of interest to be seen from the window facing the river – black plumed ibex with yellow sickle bills, rare redfan parrots with red and blue ruffles, dark green bodies and wearing spectacular white caps appeared in the Assai palm tree, and of course, the sun bittern came to fish as usual. It rained more or less without stopping for two days, and then there were just the occasional showers.

We decided to make the most of the last day in the lovely *igapó* of the Strophocactus, and as soon as we arrived on the still water we heard sounds high in the trees and a band of jet black monkeys sprang from branch to branch. They were certainly not the howler monkeys which I had heard that morning at dawn, roaring in chorus – an unforgettable sound without which none of my journeys in Amazonas are complete.

No sooner had the black monkeys departed, leaping through the treetops, than there was a loud splash from a green iguana which was swimming across the lake. At first it seemed to be a snake by the extraordinary length of the tail and serpentine movements. The canoe was moored to a small leafless tree in the middle of the water, which the iguana climbed with incredible agility, so I was able to observe it at close quarters. Rapidly I sketched this beautiful reptile and made notes in my sketchbook before it decided to continue on its course, swimming to shore and disappearing into the shades of the *igapó*. It was an intense green, the immensely long tail merging from green to rust brown, the body markings and tail rings dark grey graduating to white, the ears with a fine mother-of-pearl membrane. From the crown of the head and all the way down the spine were saw-like projections of a darker green. An elegant ruffle hung from its lower jaw. The five digit feet and delicate hands were long and bony.

The storms of the last two days brought up the water level so that the ants which had prevented me from collecting the bromeliad *Streptocalyx longifolius* had left their refuge. Although the flower was all but submerged it was easy to secure a specimen in relatively good condition.

Selenicereus wittii

Rio Negro

All too soon we had to return to Manaus. We told Paulo a few days before, but since every day was the same to him, the arrangement was that we would go to fetch him on the day of departure. We paddled to his hut to tell him we were ready to leave, and he was soon round to pick us up, with Maria and the grandchild accompanying him. and we left immediately. It was 9 o'clock, and a glorious sunny day with a ripple of wind. The Reserva das Anavilhanas drifted along beside us for hours, green and tranquil. We proceeded calmly until early afternoon when we ran into a stiff wind and choppy water, in the widest part of Rio Negro where, until late afternoon, it is always turbulent. Since we were making little headway with great difficulty, Paulo took refuge in the mouth of a small river, where we moored by a sandy beach. It was a lovely spot and I explored its fascinating vegetation with interest. Meanwhile, Paulo and Maria had cooked themselves a large fish meal and were sleeping deeply. But I felt that we should press on, so awakened the sleepers and we set off for the last stretch. The turbulence had died down by this time leaving the water only slightly choppy.

Suddenly there was panic aboard when the steering went haywire: the steering chain had snapped in two. We were heading straight into a large tree, the spreading canopy of which was half immersed. Branches cracked and crashed and we were well tangled in the twigs and foliage. Paulo managed to stop the motor just before we hit the powerful trunk, and with superhuman force pushed the *Secorro* clear and moored her to the tree. I had visions of spending the night in the treetop, for the light was fading rapidly and the steering might prove impossible to repair. However, Paulo and Maria worked on it together, sometimes under water. Eventually we got under way and after a while night surrounded us. So we sailed along a shining path lit by a great full moon towards the distant lights of Manaus.

Back in the world of turmoil, pollution and politics I wondered when I would be able to return? I couldn't get out of my mind our last night in Gilberto's house and the moment when the sun sank and a pink glow spread over the sky and was reflected in the black water – and the sun bittern appeared to do some late night fishing.

We moored by a sandy beach

Zygosepalum labiosum
"*L.C.Rich.*"*Garay.*
Para

Margaret Mee

1984

ORIXIMINÁ AND RIO TROMBETAS
GOLDMINERS, ENCHANTING LAKES, DESTRUCTION

In June, two years after my return from Anavilhanas, I was invited by the Federal University of Rio de Janeiro to stay and work at their outpost in Oriximiná on Rio Trombetas.

After flying over range upon range of mountains cut by streams and narrow valleys, the nearer we came to Amazonas it was a visual shock to see kilometre after kilometre of devastated land. Never had I seen such wanton destruction of forest and such enormous expanses of man-made desert. I was only thankful when the clouds hid this grim scene. After a brief stop in the pleasant town of Santarém, it was reassuring to see that some and typical landscape still existed, as we flew above stretches of dense, steaming forests until the majestic Rio Trombetas came in sight.

River launches, Oriximina

The outpost in the little town of Oriximiná had recently been established to accommodate university medical students and doctors who worked for some months in the local hospital, and also visited surrounding villages giving medical treatment and advice to the inhabitants. It was on these expeditions that I was to accompany them to study the local flora and the effects on it of the massive deforestation programmes taking place in the area. I was provided with a pleasant bungalow standing in its own grounds where mature native trees provided shade and fruit in season. A large cashew was home for a red and blue macaw, one-eyed since a fledgling when it had been captured and sold in the street before a doctor rescued it.

The great Rio Trombetas debouches into the north side of the lower Amazon, and the port of Oriximiná at its mouth was a mooring station for many and varied boats. These were mainly used for fishing or carrying cargo and plied their trade on the many lakes, waterways and tributaries in which the region abounds. Consequently, nearly all the the trips which I made were by water.

Huts built of posts and straw

On the first of these journeys I left for the port at crack of dawn to embark on the *Sacuri*, bound for the village of Sacuri. The battered craft was cramped and so heavily loaded with passengers, doctors and students and their medical equipment that the water came well above the Plimsoll line. Behind the launch the university team's canoe was in tow.

Having passed Lago Jatoba, the nearest lake to Oriximiná, we sailed for two hours past distant forest until we reached Sacuri, a village scattered through swamp land. We moored in view of the tiny church and a group of three huts built of posts and straw, around which Bacaba palm leaves lay drying in the sun to be used for repairs to roofs and walls. Here the medical personnel went ashore to work in a large open barn, while I continued in the *Sacuri* together with a veterinary surgeon and two health inspectors who were going to visit outlying areas. In Sacuri we transferred to the canoe in order to penetrate the *igapó* more easily, so I could search for plants and the men reach some of the more remote villages. Their duties led them to many huts where the hospitality of the owners meant we were invariably

Memora schomburgkii

Zygosepalum sp.

offered coffee, oranges and even cooked fish. I found the last visit harrowing. Having moored the canoe in a well wooded part of the stream beside a steep bank, up which we scrambled on rickety steps, leading to a wattle cabin, a horrifying scene came in view – a *caboclo* cutting up the head of a bull on a rough wooden table. The animal had been tame and friendly, but had grown too fat, we were told. That had sealed his fate, and his bloody head, almost stripped of flesh, lay on its side with one dark eye looking at me from its socket with a reproachful gaze. I was sickened by the macabre scene, thinking of the poor beast's suffering, and the grim impression lingered until we got into the canoe and skimmed the still waters, returning to the river by devious channels. But a wonderful sight soon put the horror out of my mind, for in one shady copse, massed on the mossy trees gleamed the white delicate flowers of a rare orchid, *Zygosepalum labiosum,* and I eagerly collected a couple of plants.

Still gliding silently, we passed unnoticed by a handsome green, black and grey iguana, fully a metre long, gracefully draped over the thick foliage in the canopy of a tree. Nearby three of its companions, basking on branches in the dappled sunlight, were startled by the canoe, and one fell with a loud splash into the water, while the other two hastily rustled away through the leaves.

When we got back to Sacuri, to our dismay the launch had disappeared from her moorings. We looked up at the blackening skies in trepidation, for we had no cover in the canoe and were still some way from the village itself. Paddling rapidly for any shelter we could find, we were greatly relieved to see our companions faces looking from the windows of a hut on the opposite shore where they had moored the *Sacuri*. At the same time the heavens opened.

There were many such journeys to the waterways and lakes of the Trombetas region. A voyage to Lago Sapuacua meant we had to embark in the small hours of the morning. Like a sleepwalker I hung my hammock in the darkness of the lower deck, away from the noise above, for the upper deck was crowded and the ship's bell clanged incessantly as the pilot navigated the bays and passengers and cargo disembarked at isolated villages. The return next night led through overshadowed waterways under a full moon where the kapok trees (*Bombax munguba*) appeared to be one mass of white flowers, but in fact were the crowded roosting sites of white herons.

It was a change to travel overland, in a jeep driven by a competent driver, Guara, to the distant village of Poção. The journey was a bitter disappointment, as I had read the glowing accounts of nineteenth century scientists who explored the rich forests that clothed the country in the area. But I was in a state of visual shock after a few miles along the 'road' between Oriximiná and Óbidos. Road it was not, but a track so dangerous and eroded that it defied imagination, and the landscape (what was left of it) a sad stretch of brushwood, and where once existed virgin forest, we saw a blackened sea of giant skeletons. There were a few successful monocultures – created by nature – Embaubas, which were struggling to regenerate the almost exterminated jungle trees. In spite of the decimation and fencing in of the land, I found a survivor, a marvellous woody vine, *Memora schomburgkii* – first I saw a flash of brilliant orange as my driver sped along the awful track, then another, at which I stopped to get a glorious orange Bignone, a trumpet vine. I had to sketch it in an old notebook as soon as we arrived in Poção as it was already starting to wilt and lest I should not find another.

We saw a blackened sea of giant skeletons

One of the goldminers who shared my boat

Poverty and sickness in the village were very evident – children with swollen stomachs and thin limbs, dull eyes and yellow skins. The village 'nurse' told me that worms were the main affliction, but that malaria was very prevalent, too.

Another day, whilst waiting for news about a long postponed visit to Reserva Trombetas, I was invited to a picnic at Lago Caipuru. Transport turned out to be a noisy, crowded boat with a load of excited children and rowdy parents, who ate too much and certainly drank too much and then danced it off on the white sands and in the river. As for the picnic, on the grill above the embers were not only the usual fishes but three large turtles. The wretched creatures were being cooked alive and I was so disgusted at this cruelty that, when offered to partake of this gruesome roast, I refused it. So developed a heated argument with the *caboclo* in charge of the barbecue. But I realised my opinions and feelings on this barbarity made no impression and indeed as far back as 1962 in the Mato Grosso I knew turtle eating was a mania along the Amazon, though I had never seen live turtles cooked before.

A three-day journey up Rio Cuminá-Mirim had been arranged for me. Students helped me carry my luggage and basket of provisions for the journey to the *Santana*, a launch berthed at the far end of the port, the last mooring and quite a lonely spot. Embarkation was arranged for 10p.m., rather a strange hour to start a journey I thought. When we arrived, an unsavoury and insolent youth sitting on a wall told me that the *Santana* was in fact a passenger boat and that he and six others were to embark that night and had already hung their hammocks on deck. I was most annoyed, not only by the fellow's manner, but also because I had hired the boat exclusively for my work and had no intention of carrying other passengers. When the young man told me that they were goldminers all bound for a gold mine near spectacular falls on Rio Cuminá, I really saw red, and even thought of cancelling my trip. But at this threat the captain, who had just arrived from a bar in the port, became conciliatory, and promised that I would be the only passenger, and the six hammocks were removed. However, when I stepped aboard, the captain's manner changed and be became far from pleasant and outraged that I had not brought meat amongst the food which I had handed over to him. At this outburst, my student friends, who luckily had stayed in the background while all these altercations were taking place, intervened, advising me to abandon the journey. I had only a few days of my visit to Oriximiná left, and was eager to accomplish more research before returning to Rio, so decided to brave it out. Besides, the attraction of Rio Cuminá-Mirim was strong for I believed that I should find new plants in that area. So I bade farewell to my somewhat anxious companions and hung my hammock, but could not sleep believing that the youth, who had been allowed to come back on board, this time as 'crew', was in fact one of a group of ruffians, as were many of the goldminers.

We sailed at a good speed through the night, although I was somewhat uneasy. However, the tranquillity of the dawn calmed me, and I watched the landscape sliding by from the depths of my hammock. A waxing moon still hung in the sky above golden streaks of cloud, heralding a magnificent day. Then the red sun rose behind the arabesque of forest trees and the black fringes of the Jauarí palms. My frugal breakfast consisted of a cup of tea as all my supplies were with the captain.

Later in the morning the captain, who also acted as pilot, and whose name I never discovered, announced we were nearing the Cachóeira de Verão (Summer Waterfall). These impressive falls, which spanned the complete width of the river, were hidden from view by a forested island, which divided the river into two arms. The lofty shore on the north bank was composed of many strata of rocks in varied colours and crowned by palms and hardwood trees. A narrow *igapó* masked many of the hanging ferns and plants growing between the cracks of the stratified stone. On the margin of the river giant trees stood like sentinels before a castle wall. Could this be an extension of the Guyana Shelf, I wondered? I was eager to see more of the raging falls at closer quarters and, as we had disembarked, I made my way through bushes and over rough ground towards them. The pilot and his mate walked ahead and, hearing voices, I was suddenly aware that we were near the goldminers' camp. Under a blue tarpaulin suspended on poles sat a motley collection, surrounded by saucepans, hammocks and a mass of jumbled equipment. In the water nearby a dredge dangled long white tubes.

The captain introduced me to the 'Boss'. To this sinister looking crowd who were destroying this beautiful spot, I must have appeared as cold and unfriendly as I was feeling. The 'Boss' stared at me with a hard, antagonistic gaze, whilst the goldminers glowered at me sensing my enmity, doubtless suspicious that I was spying for another gold-prospecting company. A short, elderly white-haired man, with a red skin, bristly chin and brushcut, a belt holding up his paunch, he spoke to me as though I were a small child. Indicating the pump with a wave of his hand he explained that the machine was used for looking at the river bed, 'and of course, gold', I added. I assured him I was not interested in walking on my own for two hours through wasteland and forest to the Serra de Canauba, as he suggested.

Under a blue tarpaulin suspended on poles sat a motley collection

The Boss of the goldmining camp

Rodriguezia lanceolata

I remembered reading Richard Spruce's description of his journey to the Serra de Canāu – one of the toughest and most frustrating of all his expeditions in the Trombetas region. The Serra Canauba may have been the same mountain range as that described by Spruce. I felt sure that an attempt to walk there alone would have meant a walk into oblivion, or that on my return the boat would no longer be there. So I spoke sharply to the captain, telling him that I wished to go and collect in the *igapó* instead of wasting my time which was short enough. After a lengthy whispered conversation between the group the captain and I left, but not the 'crew member', who, as I had already guessed, stayed behind with his fellow gold goldminers.

Plant hunting along the river banks was well nigh impossible in a large clumsy boat like the *Santana*, and to enter the *igapó* out of the question. I had requested that a canoe in tow was essential to my work, but this had not been provided, and I was very upset to pass by fascinating plants without a hope of getting near enough to identify them. I decided that at the first opportunity I would borrow a canoe and collect alone. My chance came when the captain moored the *Santana* near a hut belonging to a friend, where he remained for the rest of the day and all night.

A friendly *cabocla* who lived in the hut arranged to take me in her canoe into the nearest *igapó* to collect. She was a pleasant, communicative woman, and from her I learned that we were in Rio Cuminá, not in Rio Cuminá-Mirim, which it was only possible to enter by navigating the falls. We paddled among trees and bushes recently devastated by fire though their wounds had begun to heal, finding several plants which had escaped the conflagration.

There were orchids in plenty, the prize of them being *Ionopsis utricularioides,* with a mass of fragile violet flowers. The bromeliads were more of a problem, and I was hacking away at the roots of one with my bush knife, surrounded by branches and twigs, when the canoe, unsecured, slipped forward and landed me in its bilge, legs in the air. With a struggle I managed to extricate myself without injury.

When we got back to the *Santana*, the pilot seemed to be enjoying a holiday with his friends for he completely neglected me. Consequently, since he still had control of my provisions, I lived on a packet of biscuits and a few tangerines, receiving only a plate of thin soup and hot water for tea which I had to ask for. Famished, I lay in my hammock and heard the captain and his friend eating noisily, late and long into the night, but no offer of a plate for me.

At daybreak the next morning the captain decided to return (a day early) and by 10a.m. we were within sight of Oriximiná. I paid the rapacious man for three days, in spite of being one day short, and he lost no time in getting rid of me. At the outpost, everyone was surprised at my early return, and annoyed that I had been treated so badly. And I learned that the Cachóeira de Verão, where the goldminers had their camp, was the limit for a boat of any size, and that in the *Santana* it would have been out of the question to reach Rio Cuminá-Mirim.

From Oriximiná I returned to Santarém and thence home for two months to attend to some business, but during that time I was able to devote much time to painting the plants I had found on Rio Trombetas. In early September I found myself once again in Oriximiná. The University Outpost had been repainted while I was away and looked spick and span, but the absence of friends I had made on my previous visit gave the place a slight feeling of sadness, for a quick turnover of staff and students was one of the policies and among those who remained there were many new faces.

However, one good piece of news was that the goldminers' camp near the Cachóeira de Verão had closed having yielded no gold. Unfortunately, I also learnt that another very destructive mine on Rio Nhamundá was still functioning, many wild animals in that area

Ionopsis utricularioides

Ionopsis utricularioides

Sophronites pumila

had been killed for their skins, and that the falls on Rio Trombetas were swarming with prospectors who were fast destroying the surroundings.

When Sunday came doctors, students and I sailed to Lago Caipuru to enjoy the sun and to swim in the clear, dark water of the lake. Whilst strolling along the beach I noticed many epiphytes growing in the trees which fringed the forest and determined to return, so the next day a young dentist, João, and I hired a boat from one Dido, and set out for the lake.

Streptocalyx poeppigii, a bromeliad with a flame-like inflorescence and protected by a multitude of thorns, was difficult to detach from its host, the Monkey Cup tree (*Cuia de Macaco*). Further afield in old forest the smoky-purple flowers of Erisma trees sheltered orchids, and in the branches grew a dainty Galeandra, whilst *Schomburgkia crispa* encircled the huge trunk with a wreath of golden-brown flowers.

João acted as main collector until he cut his foot on the sharp wood of a dry tree at which Dido took over. Dido tired quickly, and after a snack I suggested that we should return. As we left the stillness of the *igapó* a black sky was lowering over the landscape. But we were too late to escape the storm and the rain poured into the open canoe until everyone and everything were soaked and dripping. Then the wind whipped up the waters of the shallow lake into foaming waves which made sailing in a small canoe hazardous. We made little headway against the lashing wind and the boat was filling up with water for we had nothing to bale with. Eventually, exhausted, we landed in the darkness like three drowned rats, and João and I hurried through the torrential rain to the welcome shelter of the outpost.

The main objective of my visit to Oriximiná this time was to be a journey to the Trombetas Reserve and the great lake of Eripucu, where I hoped to stay and work for some days. I had applied for a permit well in advance, but the delays and bureaucracy and the failure to get transport proved an ongoing frustration. When at last the permit arrived, the reserve boat was out of action due to lack of funds and I had to devise other means of transport which further delayed the journey.

In the meantime I was invited to accompany two visiting botanists, Klaus and Lais, to the Paraná Yamundá, which flows into the Lago de Faro. This journey had particular appeal for me since I had visited the lake and Rio Nhamundá in 1977. We planned to collect specimens from trees in flower. João the dentist was also to accompany the expedition, and the hired boat was a trifle small for the four of us, and, as we discovered only after we were underway, somewhat inadequate, for there was no lighting whatsoever and the gas stove of two burners did not always function. Nevertheless, every moment of the journey was a pleasure.

The Paraná Yamundá is not to be recommended for spectacular Amazon scenery, with cattle mainly responsible for the somewhat shabby landscape. Small, uninviting huts of farmers sprinkle the river banks. Trees are almost confined to a dozen or so species – Couroupita (the Cannonball Tree), *sapucaia*, Ficus, and Jauarí palms being preponderant.

In spite of the rather sterile surroundings I collected from an enormous *sapucaia* tree flower sprays which grew direct from the trunk. It was a spectacular sight for the tree was full of white flowers and at the same time bore fruit like cannon balls. I also found a lovely white *Phryganocydia corymbosa* which I sketched in on board, working far into the night. It is one of the trumpet vines. Apart from these two specimens, there was little to be found in this area, which formerly must have been rich in many species of Amazon plants and trees. We wandered through pathless fields and there sighted Clusia flowers on a large bush, but the bush was owned by a snake and we decided not to dispute his territorial rights.

On reaching the end of the *paraná* the scenery began to improve – more trees and in greater variety lined the banks, and the botanists became animated and stopped the boat many times to gather specimens. Eventually we reached Faro, one of the oldest towns on Rio Trombetas, a quiet, peaceful settlement, sleepy apart from the very vocal and lively children who mobbed the 'Padre' as they insisted on calling Klaus, the older of the two botanists.

We wandered past the church and through the village, searching for a restaurant, as our supplies were giving out, but there was a dearth of them as Faro is not on the tourist map, although it is one of the most charming towns I have visited in Amazonas and Pará. Near the church we found an unpretentious café where the owner managed to arrange a satisfying meal. The villagers were unassuming and friendly, as we discovered when we swam in the little port – the only way that we could take a bath.

When we returned to the boat the light had faded and with some difficulty I managed

Heliconia

Margaret Mee
September, 1984

Phryganocydia corymbosa (Vent.) Bur.
Rio Yamunda, Pará

Probably a silk cotton tree (*Ceiba pentandra*)

Urospatha sagittifolia

Opposite. *Symphonia globulifera*

to hang my hammock in the shadowy boat. We set sail for the lake early in the morning as the days were sunny and warm, and soon reached a beautiful shore where we avidly collected and then pressed tree flowers. The work was not without its perils, as the specimens had to be dried in a stove placed by the motor for lack of space, where it caught fire which was only quenched by the prompt action of João.

Landing from time to time on the rocky shore I was entranced by the vegetation: a swamp plant, Rapatea, which I had found and painted on Rio Uapés in the 1960s, had a close relative growing in profusion and the lovely Aroid, *Urospatha sagittifolia*, flourished in the marshy land. The most spectacular of the trees was a tall Guttiferae, *Symphonia globulifera,* with a trunk clear of branches up to the crown. Seeking light, the flowers grew in clusters above the spreading branches, brilliant scarlet-cerise in colour. I remembered having seen one or two groups of these impressive trees as I sailed up Rio Nhamunda in 1977 and realising, with a feeling of frustration, that they were far out of reach. Here a tree had been felled and lay on the ground and I gathered some of these rare flowers.

I could have spent many days on this enchanted lake with its wealth of plants, new delights appearing as the journey progressed. The forested slopes gave way to low *caatinga* trees, growing in dazzlingly white sand, and small inland lakes of clear dark water in the depths of which ornamental fungii flourished, firmly attached to twigs on the sandy bed. They were to be avoided when swimming, as they produced a skin irritation.

My botanist companions took the canoe and paddled far up one of the small lakes, often crouching down to avoid the mass of low branches, whilst I remained on deck sketching sculptural forms of dried trees growing in the then hot sand. Hearing loud shouts, I looked up from my sketch book to see a strange sight. The canoe was approaching with Lais paddling rapidly, and beside it swam Klaus, a white linen hat and dark glasses on his head, and fully clothed. The canoe had capsized far away from the shore and both had fallen into the lake, but Lais, apprehensive of the underwater fungi and snakes, had scrambled in again whilst Klaus heroically swam alongside.

Too soon our expedition came to an end. It had been short but stimulating, relieving the tension and frustration of my postponed visit to the Forest Reserve of Trombetas.

On my return to Oriximiná I got the news that a passenger boat, the *Elo*, would be leaving for Mineração, the nearest stop for the Reserve, at 9p.m. that night. From there

Catasetum appendiculatum
Rio Negro, Amazonas

Margaret Mee
May, 1985

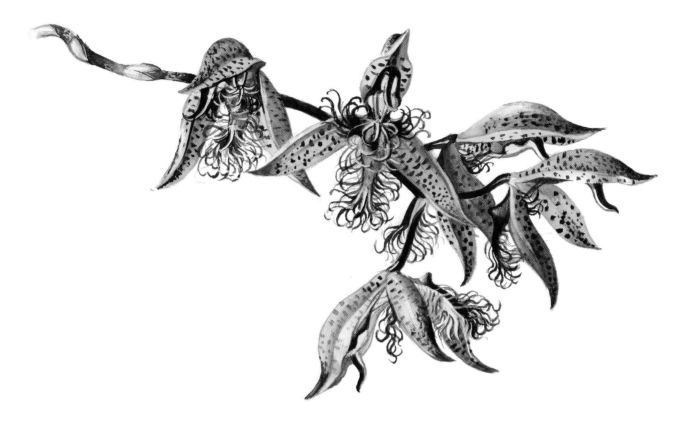

the launch *Perola de Nhamundá* would land me on the reserve raft on Lago Eripucu. I was to stay in the small cabin on the raft. It was already 6p.m. when I got the news, so I packed hastily, realising that there would be no time to purchase supplies before leaving. João the dentist was to accompany me but got caught up with fifty pregnant women seeking advice about their teeth. When I arrived at the port, it seemed that the outpost was being deserted, for there I found Klaus heading for another boat bound for Mineração on which three vets were passengers, on their way to vaccinate dogs at a bauxite mine.

Arrangements had been made to hang my hammock before I arrived on the boat which was full to overflowing when I arrived. After sailing for five hours the *Elo* moored at Mineração and I disembarked, bemused with sleep. As dawn broke in Mineração I had time to observe the bauxite company's destruction of the Amazon forests. It came as a shock, having been told in Oriximiná of the care that had been taken not to damage the ecology and to replant trees for those that had been felled.

A red-brown sea of bauxite residue swamped the most glorious virgin forest. Great trees, species extinct in many areas, were being grubbed out, for this sea, as dead as the Red Sea, extended for ten kilometres down a valley of considerable width. Where this residue had drained into the earth it destroyed the humus with a coating of a noxious substance, suffocating all life. Dead and bleached trees stood by the thousand, deathly warnings of what is to come, when the seeping tide envelops other areas. Not only the trees, but with them birds, animals and plants had perished. It was a valley of death. I was to see more of this destruction a few days later, for passing a padlocked and chained gate I saw what no journalist had been allowed to see and report, the transformation of the large Lago Batata into solid red mud. The natural barrier between this lake and Rio Trombetas threatened to break through with the weight of the mud. Formerly, Lago Batata was teeming with life, fish, turtles and aquatic birds, but the deadly residue had killed all life in and around the lake and was seeping further afield, evidenced by yellowing leaves and rotting branches.

Catasetum barbatum hindl.

Dead and bleached trees stood by the thousand

Opposite. *Mormodes buccinator*

The transformation of Lake Batatá into solid red mud

Japim's nest

An *igarapé* with a riverine population living on its banks, once used for fishing and canoe transport, was virtually dry and what water was there was polluted – another victim of the bauxite mine. Unless measures were taken in time the next victim could be the beautiful Rio Trombetas.

The *Perola da Nhamundá* arrived at 8a.m. – almost at the time I was told to expect it. Within sight of the reserve it developed engine trouble and my journey to the reserve ended in a canoe paddled by a forest guard, who landed me at the raft.

The cabin on the raft consisted of a main room used for living and cooking. Partitioned off from it were a small shower room and a dormitory where I was able to hang my hammock. The raft was moored close to the protecting forest, but at night the glow from the bauxite mines could be clearly seen.

Under the wise guidance of Alberto Guerreiro, three guards lived there – young vigorous men who were authorised to challenge and search any craft arriving inside the reserve. They were kind and friendly and treated me with great consideration, taking me over the lake in the canoe with its noisy outboard motor – hence its name *Perereca* (frog) – where I would sit and sketch by the hour. Unfortunately, when my permit to stay and work in the reserve finally arrived, it contained the usual clause that no plants were to be removed, which precluded scientific painting, and I had to content myself with drawings made from some distance, suitable only for showing the habitat. It was an exacting task, seated in the canoe under a burning sun, but so satisfying that I longed to do more than my limited time allowed.

The forests of the Trombetas Reserve had been little disturbed since the days of Richard Spruce and other exploring scientists of the nineteenth century. Nature still flourished in and around the great lake of Eripucu where turtles and various aquatic creatures thrived unmolested.

Although it was already September, the level of the lake had scarcely fallen and trees stood deep in the water, strangely weathered shapes, many heavily laden with bromeliads in flower. Seated in the canoe I had the unique opportunity to sketch a colony of *japims'* hanging nests in a small acacia tree, in their midst a white, bell-shaped wasps' nest, frequently found in the proximity of these purse-shaped dwellings. The birds were very vocal and scolded so loudly and in such varied tones (they are great imitators), that the toucans joined in their cries, at the same time defending their territory against invaders. The cacophony grew so loud that we left the spot.

With the fading light, black ducks flew low above the lake's surface moving into arrow head formation as they rose. I was told that the spotted jaguar and the red jaguar had increased and continued to increase in numbers in the reserve, that howler monkeys and other primates were more numerous since steps had been taken to expel hunters from these forests and that life in the reserve was returning to its former state.

POSTSCRIPT

Selenicereus wittii

Margaret Mee's last Amazon expedition had a specific aim – to find *Selenicereus wittii* and draw its flower. The plant takes its generic name from the Greek word for moon, *selene*, and is also known as the Moonflower, for it flowers only at night, and then only for a few brief hours. It is named for the collector N.H. Witt who lived in Manaus in the early years of the twentieth century and sent specimens to Europe for identification. The flattened stems of this curious epiphytic cactus, which twine themselves round trees, look more like leaves, while the flower is a long tubular form which bursts into white blossom at its tip. The flower's unusual shape and night-flowering habit suggest that pollination takes place by long-tongued hawkmoths.

Margaret had first seen *Selenicereus wittii* as early as 1964, and on three subsequent occasions, but she had never seen it in flower, and she was determined to capture it in full bloom in its natural habitat. Through her extensive network of friends and contacts she gathered information about the most likely location in which to find *Selenicereus wittii* during its brief flowering period of a couple of weeks at the very most, probably some time during the month of May

In May 1988, together with her friend Gilberto, his boat and boatman Paulo (both had been put at her disposal by Gilberto during her journey on Rio Negro in 1982), and accompanied by a handful of English friends, Margaret left Manaus and headed for the Arquipélago das Anavilhanas, the nature reserve on Rio Negro which she had visited and passed many times on previous expeditions.

Margaret Mee
June 1988

Selenecereus wittii
Rio Negro, Amazonas

For a few days in that area, in permanently flooded swamp forest, the party spent time searching out possible sites where it was thought, and hoped, that Moonflower plants would most likely be found. Eventually, a thriving plant bearing several buds was located. Then came the exciting evening when it was thought the plant might flower. Margaret returned to the spot for an all-night vigil during which she had the thrill of witnessing the buds slowly open to large white many-petalled blossoms which released a delicate fragrance. By dawn the flowers had withered. Throughout the night, sketching by torchlight from the deck of the riverboat, Margaret's long-held wish was realised, and she was able to capture each stage in the life of the Moonflower, from opening bud, to full bloom, to withered end.

While on the trail of the Moonflower, as if to highlight her determination and eventual success in finding the Moonflower in flower, on 22 May Margaret celebrated her birthday on the Amazon.

She completed several magnificent paintings of each stage of the Moonflower's development – at the time her series of paintings of the ephemeral flower of *Selenicereus wittii* were the only known images of the plant in its natural habitat. The paintings were her last major project.

In the autumn of 1988 recognition of her pioneering spirit and work in botanical art came in the form of accolades from two distinguished institutions. Margaret came to England to lecture to the Royal Geographic Society and attend the opening of an exhibition of her paintings, *Margaret Mee's Amazon*, at the Royal Botanic Gardens, Kew.

It is ironic that this enthusiastic lover of the Amazon, who had braved so many hazardous and alarming situations, was killed in a car crash in England. She was seventy-nine, keen to return to the Amazon, and still producing fine work. There is every reason to suppose that more passion and more painting would have been forthcoming. As it is, her legacy is incalculable.

Selenicereus wittii
Rio Negro Amazonas

Margaret Mee
May, 1988

EPILOGUE

Much of my professional life was spent interviewing people for television, in Canada, the U.S., and Britain, and I have encountered people of all qualities, some famous, some not. Many of them – some deservedly – have vanished from my memory, but one who remains absolutely vivid is Margaret Mee.

I met her in New York, in November 1988, for an interview about her book, *In Search of Flowers of the Amazon Forests*. The interview was broadcast on PBS (the Public Broadcasting Service) on America's Thanksgiving Day and afterward we were deluged with calls and letters. Six days later, we heard that Mrs. Mee had died in a car accident in Britain, so we re-ran the interview, to an even greater response.

I treasure the book, which she autographed, and many times over the years since I have studied her exquisitely detailed renderings of the exotic Amazonian plants. On the day of our meeting, however, what struck me was her extraordinary personality. Margaret Mee had personality, as some Americans say, to da max! At seventy-nine, she was brimming with seeming youth and vitality, sparkling with energy astonishing in a woman about to enter her ninth decade.

She was seductive. In fact, to the amusement of my wife and colleagues, I was obviously smitten by this woman, as though she had been decades younger. They ribbed me about falling in love with her, claiming that it showed in the rather goofy smile that played over my face in that interview. After sixteen years I have just viewed it again and I'll concede some of what they claimed. And if that happened to me, at fifty-seven, in one meeting of an hour, think how many hundreds of people Margaret Mee must have captivated over the years! Her personality must have opened many doors as she insisted, from girlhood onwards, on always doing the unconventional, the unexpected, the idiosyncratic, with that obsessive certainty of purpose that is often the mark of genius. But few geniuses can have had their way eased with a personality so winning. Whatever the difficulties of the journeys she took – the risks, the insects, the crushing heat and humidity (all pooh-poohed in our interview) – her personality must have made her great fun to be with.

It was like a light that shone around her, a childlike quality of wonderment, undimmed by the cares that wear most people down if they have lived so long. In her, youth's a stuff that did endure. That was part of her seductiveness: one felt in her presence that she had tapped into a mysterious supply of vitality.

There was a theatrical side as well and it's not surprising that she briefly flirted with the idea of acting as a career. She made up her eyes with heavy black eye-liner and she could use those very dark eyes dramatically, flicking them upwards in an eloquent appeal to the heavens, as teenage girls do, as distressed heroines did in genre paintings. She wore her hair, luxuriant and richly-textured grey-white, in a theatrical twist tied with a black ribbon. And she could pitch her voice in the most artful way when telling a story about her adventures, as one tells stories to children, telling it as though for the first time, fresh and vibrant with the experience just then recalled in all its terror and excitement.

Behind this, of course, was the serious core of her personality, the essential core, the woman who had demonstrably solved the essential mystery that confronts us all: what are we put here to do? Many of us spend our lives not quite finding out, so we envy, we are fascinated, by people who know, and she certainly knew.

Part of her attraction to me was her absolute commitment to what she had chosen to do (perhaps *been* chosen is more accurate), the conviction she conveyed of having lived absolutely the life she was supposed to live. To have one's mission so clear, and such an inspiring mission; to have the gifts of talent and of character to fulfill it; to be able to convey it all so guilelessly and so modestly made her enchanting. And it was clear that all this prodigious stuff, had overflowed the limits of one life.

At the end of our interview I asked Margaret Mee what she had yet to do, what left her still unsatisfied. She replied that she had done 'quite a collection of Amazon plants, but there are still so many, so many to be recorded, and this has to be done before they're destroyed, if it's humanly possible. Well, I shall need another six lives, which won't be granted, to really do enough to satisfy me.'

It was said cheerfully, yet wistfully, and in the tone in which she said, 'which won't be granted' I felt there lingered a child's half-belief in magic, in another world, in which, conceivably, another six lives might be granted, as in children's stories, where anything can be granted. Alas!

Robert MacNeil

Robert MacNeil was a journalist for forty years with, successively, the Canadian Broadcasting Corporation, Reuters News Agency, NBC News and the BBC, culminating in twenty years as Executive Editor of the MacNeil-Lehrer NewsHour on PBS.

BOTANICAL HISTORY

We are grateful to Ruth Stiff and Simon Mayo of the Royal Botanic Gardens, Kew
for providing botanical descriptions of some of the flowers Margaret painted

Aechmea fosteriana
(family Bromeliaceae)

Aechmea huebneri
(family Bromeliaceae)

Aechmea meeana
(family Bromeliaceae)

The genus *Aechmea,* comprising almost 200 species, was named in 1794 by the Spanish naturalists and explorers Hipolito Ruiz and Sebastian José Pavon. Aechmeas are well known for their vividly coloured foliage and long lasting, prominent flower crowns. Attracted by the nectar of the flowers, hummingbirds are known to pollinate many species of *Aechmea.* Although they are native to central Mexico south to Argentina, the main area of distribution for these plants is Brazil, where they grow epiphytically on trees in tropical cloud and rainforests and rarely on the ground. They have also been found in dry regions.

The Brazilian species *Aechmea fosteriana* was collected by and named for the American bromeliad collector and explorer Mulford B. Foster, who co-founded the Bromeliad Society in 1950. Its beautifully variegated leaves and striking inflorescence, with dark red bracts, combine to make this bromeliad one of the most outstanding *Aechmea* plants. The plant in this painting came from the well-known gardens of Dr. Roberto Burle Marx, Brazil's most celebrated landscape architect.

Aechmea huebneri was discovered by and named after the German botanist and collector, G. Hübner, who first encountered it in 1927 along the banks of the Rio Taruma-Mirim, a tributary of the lower Rio Negro in Amazonas. A large plant reaching approximately 1.3 metres high, *A. huebneri* grows terrestrially on open ground and epiphytically in the igapó (permanent swamp forest) to 135 metres altitude. It has an interesting geographical distribution in that it jumps from Amazonia to the eastern coast of Brazil. With its formidable thorns, it is a difficult plant to collect.

Lyman B. Smith (1904-), long considered the world's leading authority on Bromeliaceae, named *Aechmea meeana* in honour of its discoverer, Margaret Mee. During Margaret's early years in Brazil, when she was employed at the Instituto de Botanica of São Paulo, she collaborated with Smith on the preparation of a large series of paintings depicting bromeliads of the whole of Brazil. The knowledge she gained from this experience enabled her to discover several previously unknown Amazonian species.

Aechmea meeana grows to approximately 70cm high, with many strap-shaped leaves rising to form a conical vase. Each leathery leaf narrows to a point ending in a woody black spine and is notched along its margins with large, deep purple spines. The leaves are densely covered with water-absorbing scales, a characteristic common to all bromeliads. This rare bromeliad was collected from the Rio Maraú, near Maués, Amazonas, and remains scientifically known only from Margaret Mee's collections.

Aechmea polyantha
(family Bromeliaceae)

Aechmea rodriguesiana
(family Bromeliaceae)

Aechmea tillandsioides
(family Bromeliaceae)

This species was first discovered by Margaret Mee in 1972, growing as an epiphyte in igapó forest (permanent swamp forest) on the Rio Maraú, near Maués, Amazonas. A splendid bromeliad, reaching nearly one metre in height, *Aechmea polyantha* forms a remarkable ellipsoid tank with its many leathery leaves, edged with spines. Its coral inflorescence is borne on an erect stalk, 25cm long. This rare species is known scientifically only from Margaret Mee's collections.

Aechmea rodriguesiana was named in honour of William A. Rodrigues, the notable Brazilian botanist who first discovered it in the area of the Ducke Reserve near Manaus. Margaret collected this plant along the Rio Maraú and depicted it within its rainforest habitat, inserting a twig from a young *Clusia* epiphyte as well as the curious leaves of the aroid, *Philodendron goeldii,* in the background.

Aechmea rodriguesiana grows epiphytically in the region of the lower Amazon and Rio Negro. Its leathery leaves, reaching up to 1.4 metres in length, are edged with thin dark thorns and tipped with red at the apex. The inflorescence rises dramatically above the leaves to a height of 60cm on a thick floral scape, covered with scales.

Aechmea tillandsioides, reaching a height of 50cm when in flower, forms an upright funnel-shaped rosette with leathery greyish green leaves edged with spines, each leaf being pointed at its tip. Its small yellow flower petals are followed by long-lasting, ornamental berries which are first white in colour, then blue. This species was discovered on the Rio Japurá in Colombia in 1820 by the distinguished German botanist, Karl von Martius (1794-1868). His monumental, fifteen volume work on Brazilian flora, *Flora Brasiliensis,* was completed thirty-eight years after his death by a team of international botanists.

Aechmea tocantina
(family Bromeliaceae)

Billbergia decora
(family Bromeliaceae)

Catasetum appendiculatum
(family Orchidaceae)

Widespread in South America, *Aechmea tocantina* can be found at altitudes ranging between 100 and 700 metres in Venezuela, Guyana, Bolivia and Amazonian Brazil, where it grows epiphytically to a height of 1-2 metres. It was first discovered by the British botanist Hugh Weddell on the Rio Tocantins, the easternmost major river of southern Amazonia.

Billbergia, a genus of approximately sixty species, is named after the Swedish botanist Gustav Johannes Billberg (1772-1844). These plants are tall and tubular and thus easily distinguishable from the characteristic rosette shape of the Aechmeas. Its five to eight leaves, fewer in number than most bromeliads, are usually mottled, banded, or variegated with contrasting colour. Although its colourful, pendent inflorescence is short-lived, lasting only three to five days, it can bloom up to three times a year.

Billbergia decora was first collected in 1831 by the German botanist and explorer Eduard F. Poeppig. Its name is derived from the Latin *decoratus* (ornate), referring to the decorative nature of this plant so beautifully illustrated in Margaret Mee's painting. It grows as an epiphyte in the forests of Amazonian Peru, Bolivia, and Brazil. This species had not been recorded from the Rio Negro region until Margaret collected it in the Arquipelago das Anavilhanas, a network of river islands on the Rio Negro close to Manaus.

The genus *Catasetum* confused taxonomists for many years mainly because of the dimorphic flowers of many of its species. Plants that produced female flowers and a number of others that produced hermaphrodite flowers (both male and female organs in the same flower) were placed in different genera from those that produced only male flowers. After much study, Charles Darwin, in the *Journal of the Linnaean Society* (1862), concluded that they all belonged to the same genus and in certain instances to the same species.

This rare Brazilian orchid belongs in the *Catasetum cristatum* complex, being characterised by the lip, which is ciliate or covered with fleshy hairs. It is easily distinguished from the better known *C. cristatum* and *C. barbatum* as its flowers are rose red, rather than the green of the former. The species was first described by Rudolf Schlechter in 1925.

Margaret is exquisitely precise in her treatment of the flowers. In addition, she has most successfully depicted the weight of the pendulous inflorescence upon the fragile stem.

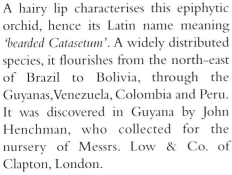

Catasetum barbatum
(family Orchidaceae)

Catasetum discolor
(family Orchidaceae)

Catasetum fimbriatum
(family Orchidaceae)

A hairy lip characterises this epiphytic orchid, hence its Latin name meaning *'bearded Catasetum'*. A widely distributed species, it flourishes from the north-east of Brazil to Bolivia, through the Guyanas, Venezuela, Colombia and Peru. It was discovered in Guyana by John Henchman, who collected for the nursery of Messrs. Low & Co. of Clapton, London.

In the 1836 issue of the *Botanical Register,* John Lindley initially described the male flowers of this species as *Myanthus barbatu,* but upon the realisation that this species produces both male and female flowers he transferred it to the *Catasetum* genus in 1844.

This beautiful species of the *Catasetum* family, described by the orchidologist John Lindley in the *Botanical Register* in 1854, is a medium-sized plant that can be either terrestrial or epiphytic in its habit of growth. It has strap-shaped leaves and produces up to twenty-five flowers on a gently arched inflorescence. The flowers of both sexes appear to be quite similar. However, the male flowers are known to be smaller than the female in this species.

Distributed throughout Colombia, the Guyanas, Venezuela, Peru and Brazil, *Catasetum discolor* flowers from February to July. The flowers are commonly yellowish~green, often tinged with lilac, but occur in a range of colour forms, with each variety having its own names, e.g., *C. discolor* var. *roseo-album*. Margaret collected this plant from the Rio Maraú, near Maués, Amazonas.

Discovered in the Brazilian State of São Paulo, near Villa Franca, *Catasetum fimbriatum* was first introduced into cultivation by J. de Jonghe in 1847. Based on the identification of the male flowers, the orchidologist C. Morren first described the plant as *Myanthus fimbriatus* in 1848, but it was subsequently transferred to the genus *Catasetum* in 1850 by John Lindley in Paxton's *Flower Garden*.

This epiphytic plant is distributed throughout Venezuela, Paraguay Argentina, Bolivia, and Brazil, where it flowers with an arching spike up to 45cm long, supporting seven to fifteen variable blooms. The plant in this painting, collected from the upper Rio Juruena in Mato Grosso, depicts the dull, yellow-green female flowers, rather outshone by the more handsome male flowers that are pale green and streaked with red-purple markings, with deeply fringed lips.

Catasetum galeritum
(family Orchidaceae)

Catasetum macrocarpum
(family Orchidaceae)

Catasetum macrocarpum
(family Orchidaceae)

This species was first described in 1886 by the eminent orchidologist H.G. Reichenbach, from whom is quoted, 'I have at hand an inflorescence of seven flowers, which are nearly half as large again as *Catasetum atratum* … the flowers are conspicuous in their bright colour and look rather pretty for those of *Catasetum*'.

This species was first illustrated in *Lindenia* in 1886 from a plant introduced by *Continentale d'Horticulture,* probably originating from Brazil. It is a rare species about which very little has been recorded.

Possibly the most common species of Catasetum in cultivation, *Catasetum macrocarpum* is distributed throughout Columbia, Venezuela, the Guyanas and Brazil. This specimen produced exclusively male flowers of dark green to yellowish-green, spotted with maroon, with the interior surface of the helmet-shaped lip being particularly eye-catching in its coloration.

The genus Catasetum, first described by Carl Kunth in 1820, contains over sixty known species distributed in Central and South America and the West Indies. Its name is derived from the Greek *kata* (down) and the Latin *seta* (bristle), referring to the two antenna-like projections on the column of the male flower. These antennae are sensitive to touch, releasing the pollinia (pollen masses) explosively on to the back of specific bee pollinators. Through a complex process, often involving mimicry, pollination occurs when the insect visits another flower and the pollinia is deposited on its stigmatic surface.

This plant, also a *Catasetum macrocarpum* as in the previous painting, depicts the more fleshy greenish yellow female flowers. Margaret has been particularly successful in capturing the high gloss characteristic of the lip of the female flower.

Catasetum punctatum
(family Orchidaceae)

Catasetum saccatum
(family Orchidaceae)

Catasetum sp.
(family Orchidaceae)

Catasetum punctatum, a rare epiphytic orchid, was introduced into cultivation by Messrs. Linden's *L'Horticulture Internationale* and flowered for the first time in the company's greenhouses in Brussels. Jean Linden (1817-98) had spent ten years as a collector of rare orchids and other plants for both the Belgian government and private individuals before establishing his own nursery in Ghent with his son Lucien in the mid-1800s. After moving to Brussels, this firm became one of the most successful in Europe, and Linden went on to support exploration of South America by financing a number of profitable expeditions in search of new and rare orchids.

This striking species was first illustrated in *Lindenia* in 1895. Its flowers, prominently carried on an arched inflorescence, are relatively large with a diameter up to 6cm, and are reported to be highly fragrant. Margaret's painting is of a plant collected along the Rio Mamori, near Manaus, Amazonas.

Note the yellow-green female flowers and the more numerous maroon to brown male ones. With her skilful use of highlights and shadows, Margaret allows one to understand the thick texture of the flowers and the gentle curves of the leaves. This highly variable species is distributed throughout Peru, Brazil, and the Guyanas.

Note the weathered branch on which this unnamed *Catasetum* orchid from the Rio Negro is perched. Margaret was clearly fascinated by the curious shapes and textures of the trees and branches in the igapó (flooded forest), home to many of the epiphytic plants that she collected and portrayed in her paintings. A number of her exquisite field sketches are detailed pencil studies of these weather-sculpted structures. Margaret Mee's drawings are now considered as impressive a part of her artistic legacy as her finished paintings.

Cattleya violacea
(family Orchidaceae)

Clowesia warczewitzii
(family Orchidaceae)

Clusia grandifolia
(family Clusiaceae)

The genus *Cattleya*, containing approximately sixty species of beautiful tropical American orchids, is one of the most widely grown genera in the orchid family. The plants were first introduced into England in 1818, arriving in a crate from Brazil with the leaves of Cattleya orchids serving as a protective outer wrapping for lichens and mosses. It was William Cattley, the notable British horticulturist, who recognised the plants as unusual, nurturing them until they flowered in 1824. The distinguished botanist John Lindley later established it as a new genus and dedicated it to Cattley.

Cattleya violacea was first discovered on the Rio Orinoco in Venezuela by Alexander von Humboldt and his companion Aimé Bonpland during their celebrated journey to the Americas between 1799 and 1804. The striking, rose-purple flowers of this orchid are delightfully fragrant and long lasting. This painting is a fine example of Margaret Mee's ability to combine botanical accuracy with her remarkable flair for composition. The *Cattleya*, shown in its natural habitat of igapó forest, is accompanied by the aquatic aroid, *Urospatha sagittifolia*, the epiphytic *Clusia* in the foreground, and down below the new inflorescences of *Heliconia* plants.

The genus *Clowesia*, containing only five species, was named in honour of the British horticulturist the Rev. John Clowes by John Lindley in the *Botanical Register* in 1843. Similar to *Catasetum*, it is distinguishable from that genus by its bisexual flowers and differing pollinating mechanism.

Clowesia warczewitzii, distributed from Costa Rica to coastal Ecuador and eastward to Colombia, Venezuela and Brazil, was named after the celebrated orchid collector Josef Warscewicz (1812-1866). This epiphytic orchid produces pale green, frilled flowers with darker green lines, borne on pendent inflorescences.

In the Amazon region, the common name for the genus *Clusia* is 'Rosa da Mata' (Rose of the Forest). Several species are cultivated for their striking ornamental flowers and foliage, yet they have a more sinister side. As members of the well-known group of rainforest plants commonly known as stranglers, the *Clusia* seedlings and juveniles begin life as epiphytes on a host tree. After some time their aerial roots reach the ground and thereafter join laterally. Despite the name of strangler, the roots themselves do not actually kill the enclosed host tree. Rather the *Clusia* overtops and shades outs its host as it grows.

Clusia grandifolia was first discovered by the nineteenth century Yorkshire botanist, Richard Spruce, who found it in 1852 on the Rio Uaupés, a tributary of the Rio Negro in igapó (flooded) forest. It has also been collected on occasion from neighbouring regions of Venezuela.

Clusia nemorosa
(family Clusiaceae)

Clusia sp., possibly **C. grandiflora**
(family Clusiaceae)

Cochleanthes amazonica
(family Orchidaceae)

The geographical distribution of the small tree *Clusia nemorosa* is interesting in that it is one of a large group of species to be found both in Amazonia and eastern Brazil, but not in the seasonally dry region in between. Its habitat includes the Guyanas, the narrow natural channels of the upper Rio Negro and the edge of rivers such as the Xingu, where it is more widespread and better known than *Clusia grandifolia*. In eastern Brazil, it is known to occur along the coastal forest region known as the 'Mata Atlantica'.

The Clusiaceae family includes trees, shrubs, or lianas which are known for their viscous sap, with several species yielding resins and valuable timber. The largest genus, *Clusia,* is found solely in tropical America.

Although this plant, which Margaret collected along the upper Rio Negro, has not yet been positively identified, it is thought to be *Clusia grandiflora*. The habitat of this species, with a somewhat restricted range, also includes eastern Amazonia, and has been found in Surinam, Guyana, and the Brazilian state of Pará in the region of Belém.

The genus *Cochleanthes* was first described by Constantine S. Rafinesque in 1838, who derived its name from the Greek words *cochlos* (shell) and *anthos* (flower), in reference to the shell-like appearance of its flowers. The approximately fifteen species that comprise this genus grow as epiphytes in cloud forests at elevations from 500-1,500 metres, and flower in succession throughout the greater part of the year.

The species *Cochleanthes amazonica* produces the largest flowers in the genus, reaching up to 7cm in diameter. Its distinctive, single-flowered inflorescences, white with blue vein-lines on the lip, are often hidden among the leaves as the plants tend to form large clumps. A little known species, its distribution seems quite restricted, with records from the Rio Marãnón in Peru and western Amazonas in Brazil. No specimens exist at Kew.

Couroupita subsessilis
(family Lecythidaceae)

Encyclia randii
(family Orchidaceae)

Galeandra devoniana
(family Orchidaceae)

Flowering throughout the year, *Couroupita subsessilis* displays cauliflory in a sensational manner, particularly amongst the older trees whose trunks and large branches become heavy with fleshy flowers and massive fruit. *C. subsessilis* is widely distributed in the várzea (seasonally-flooded) forests along the primary white water rivers of western and central Amazonia, from Iquitos to Manaus and also further east in the areas near Santarém.

Known as the cannonball tree genus, it is aptly named for its cylindrical fruits which fall to the ground when mature. The native people along the Amazon use the foul-smelling pulp as fodder for pigs and chickens. Wild pigs are also thought to feed on the pulp, thus helping to disperse the seeds enveloped within the indehiscent fruits.

The distinguished explorer and botanist Joseph Dalton Hooker, who later became Director of the Royal Botanic Gardens, Kew, established the genus Encyclia in the *Botanical Magazine* in 1828. He derived its name from the Greek *enkyklein* (to encircle), referring to the way in which the lip encloses the column. It is a genus of more than 240 species of mostly epiphytic plants, usually found in seasonally dry forest from sea level up to 1,000 metres elevation and distributed throughout tropical America.

Encyclia randii, a Brazilian species, was discovered in the last century by Edward Rand on the Rio Solimões and subsequently named by the celebrated Brazilian botanist, João Barbosa Rodrigues. Its distribution extends from western Amazonas to the eastern state of Pernambuco.

Exploring in South America on behalf of the Royal Geographical Society, Sir Robert Schomburgk first discovered *Galeandra devoniana* near Barcelos on the Rio Negro, and named it in honour of the Duke of Devonshire, an ardent collector of orchids. The genus *Galeandra,* containing twenty-six species, is distributed from Mexico to Bolivia, with the strongest occurrence in the Amazon region, where it grows on trees along waterways or on flood plains at elevations ranging from sea level to 500 metres.

Galeandra devoniana bears deciduous leaves and fragrant, long-lasting flowers, varying in colour from brownish-green and veined with maroon stripes to deep purple-brown and edged with green. This tall, elegant plant was collected from the Lago Sapuacá in Oriximiná, Rio Trombetas, Pará.

Galeandra dives
(family Orchidaceae)

Gongora maculata
(family Orchidaceae)

Gustavia augusta
(family Lecythidaceae)

Galeandra is a genus of approximately twenty-six species, distributed from Mexico to Bolivia but most strongly represented in the Amazon region. The species *Galeandra dives* is distributed in the Guyanas, Venezuela, Colombia, and Brazil. This little known orchid is not known in cultivation, while in the wild it has been reported growing epiphytically on trees over river banks.

The flowers of this delicate orchid are golden brown with an unusual maroon tinge. The lip together with the spur measure around 6cm long. Margaret's painting was drawn from a plant collected from Lago Caipuru, Rio Trombetas, Pará.

Gongora is a small genus with upwards of a dozen species, with flowers of extremely variable coloration. Not widely hybridised, they are often grown for their unique flowers that are both attractive and lightly fragrant. The plants grow epiphytically, inhabiting ant nests in wet forest, with all species being pollinated very specifically by male euglossine bees. It is widely distributed from Mexico to Peru and Brazil, with this plant collected along the Rio Gurupi on Margaret's first journey to Amazonia.

Gongora maculata, also known as *Gongora quinqenervis,* was first described in 1798, with the genus named in honour of Don Antonio Cabballero y Gongora, viceroy of New Granada (Colombia and Ecuador) during the eighteenth century.

The delicate balance of this plant and its placement on the page clearly illustrate Margaret's remarkable sense of design. The succulent pseudobulbs and crisp dark leaves, while seeming to float near the top of the page as if caught on a tree limb, securely anchor the pendulous inflorescence: grace and gravity at work in perfect unison.

In 1775, the genus *Gustavia* was founded on the type species, *Gustavia augusta,* by the Swedish botanist, Carl Linnaeus, whose work, *Species Plantarum* (1753), established the universal scientific language for the formal naming and describing of plants – the binomial system of nomenclature. Linnaeus dedicated the new genus, which now includes about forty-one species, to Gustavus III (1746-92), King of Sweden, who supported him in his botanical guests.

Gustavia augusta, a medium-sized tree that reaches a height of about 20 metres, can be found along river margins and other habitats with periodically flooded soil. It is widely distributed throughout the Guyanas, Surinam, Venezuela, Peru, and Brazil. In a complex, aesthetically pleasing arrangement, Margaret has depicted *Gustavia augusta* within its natural habitat of epiphytic aroids, orchids and bromeliads, together with the symmetry of the hanging nests of the oropendula bird, the graceful arches of the *Mauritia* palm, and the elegance of the white egret.

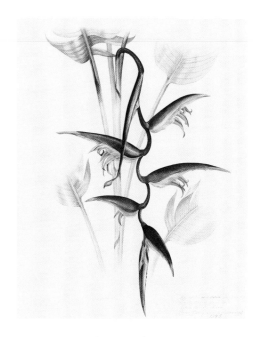

Gustavia pulchra
(family Lecythidaceae)

Heliconia adeliana
(family Heliconiaceae)

Heliconia chartacea
(family Heliconiaceae)

Gustavia pulchra, a striking species restricted to the upper and middle Rio Negro as well as nearby regions of Venezuela, occurs in the understorey of periodically flooded lowland forests. It produces spectacular snow-white flowers up to 12.5cm across. Born below the leaves, the blooms sprout directly from the branches, a characteristic trait known as cauliflory, common among rainforest trees. *G. pulchra,* normally 8-10 metres, can reach a height of 18 metres. Like numerous other Amazonian species, it was first discovered by the indefatigable nineteenth century English explorer, Richard Spruce, during his extra-ordinary journeys throughout Amazonia and the Andes between 1810 and 1864.

During her many years of exploration. Margaret Mee observed the steadily growing threats to the Amazonian forests. Compelled by the need to convey a conservation message through her work, she began to draw the plants in their forest background in a number of her paintings. From the *Leopoldinia* palm in the background, to the hummingbird alighting on the inflorescence of the *Gustavia* in the foreground, Margaret seeks to impress on the observer the interdependency of forest species and the importance of preserving their natural habitats.

Native to Central and South America and a number of South Pacific islands, heliconias are robust, fast-growing, forest-floor herbs. Like the bananas to which they are related, they may reach vast sizes, but their elegant flowering shoots give them a characteristic beauty all their own. The flowers are small and borne within the large, often vividly coloured bracts (modified leaves), whose shapes often resemble birds in flight. Although the inflorescences are pendent in many species, they may be erect in others. These remarkable plants rely on their distinct and brilliantly coloured inflorescences to serve as strong visual signals for attraction, the result of adaptation to pollination by birds.

Described as recently as 1972, *Heliconia chartacea* occurs in western Amazonia. It is conspicuous in the understorey of the forest because of the cinnamon red bracts enclosing the much smaller flowers. Attracted by the intense red colour, hummingbirds are commonly seen hovering over these plants.

Margaret's painting is of a cultivated plant from the gardens of the late Robert Burle Marx, Brazil's most celebrated landscape architect and artist. Marx had an outstanding collection of the genus, and frequently used many different species of Heliconia in his designs for tropical gardens. He was a great friend of Margaret's and on occasion would journey with her to collect rare plants. In the preface to her diaries, Marx professed his fascination with the Heliconia genus. 'In hollows near the rivers the heliconias develop a theme of extraordinary richness and variety…I see them as sculpture, as forms projected in space, shapes enriched by the tension between flowers and leaves.'

Heliconia chartacea var. meeana
(family Heliconiaceae)

Heterostemon mimosoides
(family Leguminosae)

Ionopsis utricularioides
(family Orchidaceae)

Since the founding of the Heliconia Society International in 1985, heliconias have become increasingly popular as landscaping plants throughout the tropics and subtropics. In regions where they cannot be grown in outdoor gardens, they are grown as potted plants and cut flowers.

Margaret collected this plant along the Rio Uaupés, a tributary of the Rio Negro. The drawing presents a fine and finished example of her ability to combine botanical accuracy with superb compositional arrangement. The delicate wash of foliage conveys a knowing understanding of the leaves even as they fade off into the distance. The inflorescence is captivating in its subtle coloration and striking precision of curves and angles.

Heterostemon is a small genus of less than ten species restricted in its distribution to north-west Brazil and the bordering areas of Colombia and Venezuela. Although it was first described as early a 1818, it is poorly known with the exception of the species *Heterostemon mimosoides.*

With its abundant, orchidlike flowers and splendid foliage, *Heterostemon mimosoides* is one of the most lovely of all American leguminous plants. It is a low growing shrub or small tree ranging from 2–10 metres tall, commonly found in the igapó and várzea forests (permanent seasonal swamp forests) of the Uaupés and Rio Negro rivers, particularly in the vicinity of Ega and Manaus. Margaret's plant was collected from the Rio Cueiras, a left bank tributary of Rio Negro near Manaus.

Related to *Oncidium,* this elegant species has been known to botanists since the eighteenth century, when it was first described in 1788 as *Epidendrum utricularioides.* Some thirty years later, in 1821, the British botanist John Lindley transferred it to the genus *Ionopsis,* whose name was derived from the two Greek words *ion* (violet) and *opsis* (appearance), referring to the similarity of its delicate flowers to violets. Although there are approximately ten species in this genus, *Ionopsis utricularioides* is the only one that is widely recognised.

Though it is widespread throughout tropical and subtropical America, even reaching as far as Florida, *Ionopsis utricularioides* is not known from western Amazonia. Usually epiphytic, these plants can commonly be found growing in maté and guava trees up to 800 metres elevation. It produces flower spikes typically about 40cm long, carrying flowers that are variable in colour from white to lilac to rose-red, with a striking magenta blotch on the lip. Margaret collected this plant on the beautiful Cuminá-Mirim river in the state of Pará.

Memora schomburgkii
(family Bignoniaceae)

Mormodes buccinator
(family Orchidaceae)

Mormodes buccinator
(family Orchidaceae)

The Bignoniaceae is a predominantly woody family that includes numerous large trees and many striking lianas, woody climbing plants that form a characteristic and important element in tropical rain-forests. The nineteenth century English explorer, Richard Spruce, described them memorably with his characteristic dry wit: 'there is scarcely any family of plants which does not include some members who get up in the world by scrambling upon their more robust and selfstanding neighbours. Where two or more of these vagabonds come into collision in mid-air, and find nothing else to twine upon, they twine around each other as closely as the strands of a cable, and the stronger of them generally ends by squeezing the life out of the weaker.'

Memora schomburgkii is found in the Guyanas and Amazonia. The handsome trumpet-shaped flowers are characteristic of this plant, and their leaves tend to be subdivided pinnately like those of an ash tree. The long pendulous pods that form its fruit initially appear very similar to those of legumes. Margaret collected this plant in Oriximiná, Pará, near the mouth of the Rio Trombetas, one of the largest northern tributaries in lower Amazonia.

The unique twists of the column and lip of the genus *Mormodes* amazed the eminent taxonomist John Lindley in 1836, prompting him to coin its generic name from the Greek word *mormo* (phantom, frightful object). Distributed from Mexico to Bolivia and Brazil, these epiphytic orchids, also known as *Mormodes amazonica,* often occur on dead limbs of trees in moist or wet forests, at elevations from sea level to 800 metres. Like their relatives the *Catasetums, Mormodes* flowers may be unisexual and the shape of their flowers may be extremely variable within a single species.

Mormodes buccinator was first described by the distinguished British orchidologist, John Lindley, in 1840 and is distributed from Mexico to Equador, Venezuela and Brazil, where it is restricted to the state of Amazonas. It can often be found growing on dead trees up to 1,500 metres above sea level. Flowering from winter to spring, it produces an erect to arching spike 15-40cm long on which numerous fleshy flowers are borne. They appear in a variety of colours, from white – like the plant pictured here – to greenish-yellow, yellow, pale pink, or brownish-purple, and may also be striped or spotted.

Neoregelia concentrica
(family Bromeliaceae)

Neoregelia eleutheropetala
(family Bromeliaceae)

Neoregelia leviana
(family Bromeliaceae)

The family Bromeliaceae, consisting of approximately 2,000 species, is exclusively of the Americas, with the exception of Pitcairnia feliciana, which is found in West Africa. The Swedish naturalist Carl Linnaeus formally established the genus *Bromelia,* honouring Olaf Bromel, a distinguished nineteenth century Swedish botanist.

Neoregelia concentrica grows epiphytically on trees in the forest and is found in the Serra dos Orgaos, State of Rio de Janeiro. Its name refers to the arrangement of its violet flowers, clustered in concentric circles in the centre of the rosette.

Neoregelia eleutheropetala, first discovered in Peru in 1902, is the most widespread of the Amazonian neoregelias, distributed throughout the Amazonian regions of Colombia, Venezuela, Peru and Brazil. It can be found growing as an epiphyte or terrestrial in rainforests at altitudes ranging from 100-1,650 metres.

The plant depicted in Margaret Mee's painting is from the Rio Urupadi, which flows across the border between the states of Pará and Amazonas. The compact rosette is formed by thirty or more red and green banded leaves, creating the water tank or reservoir common amongst several genera of the Bromeliaceae family. Cupped in the centre of its innermost leaves is the inflorescence, containing numerous tiny white flowers.

Neoregelia leviana is known scientifically only from Margaret Mee's collection of 1967 from the banks of the Rio Cauaburi, a left bank tributary of the Rio Negro. Her discovery of this species occurred during her attempted ascent of the famous Pico da Neblina mountain, which lies on the border with Venezuela. As long ago as the mid-1800s the British explorer, Richard Spruce, had reported sighting a vast mountainous formation during his exploration of the upper Rio Negro. The first recorded ascent, eleven weeks of laborious trail cutting, did not occur until 1953 when it was led by Bassett Maguire, Curator of the New York Botanical Garden.

Intrigued by this mountainous region and assisted by a scientific grant from the National Geographic Society, Margaret Mee became, in 1967, the first woman to attempt a southern approach to this mountain. Torrential rains, however, obliterated the trail and the expedition had to be abandoned. An account of the journey with its botanical discoveries, including *Neoregelia leviana,* was presented in a special National Geographic Society Research Report.

Neoregelia margaretae
(family Bromeliaceae)

***Neoregelia* sp.**
(family Bromeliaceae)

Nidularium antoineanum
(family Bromeliaceae)

During her journeys, Margaret Mee collected four of the five species of *Neoregelia* known from Amazonian Brazil, and is credited with first discovering three of them herself – *N. margaretae, N. leviana,* and *N. meeana.* Margaret's significant contribution to the knowledge of this genus helped establish her reputation as both a scientist and a botanical explorer. As *Neoregelia margaretae* has not yet been recollected, it is known only from Margaret's collections.

The plant in her painting was found in January of 1965 in a remote region of Amazonas – on the banks of the Rio Içana, a right bank tributary of the upper Rio Negro. The painting accurately depicts the splendour of *N. margaretae.* At its centre are tiny blue and white flowers, set in a sunken cluster, surrounded by the brilliant, rose-coloured inner leaves of the rosette, which retain their flush of colour long after the flowers have died. The reservoir or tank formed by the leaves of the plant becomes filled with rainwater, providing a home for a myriad of animal life, from tiny insects to small vertebrates such as frogs or lizards. Those that die serve as a source of nutrition for the plant as it absorbs the water and dissolved salts by means of its leaf scales.

The genus Neoregelia was named in honour of the German botanist A. von Regel, superintendent of the imperial Botanic Gardens, St. Petersburg, Russia. It has become a favourite indoor plant, particularly in Germany and Japan, as it is easy to maintain and produces dramatically coloured foliage, often lasting months after the flowers have withered. In the wild the plants grow epiphytically on lower branches of trees, seeking a shaded place with good air circulation.

This painting of a plant from the Rio Uaupés, Amazonas correctly depicts the tentacle-like nature of its pale green, spiny leaves, delicately edged in rose, encompassing the more vibrantly red, inner leaves which border the inflorescence. Known from eastern Peru and Colombia, this genus is most abundant in eastern Brazil, particularly in the area known as the 'Mata Atlantica', the coastal forest region.

The genus *Nidularium* derives its name from the Latin *nidulus* (small nest), referring to the nest-like shape of the flower clusters. Like *Neoregelia* species, *Nidularium* form a water reservoir with their rosettes. It is distinguishable by virtue of its funnel-shaped tanks as opposed to the tubular shape of *Aechmea* and *Billbergia* genera. *Nidularium* are exclusive to Brazil.

The species is named in honour of the Austrian horticulturist Franz Antoine Jr., Director of the Schönbrunn Gardens, Vienna. This epiphytic plant is from Boracéia, Estado de São Paulo. Margaret Mee's painting succeeds in capturing the delicacy of this plant with its cluster of blue flowers surrounded by brilliant wine-coloured bracts.

Nidularium innocentii* var. *wittmackianum (family Bromeliaceae)

Nymphaea rudgeana
(family Nymphaeaceae)

Oncidium lanceanum
(family Orchidaceae)

This species was named after the Marquis de St. Innocent, the French publisher and bromeliad enthusiast, with the variety name honouring Ludwig Wittmack, the German botanist. Margaret Mee painted this plant portrait during her early years in Brazil, when she was working closely with Dr. Lyman Smith to depict the bromeliads of eastern Brazil. A common epiphyte in tropical rainforests, it is distributed along the eastern coastal regions from São Paulo to Santa Catarina.

Nidulariums, like the Neoregelias, make superb indoor plants with their small to medium size, easy maintenance, and striking leaf colour. They. do, however, require more light than Neoregelias. There are thirty-five species in the genus *Nidularium,* all of which are located in eastern Brazil.

Rarely seen in cultivation, this tropical night-blooming waterlily is a smaller relative of the well-known *Victoria amazonica,* the giant Amazonian waterlily that has, since the last century, remained a coveted show plant of botanic gardens worldwide. Distributed throughout the West Indies and the Amazonian regions of Brazil and its neighbouring countries, *Nymphaea rudgeana* often makes its home in the slow flowing waters of lowland coastal habitats.

The intrepid English explorer and botanist, Richard Spruce, first discovered this species in 1849 at Óbidos, on the Rio Amazonas near Santarém. Its greenish-yellow flowers, 8-9cm in diameter, reportedly open at dusk for two or three successive nights, emitting a pleasing lemon scent that attracts its pollinator, a scarab beetle. Among the new hybrid waterlilies are several with *rudgeana* characteristics.

As a member of the so-called 'Mule-ear' orchids, this plant is distinctive for its erect, leathery leaves, finely mottled with red to chocolate-brown colouring. The genus *Oncidium* is extensive, containing over 400 species of epiphytes, and has remained one of the most widely cultivated and popular genera throughout the years. John Lindley described this species in 1836, dedicating it to John H. Lance, who introduced it into cultivation from Surinam.

Collected along the banks of the upper Rio Negro, this plant bears twenty or more long-lasting, intensely fragrant flowers, whose scent is reminiscent of cloves. These striking flowers, with a diameter of about 4cm, vary in colour from yellow to yellow-green and can be found in Venezuela, Trinidad, the Guyanas, and Amazonas state in Brazil.

Oncidium sp.

The name *Oncidium* is derived from the Greek word *onkos* (swelling or mass), undoubtedly referring to the characteristic warty callus on the lip of many of the species. It was described in Stockholm by the Swedish botanist Olaf Swartz in 1800. Swartz authored several seminal works on orchid morphology in the late 1700s, having been educated at Uppsala as a student of Linnaeus' son.

Margaret Mee's painting of this delicate orchid is based on a plant from Amazonas state. The species remains undescribed by taxonomists.

Ouratea discophora
(family Octinaceae)

Margaret Mee collected this plant along the Rio Urubaxi in Amazonas. The red, bell-shaped fruits of the small tree, which grows to a height of about 4–5 metres, contain seeds suspended within the receptacle that change over time from green to blue-black. This plate has been previously published as 'Unknown plant'.

Philodendron brevispathum
(family Araceae)

A member of the Araceae family which includes climbers, epiphytes and hemiepiphytes, *Philodendron brevispathum* is a climbing epiphyte whose stems are coated with a thick layer of rusty-brown, coarse hairs, a peculiar characteristic also exhibited in other species. Although it is not well known, *P. brevispathum* is quite widespread throughout western Amazonia, Bolivia and the Guyanas. Margaret's painting of this species is the only colour illustration known.

Phryganocydia corymbosa
(family Bignoniaceae)

Psittacanthus cinctus
(family Loranthaceae)

Rudolfiella aurantiaca
(family Orchidaceae)

Phryganocydia corymbosa, a widespread tropical American liana, blooms throughout the year producing fragrant flowers which are typically rose, lilac or magenta in colour. In addition, white-flowered plants may also be found, but only in select areas. As the most common species of the Bignoniaceae family in the Canal Zone and eastern Panama, its range extends southward to include Brazil. Margaret collected this plant near the mouth of the Rio Trombetas, not far from Santarém, the area where Spruce collected it one hundred and thirty years previously.

Psittacanthus cinctus belongs to the largest family of mistletoes, Loranthaceae, comprising approximately 65 genera and 900 species. As woody plants, mistletoes develop a parasitic attachment to their host tree. However, they are not totally reliant on their hosts as they are photosynthetic and thereby able to synthesise sugars using sunlight. The flowers of many of these plants are especially showy, attracting the attention of birds and insects for pollination.

Margaret Mee's painting accurately depicts the bulging upturned tips of the flowers, characteristic of this species. Its range extends along the Rio Negro from Manaus in Brazil to the Amazonian region of Venezuela. Richard Spruce is known to have collected this plant in 1851, growing on lecythid trees (brazil nut family) near Manaus, known at that time as Barra do Rio Negro.

In 1836 the celebrated British botanist John Lindley described *Rudolfiella aurantiaca* from a plant collected in Guyana, which flowered in the collection of the Duke of Devonshire at Chiswick, London. The Duke, a man of tremendous wealth, was well known at the time for his conservatory at Chatsworth, Derbyshire, home to one of the largest orchid collections of that time.

This painting depicts the plant as Margaret Mee observed it, perched on a Jará palm in the igapó (flooded) forests of the Rio Negro, a common habitat for this epiphytic orchid. Bearing up to twenty golden yellow, red-spotted flowers, the inflorescence of this striking plant may reach 30cm long. It is widely distributed in the Amazonian area of Brazil, Peru, Colombia, Venezuela and the Guyanas.

Scuticaria steelii
(family Orchidaceae)

Selenicereus wittii
(family Cactaceae)

Selenicereus wittii
(family Cactaceae)

Scuticaria, a small genus of only five species, was described in 1843 by the eminent botanist John Lindley, who based its name on the Latin *scutica* (whip),in reference to the long, whip-like leaves that may reach up to 1.5 metres in length.

Scuticaria steelii was named after Matthew Steele, who discovered this unusual orchid in Guyana in 1836. In the wild, it occurs in the Guyanas, Venezuela, Colombia, and Brazil and produces fragrant, pale yellow flowers, blotched with reddish-brown and measuring 5-7cm in diameter. The plant in the painting was collected along the Rio Negro, where it was found growing on a Jará palm *(Leopoldinia pulchra)* in igapó forest.

The German botanist Karl Schumann (1891-1904), a nineteenth century leading expert on the Cactaceae family, named this remarkable epiphytic cactus *Cereus wittii* in 1900, working from specimens sent to him by a German collector, N.H. Witt, residing in Manaus at the time. In 1913 the plant was placed in a genus by itself as *Strophocactus wittii,* the generic name from the word *strophe* (twisting, curling) referring to the manner in which the flattened leaf-like stems wind themselves around Amazonian trees. In 1986 taxonomists determined that this extraordinary night blooming cactus belonged in the *Selenicereus* genus, which includes the spectacular, night-flowering cactus, *Selenicereus grandiflorus,* 'Queen of the Night'. The generic name is derived from the Greek *selene,* meaning moon.

Margaret Mee collected this plant in the igapó (flooded forest) of the Arquipelago das Anavilhanas, a reserve on the Rio Negro near Manaus. In this painting, Margaret's first of the species, *Selenicereus wittii* is beautifully portrayed within its forest surroundings, depicting its developing fruit and curious spine-edged, flattened stems, suffused with crimson.

After first seeing this fascinating, night-flowering cactus in 1964, Margaret began a search that eventually grew to span twenty-four years – to find and paint the 'Moonflower' in full bloom. Finally, in May of 1988, the month of her seventy-ninth birthday and barely six months before her untimely death, Margaret had the thrill, during an all-night vigil, of witnessing the beauty of the delicate, fragrant flower in full bloom, and of sketching it by torchlight from the deck of a riverboat in the igapó of the forest reserve, Arquipelago das Anavilhanas, Rio Negro.

Each flower of *Selenicereus wittii* is in the form of a very long tube that flares out at the end, creating a large, white ephemeral blossom that opens at night, lasting only till the dawn of the next morning. As with several other species of the genus, the tubular shape of the flower and its night-blooming habit has led experts to believe that this epiphytic cactus is pollinated by long-tongued hawkmoths.

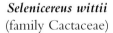

Selenicereus wittii
(family Cactaceae)

Sobralia margaritae
(family Orchidaceae)

Streptocalyx longifolius
(family Bromeliaceae)

Margaret Mee's series of paintings of *Selenicereus wittii* is the only known study of this plant in the wild. Several paintings of the related species, *Selenicereus grandiflorus,* all drawn from cultivated plants, have become quite famous. As early as 1752, the celebrated flower painter, Georg Dionysius Ehret, beautifully portrayed this cactus, entitling it, 'Queen of the Night'. A painting by the renowned Belgian artist, Pierre-Joseph Redouté, dating from the time of Marie Antoinette, also depicted this night-flowering cactus. However, this *Selenicereus* species is probably best known from the painting entitled 'The Night Blowing Cereus', included in Robert Thornton's magnificent folio, *The Temple of Flora,* published in parts from 1797 to 1807.

Selenicereus wittii occurs in the Brazilian Amazonian region, where it thrives in the igapó, permanently flooded swamp forest. Margaret had initially noted this rare cactus during her early explorations in 1964, and again on three other occasions, but always without flowers. This painting portrays plants which had flowered the previous night. As a result, the flowers are already withering.

Attractive foliage, distinctive flowers, and reedlike stems, up to 180cm tall in some species, are all characteristic of the genus *Sobralia*. It was first described by H. Ruiz and J. Pavon in 1794 in honour of their friend Francisco Sobral, a Spanish physician and botanist during the latter years of the eighteenth century. Restricted to the tropics of Mexico and Central and South America, this genus includes approximately thirty-five species.

First discovered by Margaret Mee, who saw it growing on tall trees in the igapó (flooded forest) of the Rio Urupadi in Amazonas, *Sobralia margaritae* was named in her honour by her friend Guido F.J. Pabst, Brazil's premier orchid specialist. This fine epiphyte combines shiny heavily veined leaves with large, finely-textured flowers, strongly resembling the showy flowers of the *Cattleya* genus in form. Although the flowers of *Sobralia margaritae* are short-lived, with some lasting only a day, the plant does continues to flower over a period of time.

Streptocalyx longifolius, native to the rainforests from Brazil to north-east Peru, is a typical ant-inhabited bromeliad, with thousands of biting ants living in its large leaf sheaths, making it very difficult to collect. The French botanist, Joseph Martin, discovered *Streptocalyx longifolius* in French Guyana in the early 1800s. Unfortunately for him, his prized collection ended up in the hands of the British when the ship carrying it back to France was seized by English privateers in 1803.

Growing up to 92cm in height, *S. longifolius* is a dense rosette of spiny light-green leaves with a striking, pallid pink inflorescence (cluster of flowers) borne on a short scape. These epiphytic plants thrive in the hot, humid conditions of the rainforests, occurring from Brazil to north-east Peru. Margaret collected this beautiful bromeliad along the Rio Negro in 1967.

Streptocalyx poeppigii
(family Bromeliaceae)

Streptocalyx poeppigii
(family Bromeliaceae)

Symphonia globulifera
(family Clusiaceae)

Streptocalyx poeppigii belongs to the bromeliad or pineapple family, a group of over two thousand species that are mainly epiphytes – plants that grow on other plants without feeding on them. The genus *Streptocalyx,* comprising fourteen species of terrestrial (growing in the ground) or epiphytic bromeliads, is distributed throughout Brazil, Ecuador, Colombia, and eastern Peru. It was named by the notable Austrian botanist, Johann Georg Beer, who published the first monograph devoted to bromeliads, *Die Familie der Bromeliaceen,* in 1857.

Streptocalyx poeppigii, distributed widely throughout Colombia to Amazonian Brazil and Bolivia, was collected by and named for the distinguished German botanist and explorer, Eduard Poeppig (1798-1868), who made a significant early expedition to the Amazonian area of both Peru and Brazil. This bromeliad grows as an epiphyte in the rainforest but occasionally may be seen growing terrestrially adapting to altitudes ranging from 25-1,200 metres. Its robust inflorescence, with rose-purple flowers, is replaced by pink and white berries which gradually turn purple in colour and remain for months.

Margaret Mee created two paintings of *Streptocalyx poeppigii,* completed at various points in her career as an artist. The earlier work, completed in 1962 and drawn from the Collections of the São Paulo Botanical Institute, is in the classic style with the plant placed against a stark white background. In her later painting, Margaret expressed her concern for the delicate balance of the Amazon ecosystem by setting the plant against a backdrop of rainforest trees and plants depicting its natural habitat. The latter work, drawn from the Collections of the Royal Botanic Gardens, Kew, was completed in 1985, three years prior to her death.

The genus *Symphonia* is distributed in both tropical Africa and tropical America. However *Symphonia globulifera* is the only species found in the Americas, where it is widespread in many types of forest. A medium-sized to large tree, it can reach a height of approximately 35 metres. The bright yellow sap located in its tissues, easily obtained when branches or bark are cut, is utilised medicinally by the Amazonian Indians in a variety of ways. The plant in the painting comes from the Paraná Yamundá, a tributary of the Rio Trombetas.

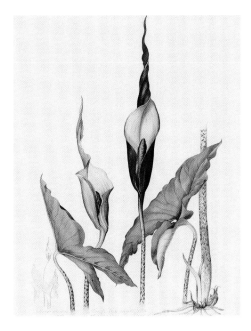

Tillandsia linearis
(family Bromeliaceae)

Tillandsia stricta
(family Bromeliaceae)

Urospatha sagittifolia
(family Araceae)

The genus Tillandsia, established in 1753 by Linnaeus, was named in honour of the Finnish botanist Elias Tillands (1640-1693). With its more than 400 species, it has the distinction of being the largest genus in the Bromeliaceae family and, to many collectors, it is also the most interesting, since it comprises numerous smaller species conducive to being grown in terrariums or small greenhouses. The most commonly known species of this genus widely distributed in the United States is *Tillandsia usneoides,* the famous 'Spanish Moss'.

Tillandsia linearis was discovered by the Franciscan monk Frei Vellozo, who laboured for eight years from 1782 to 1790 to prepare a flora of the plants of Rio de Janeiro, only to die several years prior to its publication. It has a somewhat restricted distribution, occurring in Goiás and south-eastern Brazil, from the vicinity of Rio to Paraná. Margaret's plant comes from the lovely region of Parati in western Rio de Janeiro, reportedly very close to where Vellozo first discovered this species.

Tillandsia stricta is one of the most popular species of the genus as it flowers frequently with a colourful, cone-like inflorescence 4-5cm in length. It is distributed not only in Rio de Janeiro and its immediate vicinity but has extended its occurrence north to Venezuela and south to Argentina, where it grows epiphytically on trees and shrubs. It is also commonly seen growing on telephone wires in more populated areas. Margaret Mee's plant, collected near São Paulo, is very similar in form to the original featured in the *Botanical Magazine* as early as 1813.

Urospatha sagittifolia, a striking wetland plant, is outstanding for its elongated, corkscrew-tipped inflorescences and large triangular leaves. Several species of the related genus, *Cyrtosperma,* from south-east Asia, also produce curiously twisted floral spathes, pointing to ancient contacts between the plants of the Old and New Worlds.

With a widespread distribution throughout the Guyanas, most of Amazonia, and reaching as far east as Bahia, this species grows in large stands on marshy ground along river banks.

Vriesea ensiformis var. bicolor
family Bromeliaceae)

Vriesea erythrodactylon
(family Bromeliaceae)

Vriesea guttata
(family Bromeliaceae)

The genus *Vriesea,* named after the Dutch botanist, W.H. de Vries (1807-1862), was established by the British taxonomist John Lindley in 1843, and contains more than 225 species, with new ones constantly being discovered. These plants are distributed over a large area from Mexico, Central America and the West Indies to Peru, Bolivia, Argentina and Brazil. Seeking dappled combined with good air circulation, vriesias grow epiphytically on tree branches in the rainforest at altitudes between 100 and 950 metres, forming vase-shaped rosettes with their broad leaves. Their highly coloured floral bracts remain vivid for weeks.

The species *Vriesea ensiformis,* discovered by the Franciscan monk Frei Vellozo around the year 1790, is commonly seen along the coastal rainforest, from Bahia to Santa Catarina. Its variety, however, was not discovered for yet another century and remains unknown outside its original state of São Paulo.

The twenty to thirty leaves of *Vriesea ensiformis* var. *bicolor* form the characteristic funnel-form rosette and the bicolorous character of its inflorescence is highly ornamental. Margaret's plant was collected from Paranapiacaba.

Directly translated, the name given to this species of *Vriesea* by the distinguished Belgian botanist Edouard Morren means red-fingered *Vriesea.* The single spike is striking with its colouring of green edged in red, and its leaves are noteworthy by themselves, with their dark purple and brown sheaths. Although it is not common in cultivation, Professor Morren reportedly had it growing in his gardens in Belgium as early as 1882. Distributed on the eastern coast of Brazil, it is found from Espirito Santo to Santa Catarina, thriving along the coastal areas. Margaret collected her plant at Caraguatatuba, north of Santos.

The species *Vriesea guttata* was described in 1875 from plants grown from seeds that had been brought to Europe from Santa Catarina, Brazil in 1870. Its name is derived from the Latin *gutta* (spotted), in reference to its spotted leaves. Ten years later, in 1880, the distinguished Belgian botanist Edouard Morren featured this species in the publication, *La Belgique Horticole,* which had been started by his father.

With a distribution restricted to Brazil, *V. guttata* is found in greatest concentration in Santa Catarina, the region where it was initially collected. It has also been found in various locations along the coastal rainforest, including the Organ Mountains north of Rio, where Margaret collected the plant depicted in this painting.

Vriesea heliconioides
(family Bromeliaceae)

Vriesea jonghei
(family Bromeliaceae)

Zygosepalum labiosum (family
Orchidaceae)

This painting of a plant from the Rio Demini, Amazonas depicts the spectacular *Vriesea heliconioides* in bloom, with its brilliant red flower spike edged with chartreuse and surrounded by smooth green leaves suffused with red. This species was first discovered in 1801 by the indefatigable explorers Alexander von Humboldt and his assistant Aimé Bonpland, and is distributed throughout southern Mexico to Bolivia and western Brazil.

Vriesea jonghei was introduced to European gardens by the Belgian horticulturist M. de Jonghei. Distributed in Central and South American forests, this stunning plant occurs most frequently in Brazil's southern coastal mountains, or the Serra do Mar. *V. jonghei* is valued for its striking inflorescence, with large yellow flowers and mustard-brown floral bracts, densely speckled with brown spots.

Zygosepalum, a small genus of possibly five species of orchids, was described in 1863 by H.G. Reichenbach (1823-1889), a German botanist and successor to John Lindley as the leading orchid taxonomist of the day. The generic name was derived from the Greek words *zygon* (yoke) and *sepalum* (sepal), probably referring to the fused sepals that are characteristic of the plants in this genus.

Growing epiphytically at elevations from 100-500 metres, *Zygosepalum labiosum* is frequently found in lowland forests. Its fragrant, long-lasting flowers, up to 5cm wide, are large in relation to the rest of the plant and handsome, with their white coloration and peachy-brown highlights. The painting clearly depicts the swollen stems, or pseudobulbs, remarkable adaptations that allow the plant to withstand the daily period of relative drought caused in the forest canopy by the sun.

GLOSSARY

agouti – a small rodent similar to the guinea pig

anta – tapir

anú – shiny cowbird *(Moluthrus bonairensis)*

arara – macaw

ariranha – giant otter

Baiana/o – Bahian

banzeiro – a local name for waves after a storm

caatinga – forest on very poor sandy soil, which is thinner and lets in more light

caba – wasp

caboclo/a – of mixed Portuguese/Indian blood

cacué – a bird related to the parrot

carapana – mosquito

chaga – a beetle which bites and then defecates on the wound, causing itching; when the wound is scratched a substance is released into the bloodstream, bringing the danger of heart disease

chuva branca – white blanket of rain

Crente – a Protestant

cupuaçú – *Theobroma grandifloram* – a fruit tree related to cacau

curica – a parrot of the genus *Pionopsitta*

Embauba – *Cecropia,* a fast-growing tree with conspicuous palmate leaves

FUNAI – Government Agency for Indian Affairs, successor to IPS

garimpeiro – prospectors or goldminers

graúna – cowbird *(Scaphidura oryzivora)*

guaraná – a soft drink made from *Paullinia sorbilis*

guaruba – a bird related to the parrot

hoatzin – a primitive, almost flightless bird

IBDF – Institute of Brazilian Forestry Development

igapó – forest permanently flooded by black water rivers

igarapé – a small stream

INPA – National Institute of Amazon Research

IPS – Indian Protection Service

irará – tayra *(Tayra barbara)*

itáuba – *Mezilaurus itauba,* the favourite wood for canoes

jaburu – stork

jacaré – alligator

jacu – a ground cuckoo *(Neomorphus)*

jaguatirica – a wild cat, smaller than a jaguar

japim – a yellow rumped cacique (a sparrow-like bird)

japo/japú – an oropendula bird

japusinho – a small oropendula

jararacussu – a dangerous poisonous snake

Jurupari – the devil

loro – trees of the laurel family

Macaco de Cheiro – squirrel monkeys

macumbeira – shaman, doctor-priest, follower of voodoo

maloca – communal Indian hut or huts; Indian settlement

marva – a highly inflammable fibre similar to jute

mergulha – anhinga or snake bird, a species of diving bird

mestiza/o – mixed race, usually Spanish and American Indian

molongo – *Montrichardia arborescens,* an aquatic aroid

mucuim – chiggers, South American fleas

mulato/mulata – half Indian, half European

mutucas – horseflies

mutum – curassow, a bird

paca – a small rodent, rather like a guinea pig, edible

paraná – side channel

parasitas – epiphytes

peixe – fish

pererECA – tree frog

piaçaba – palm fibre from *Leopoldina piassaba*

pirarucu – *Arapaima gigas,* type of large edible fish

pium – minute blood sucking simulidae fly

pootoo – a night-flying bird rrelated to the nightjar

Posto Indigena – agency reserve/camp

Qualea – *Erisma calcaratum*

quati – coati

saracura – a night rail

seringueiro – rubber gatherer

serra – mountain range

socco – a heron

sucuri – anaconda

tachã – southern screamer – *chauna torquata*

tercado – bush knife

tracajá – turtles

tocandira – the large black conger ant

tucanare – a beautiful fish

uirupuru – a small bird with a musical call, related to the wren

várzea – river margin seasonally flooded by white water

xoto – long basket

ACKNOWLEDGEMENTS

We should like to thank the staff and associates of the Royal Botanic Gardens, Kew, and in particular Michael Daly, Marilyn Ward and Ruth Stiff, for their most helpful contributions to this publication. We are especially grateful to Dr. Simon Mayo, Professor Sir Ghillean T. Prance, Dr. Cássio van den Berg, Dr. Gwilym Lewis and Cecília Azevedo for their invaluable advice and identification of flora, fauna and locations.

All illustrations are either by the late Margaret Mee or the property of her estate, apart from the following:

throughout – the bird, fish and animal plates which are by Alexandre Rodrigues Ferreira and taken from *Viagem Filosofica, pelas capitanias do Grão Pará, Rio Negro, Mato Grosso e Cuibá, 1783-1792*.
page 7 – Greville Mee
page 11 – Ghillean T. Prance
page 12 – World Wildlife Fund for Nature, USA

The maps on pages 20-29 are based on maps by Greville Mee, to whom we also owe a debt of gratitude for lending us text of the diaries and very many illustrations. His constructive criticism at proof stage was much appreciated.

INDEX
Page numbers in bold type refer to illustrations and captions